PRF

The idea for this book came
the Crown with whom I had
Parliamentary Counsel. When
the civil service he suggested that I mig-
various factors that influence the precise wording and gen-.
of Acts of Parliament, with a view to providing background of a kind
that might be helpful to practitioners, judges and academics.

Whether I have succeeded in producing a book along the lines that
he had in mind I do not know. I hope, however, that the book will
turn out to be a useful addition to the vast literature that has already
grown up about the process of legislation. In any event, the book has
been great fun, not to mention therapeutically cathartic, to write.

The opinions expressed in this book are mine; any resemblance to
any opinion held by or on behalf of the Government or anyone else is
(a) extremely unlikely, and (b) purely coincidental.

I have great pleasure in thanking the following. All my colleagues
who have taught me so much and given me so much support in many
different ways over the years; in particular, Christopher Jenkins who
helped me to excise much of what was wrong with the original manu-
script of this book (although doubtless much remains with which he
disagrees) and who taught me nearly everything I don't know about
legislative drafting, Philip Davies who taught me most of the rest by
example, and others whom I refrain from mentioning by name only
out of respect for their professional reputations. My new colleagues
at Berwin Leighton Paisner LLP who have been so welcoming. Sweet
& Maxwell for their publishing expertise and for being superb people
to do business with. My wife Julia and my children Yisroel, Avi, Shira
and Elisheva for their love and support. And God for giving me so
many blessings of so many kinds.

Daniel Greenberg
London, 2011

DEDICATION

To Philip and Jacky,
Euan and Mary Anne,
and Christopher and Margaret,
with love and gratitude.

LAYING DOWN THE LAW

LAYING DOWN THE LAW

A discussion of the people, processes and problems that shape Acts of Parliament

Daniel Greenberg

Parliamentary Counsel (UK) 1991–2010
Parliamentary Team, Berwin Leighton Paisner LLP from 2010
Editor, *Craies on Legislation*

SWEET & MAXWELL  THOMSON REUTERS

Published in 2011 by Sweet & Maxwell, 100 Avenue Road, London, NW3 3PF
part of Thomson Reuters (Professional) UK Limited
(Registered in England & Wales, Company No 1679046.
Registered Office and address for service:
Aldgate House, 33 Aldgate High Street, London EC3N 1DL)

*For further information on our products and services, visit
www.sweetandmaxwell.co.uk*

Printed in Great Britain by Ashford Colour Press, Gosport, Hants
Typeset by Servis Filmsetting Ltd, Stockport, Cheshire

*No natural forests were destroyed to make this product;
only farmed timber was used and re-planted.*

A CIP catalogue record for this book is available from the British Library

ISBN: 978-0-414-04693-1

CONTENTS

SECTION 1
INTRODUCTION

1 THE PURPOSE OF THIS BOOK

The purpose of this book is to offer some thoughts about how different factors influence the final shape of an Act of Parliament.

Although this book is designed primarily as an expression of opinion, I have tried to include a reasonable amount of practical information, while at the same time trying to avoid reinventing the wheel. There are already many publications that describe different parts of the legislative process, and Ch.2 directs the reader to some that he or she is likely to find particularly useful in providing the technical backdrop against which this book is written.

So I have assumed that the reader already knows the basics of how the Government and Parliament machines work in producing legislation, and I have tried to focus on adding information and opinions that will hopefully add to the pre-existing literature.

Although I began to write this book slightly doubting whether it would be of such practical relevance as the former Minister who suggested it thought, I have come to agree with him more and more as it has unfolded. It is likely that each reader of this book will already know a great deal of what I say, and will probably know more than I do about at least some aspects of the book. But it is also true that there may be few readers who have had an opportunity to observe all the aspects of the legislative process and the factors which influence it about which I write: the experience of Parliamentary Counsel may be lacking in depth in some areas, but it does give one an overview of all the factors which influence the final shape of legislation. Certainly, there is at least one recent decided case in which a more thorough understanding of how drafting is influenced by Parliamentary procedure could have saved a lot of people a lot of trouble[1]; and the same may be true of other aspects of the process.

---

[1] See *Friends of the Earth v Secretary of State for Business, Enterprise and Regulatory Reform* [2008] EWHC 2518 (Admin).

2 AVAILABLE LITERATURE

As already explained, I am assuming in writing this book that my reader is already familiar with the basic technical details of how Government and Parliament work; and so I have tried to avoid boring the reader and wasting paper by reinventing a number of already published wheels.

Since, however, some readers may be less familiar than others with the way the system works, and may therefore find that they need a little technical background in order to be able to follow some of my descriptions or to disagree with my opinions from a position of strength, this chapter provides a brief cross-reference to some of the most obvious places to go to find detailed technical descriptions.

Renton Report

Although rather out of date in some respects, in many respects *The Preparation of Legislation*[1] is timeless. So far as I am aware, no more penetrating and thorough analysis of the practical issues surrounding the preparation of legislation in the United Kingdom has been carried out before or since, and provided the reader remains aware that some of the description may have been overtaken by events, there is no doubt that the report will be compelling and enlightening reading for anyone who wants to understand the basic realities and tensions underlying the whole business of legislating.

Hansard Society Report

The Renton Committee was established by Government to conduct a careful and thorough review of the whole field of legislation, and it was given the time and resources that it needed for that purpose. It is hard

---

[1] *Report of a Committee Appointed by the Lord President of the Council*, Chairman, the Rt Hon Sir David Renton (later Lord Renton), May 1975, Cmnd.6053.

to imagine a Government today having the patience for an exercise of that kind. The production of a relatively recent follow-up to *Renton* was initiated by a non-Government body, the Hansard Society, and its 1993 report *Making the Law: The Report of the Hansard Society Commission on the Legislative Process* provided an important update on many of the fundamental issues raised in *Renton*. Although it is in turn now rather outdated, it is still important reading on a number of perennial issues.

Erskine May

Erskine May's *Treatise on the Law, Privileges, Proceedings and Usage of Parliament*[2] is often referred to as the "Bible" of Parliamentary procedure; the analogy is a good one, since the two works share a combination of undisputable authority with occasional unfathomability. Anyone who needs a blow-by-blow account of the procedures of Parliament in passing legislation will need to make *Erskine May* their starting point.

In on the Act

The workings of the Office of the Parliamentary Counsel in particular and the civil service more generally as they were in the early twentieth century are lovingly and graphically described in *In on the Act*.[3] That is a purely personal account, and most of the system described in it has changed beyond recognition. But it remains one of the best descriptions of the workings of the "old-style" civil service, and anyone who has a love for the process of law-making will find the book emotionally and intellectually satisfying.

Guide to Legislative Procedures

For many years the Cabinet Office's Guide to Legislative Procedures was a Government manual, classified for authorised use only, which

---

[2] A new edition was expected to be published shortly when this book went to press.

[3] Sir Harold S Kent GCB QC DCL, *Memoirs of a Lawmaker*, (Macmillan, 1979).

was designed to be read and used by Bill teams in Departments to help them to navigate what might be the unfamiliar waters of preparing a Bill and taking it through Parliament. It is a particular benefit of the modern movement towards openness in Government that this resource has now been declassified and is made freely available on the internet website of the Cabinet Office.

Although this work has existed for many years, its classified status meant that even many people with great expertise in legislation remained unaware of its existence, and a number have been fairly slow to find out about it since its declassification. It is an important resource both because of the level of practical detail to which it descends on issues of the Government's preparation of legislation, but also because in addition to its descriptive value it is a work of authority, as Government Departments are required to follow the procedures that it lays down. So it does not only report what happens, but provides background to the constraints and requirements subject to which those involved in producing legislation work.

The work needs to be read with a certain degree of care; despite a rolling programme of revision some of it falls out of date from time to time, and it has always contained a certain amount of material that might be described as the triumph of hope over experience. So although it is not to be relied upon entirely or without question, it remains a largely authoritative and wholly interesting guide to the technicalities of Bills.

Craies on Legislation

A relatively short and hopefully reasonably accurate overview of the legislative process will be found in *Craies on Legislation*,[4] Part 2.

Annual debates

As long as Lords Renton and Simon of Glaisdale were active participants in the House of Lords, there was a series of annual debates in that House based around a motion of a general nature to do with

---

[4] By the present author, 9th edn (London: Sweet and Maxwell, 2008).

the quality of legislation. Although normally taken as "dinner-hour" business and not attracting either the largest of turnouts or anything in the way of media attention, these were often extremely enlightening occasions for those who did take the trouble to attend and participate. I briefed Ministers for a number of these in the 1990s, and learned a lot about how senior Parliamentarians see the legislative process—anyone who wants something a bit less purely descriptive than the works referred to above, but that gives a feel for some of the more controversial issues in the legislative process, would do well to consult the *Hansard* reports of those debates.

SECTION 2
PEOPLE

3 OVERVIEW—MANY HANDS, OR TOO MANY COOKS?

Whose law?

Who is most directly responsible for the precise content of Acts of Parliament?

The short answer to this question is that it depends whom you believe.

To listen to some Ministers speaking to their Bills during their Parliamentary stages one could be forgiven for imagining that they have been personally and solely responsible for every single word of the draft. After the event too, Ministers sometimes speak of Bills for which they were responsible as though they lovingly crafted every single sentence. One hears media interviews with politicians or former politicians who speak blithely about "when I wrote the such and such Bill" as if they had not seen its contents for the first time, if at all, five minutes before rising at the Despatch Box to defend it.

In fact, of course, on most Bills the involvement of Ministers in even the details of policy, and still more in the details of drafting, is occasional and peripheral. A Bill that is of mostly administrative or technical interest, particularly if lengthy and complex, is likely to be developed with very little reference to Ministers at all; but even in the case of sensitive or highly political Bills where Ministers are directly involved at various stages in matters of policy and technical detail, they will have been assisted, in the case of a Bill of any size at all, by at least 20 or 30 civil servants, at least four or five Departmental lawyers, and two Parliamentary Counsel, each of whom probably thinks that he or she also had something to do with the process of writing the Bill. To say nothing of the peripheral involvement of perhaps as many as a couple of hundred civil servants from start to finish on a Bill of serious complexity; and not to mention the fact that the Department is likely to have consulted a number of outside interests, possibly including lawyers or other professionals whose websites may record their involvement in "drafting" the such and such Bill.

Members of Parliament and peers who speak on a particular amendment in the course of a Bill's passage may claim afterwards to have "been involved in" the drafting of the Bill; and the claim will have more or less substance depending on the circumstances of the case. A member or peer who has actually had an amendment accepted by the Minister, may feel entitled to claim to have "drafted parts of" the Bill, while even if an amendment was rejected but a later Government amendment arguably addressed the same or a similar point, a claim to have been "involved in the drafting" may be thought justifiable.

The result of all this is that, particularly for a high-profile and successful Act, the number of people who claim to have drafted it or contributed to its drafting, with greater or lesser degrees of justification, sometimes significantly exceeds the number who actually had any real influence on it, or at least on its precise language. There are some Acts in particular where if a single word had been contributed by each one of the lawyers, politicians or civil servants who tell their clients or friends that they had some responsibility for drafting the Act, the Act would have been several times its actual length.

By contrast, if listening to all the people who claim to have been involved in drafting certain Bills might lead one to believe that a very large number of cooks had been spoiling the broth, on other Bills, or at least on particular provisions in Bills that cause controversy, it is hard to believe that anybody actually wrote them at all. The Minister either denies or attempts to deny having been particularly involved in choosing the wording, or without denying it gives the general impression of never having seen it before; and nobody else seems particularly anxious to claim credit or to accept blame for the wording either.[1]

The reality is that for almost every Bill a large cast of actors are responsible to a greater or lesser extent not just for the broad social

---

[1] On one Bill which I drafted a provision was inserted in accordance with direct instructions at a time when it was not particularly controversial; between the drafting of the Bill and its consideration in Committee in the House of Commons the provision became distinctly controversial; when the objections to it were put to the Minister his response was that "nobody said that the draftsman is perfect"! This story serves vividly to illustrate the temptation in politics to blame whoever is furthest away, which in the case of Departmental meetings and Parliamentary proceedings on Bills is most often the drafter—the only problem is that occasionally he or she reads minutes or *Hansard*!

policy but for the precise language itself. Even for a Bill of apparently small political significance, it would be a mistake to assume that the language has been entirely chosen by a single drafter or even by the civil servants on their own. Equally, however, even with a Bill of considerable political significance it is a mistake to assume that Ministers rather than civil servants have been responsible for a particular choice of words, appearances notwithstanding. A relatively small or technical detail that the reader of a statute might assume was of insufficient political significance to have been considered at Ministerial level may in fact have been the subject of considerable high-level discussion for constituency or other reasons which will not be apparent from the context of the Act and which may not have been adverted to expressly during Parliamentary proceedings. A Minister's personal attention can be drawn to relatively small matters in a number of ways, many of which have nothing to do with the fundamental legal policy or intended application of a particular Act. On the other hand, one might assume that the language of a Bill of fundamental constitutional importance will have been discussed during the drafting process with Ministers and their closest advisers in great detail. Although that would have been the case decades ago, it is decreasingly the case now.

Certainly, the courts would be unjustified in assuming that the more important a provision appears to be the more likely it is that its precise form of words was chosen by politically responsible and accountable individuals rather than by unaccountable civil servants.

Parliament's role

In theory, of course, a Bill is dissected and its language examined forensically during proceedings in Parliament, particularly in Committee in each House where the Bill is notionally examined clause by clause. In reality, that almost never happens to a degree that would justify the courts in assuming that the precise choice of language, as contrasted with its overall policy and legal tenor, was the final reflection of the legislative intention as expressed by Parliamentarians.[2]

---

[2] Of course, everybody understands that when the courts search for "the legislative intention" they are not pretending that it is either possible or desirable

To begin with, proceedings in Committee generally run out of time long before even every fundamental provision of a Bill has been examined in detail. That may be because of a formal limit on the time available, taking the form of a programme motion or guillotine motion in the House of Commons; but even where there is no formal limit on the time available in the House of Commons, and even in the House of Lords where formal curbs on proceedings are unknown, the reality is that the Business Managers of the main parties even in the House of Lords agree informally how much time is to be allotted to each part of the Bill before the House, as a result of which proceedings may suddenly accelerate at one or more intermediate points, leaving important[3] and complex provisions virtually unconsidered.

Even where there is plenty of time for proceedings in Committee, that does not mean that the House will necessarily have seriously scrutinised the precise choice of language. It may have done, and it is common for opposition parties to put down a series of amendments designed to probe the significance of language used by the drafter. It is common for those amendments to be debated and for the Minister to agree to take an issue away and to invite the drafter to accommodate the point by producing a Government amendment with different wording. So there will be instances where the precise choice of language is indeed that of Parliament as a whole, and in those cases the admissibility of *Hansard* to show the care with which the language is chosen will have a particular resonance.[4] But taken as a proportion of words on the statute book, those cases are rare.

In other cases, however, the very importance of the provision is

---

to try to get inside the minds of the particular Members of Parliament and peers who happened to be responsible for, or interested in, the stages of that particular Bill. As to what is meant by the term, I discuss some of the decided cases and offer some conclusions in "The Nature of Legislative Intention and Its Implications for Legislative Drafting" (2006), *Statute Law Review* 27(1) 15–28.

[3] That is to say important for the people who are going to have to live with the Act, make it work and abide by its provisions; but not necessarily important for or interesting to politicians.

[4] See further Ch.30.

what stops its language being discussed in particular detail: a Bill of fundamental constitutional importance will be sent to a Committee of the Whole House in the House of Commons, where time is at a sufficient premium for it to be likely to be expended on Clause Stand Part debates dealing with the principle of each clause, rather than on forensic examination of the precise language. That may be compensated for in the House of Lords where there is less pressure on time in Committee of the Whole House; but the House of Lords tends to have its own set of priorities for determining what is particularly important and what is not, and there may well be other aspects of the Bill which seem more pressing to them when the Bill reaches them, rather than simply making up "lost ground" for the Commons.

How the system works at its best

When everybody with a part to play in the preparation of an Act knows what their role is, and has an appreciation and understanding of everybody else's role, the system works at its best; and a very effective best it is. It is when individual players misunderstand their own role, or try to interfere with other people's, that things start to go wrong.

The Minister with a certain amount of legal experience who fancies himself or herself as an amateur drafter, is likely not only to do violence to the execution of the Act but also to neglect his or her proper role in determining the policy. Similarly, when the drafter becomes a frustrated politician and tries to influence the policy more than is justified by his or her understanding of the issues, the result is likely to be not merely an affront to democratic accountability, but simply bad law.

That does not mean that the different players are not entitled to have views on how other people are performing their roles, or to make suggestions as to how they could perform them better. Every self-respecting professional values the opinion of others and particularly welcomes the refreshment of an objective view. A Minister who knows that he or she is not a lawyer, or an expert in how legislation operates, may make a tentative suggestion that succeeds in finding a solution where all the "experts" have failed. And the drafter who stresses that the policy is not for him or her to decide, but from the sidelines of the political impasse offers a tentative solution that cunningly snakes

between all the problems, will often also have a significant success.[5]
The key to both these situations is that the player interferes in other
people's roles with an appropriate degree of humility, consciously
offering an outsider's opinion to be taken and evaluated as such.

Understanding how the system works

The purpose of the following Chapters is to go into a certain amount
of detail about the precise nature of the proper role of each of the
many actors in the process of constructing legislation.

As well as being, hopefully, of academic interest, a practical understanding of precisely who has been responsible for what aspects of the
preparation of legislation, and how their different contributions will
have been made, could be of assistance in construing legislation.

For example, those involved in making decisions about the practical
application of the rules of Parliamentary procedure in connection with
the passage of Bills can have a distinct influence on the shape of the
final Act. But because neither practitioners in general nor most of the
judiciary appear to have a firm grasp on the impact of Parliamentary
procedure, they can be misled into attributing a legislative significance
to material that has a purely procedural explanation. Perhaps the best
example of this in recent times is the case of *R. (on the application
of Friends of the Earth) v Secretary of State for Business, Enterprise
and Regulatory Reform* [6] That case concerned the extent to which

---

[5] One of my most exciting and enjoyable experiences in drafting a Bill of
particular political importance was that of sitting between the Secretary of State
responsible for the Bill and the Opposition front-bench spokeswoman on the
Officials' Bench in the corridor "behind the Speaker's Chair", trying various
drafting solutions on each of them in turn, until after several minutes we finally
found an approach that satisfied all the different political considerations that
each of them had to keep in mind. That was a classic example of the drafter's
objectivity—perhaps better described as constructive ignorance—that enabled
me to come up with an endless series of suggestions, untrammelled by prejudging
the political reality, while the politicians kept themselves strictly away from technical considerations and concentrated on making their expert judgments about
what was likely to be politically acceptable to the different interests involved.

[6] [2008] EWHC 2518 (Admin).

a particular provision should be construed as imposing obligations on the Secretary of State, whereas in reality the entire provision was only a "sink clause" inserted for Parliamentary procedural purposes. Happily, the court was referred to an explanation of the intent—or rather lack of intent—of the provision in question, and construed it accordingly; but there must be other instances in which provisions of all kinds that were inserted, or fashioned, for purely procedural reasons are given an inappropriately substantive construction.

More generally, however, one sometimes sees judges speculating about what was or was not likely to have been in the mind of the drafter of a particular provision, in circumstances where one knows that it is extremely unlikely that anybody involved in the drafting of the Bill as a whole (including the drafter) gave more than three and a half seconds' consideration, if that, to the fashioning of that particular provision.[7] Again, the judiciary increasingly frequently analyse the form of a particular provision by reference to the stated policy intentions, or background policy documents, relating to a particular Bill: although they are of course entitled, and indeed obliged, to give a contextual construction to the legislation, a better understanding of the reality of how that provision was actually composed might sometimes lead them to lower their expectations of the extent to which each technical provision was in fact influenced by a broad understanding of the underlying policy. In more general terms, an appreciation of the circumstances in which different kinds of legislation come to be drafted, and the constraints within which they are prepared, might influence the judiciary in determining how ready they should be to assume that Parliament, or the drafter, or both, have simply made a mistake.[8]

In other words, anything that helps judicial and other readers to

---

[7] It may, for example, have survived unnoticed from an early draft having been rendered inept by changes in the meantime; or it may have been imported from another context with no time or inclination to examine whether each of its details was fit for translation to the new context (see further Ch.27).

[8] There is evidence that the courts are becoming both more ready to accept that a provision may simply be a mistake and that it lies within their power to correct it; see further Ch.28.

sharpen their understanding of the practicalities of legislation will hopefully make it easier for them to understand and apply it. It may also be of use for people who want to understand and influence the political processes by which legislation is formed, to know more about the reality of the role of each of the many kinds of person involved.

4 PARLIAMENTARY COUNSEL

Introduction

The shortest answer to the question of "Whose job is it to write Acts of Parliament" is that it is the exclusive province of Parliamentary Counsel. Like most short answers, this is superficially helpful, but not the whole story. Nevertheless, it is appropriate to start with the role of Parliamentary Counsel, which, simply speaking, is to write[1] the Bill for each Act of Parliament, to write amendments that are made to the Bill during its Parliamentary passage, and to advise Ministers and their Departments on matters of Parliamentary procedure.

A good deal has been written over the years about the role of Parliamentary Counsel and how they work. More or less accurate descriptions will be found in each of the following places: the *Renton Report*[2]; the *Hansard Society Report*[3]; and *Drafting Legislation and the*

---

[1] It is common to describe this process as "drafting" rather than "writing". In one sense, the term "drafting" is helpful, because it emphasises the fact that the qualifications and status of the civil servants who produce legislation do not fit them to do more than produce a draft for consideration and approval by substantive experts and accountable politicians. In practice, however, too often the word is used in almost the opposite sense, to attribute some kind of mystical status to the provisions that have been "drafted" by Parliamentary Counsel, as though drafting were somehow a more significant process than mere writing, and as though a "draft" deserves to be approached with reverence merely because of its name. When I very much wanted Departments to approach my drafts with constructive aggression and to knock them about without constraint born of any presumption that I actually knew what I was doing, I tended to describe them as "preliminary sketches"—sometimes that seemed to produce the intended result, but not always.

[2] See Ch.5.

[3] See Ch.5.

Parliamentary Counsel Office.[4] *Craies on Legislation* also offers some thoughts on particular drafting issues.[5] There are also a number of articles that have been written over the years about the Parliamentary Counsel Office and its inhabitants.[6] This chapter therefore concentrates on providing information and comments of a kind that are not, so far as I know, readily available elsewhere.

The Office of the Parliamentary Counsel

No attempt has been made to give a thorough insider's account of the process by which primary legislation is prepared since *In on the Act*[7] was published by Sir Harold Kent in 1979. That is a delightfully personal account of life in the Office of the Parliamentary Counsel, replete with anecdote and family context. It exudes affection both for the Office and for the majority of its inhabitants. The Office has changed beyond recognition since the times covered by *In on the Act*, and looks set to change beyond recognition again in the next few years.

Origins of the Office

The Office of the Parliamentary Counsel was established by Treasury Minute in 1869, ostensibly in an attempt to enhance consistency in the drafting of Acts of Parliament, but possibly in reality in order to save money. Before the establishment of the Office, Acts were mostly sent out for drafting by barristers in private practice with some knowledge of the relevant area of law; and one can well believe that establishing a central unit of salaried civil servants would have been expected to save the Exchequer money overall; one can equally well believe that its actual result was nothing of the kind.

---

[4] House of Commons Library, Standard Note: SN/PC/3756, as updated September 22, 2005.

[5] See Chs 5 and 8; see also section 3 of this book.

[6] See, for example, "Their Word is Law. Parliamentary Counsel and Creative Policy Analysis", (2009) *Public Law* October, pp.790–811.

[7] Sir Harold S Kent GCB QC DCL, *Memoirs of a Lawmaker*, (Macmillan, 1979).

Structure of the Office

The Office still exists, although it has changed in size and nature very considerably over the years. For many years, however, the essential system was a fairly simple constant: the instructions for each Bill, on arrival from the relevant Government Department, were assigned to a senior Counsel, who drafted the Bill with the support of one, or sometimes two, junior colleagues.

The grades of professional drafter within the Office start with Assistant Parliamentary Counsel, and proceeded through Senior Assistant and Deputy until one arrived at Parliamentary Counsel ("full Counsel"). Traditionally, the key distinction was between Senior Assistant Counsel and Deputy: promotion to the latter grade always marked the transition from being what used to be graphically described as the back legs of the pantomime horse into the front legs. While promotion from Assistant to Senior Assistant, and from Deputy to full Counsel, were marks of confidence and esteem, and carried a small increase of salary, neither involved any fundamental change in function. Full Counsel was always regarded as the career grade: and at least in the last couple of decades a typical rate of progress through the Office has been four or five years as Assistant, the same as Senior Assistant, and the same, or maybe a little bit more, as Deputy.

With the exception of the Finance Bill team, which has always been overseen by a full Counsel of considerable experience and aptitude, with anywhere between three and five juniors to help him or her, almost all the other teams were pairings, with the occasional troika occasioned by circumstance. The result of this was that a new drafter's training primarily consisted of sitting with eight senior Counsel in turn, watching how each of them drafted, and becoming increasingly self-reliant during the process. Training was achieved not by attending courses or reading sterile manuals, but by a constant flow of observation and discussion of each other's work. It was possibly one of the most intensive and effective training programmes in the world; and it was certainly, at least in my case, the most enjoyable and enriching professional experience it is possible to imagine.

This structure has now been changed, with the Office being divided into a smaller number of larger groups. Each is to be overseen by a full

Counsel, who will be ultimately responsible for all the work produced by the group, and for the professional development of each person within it.

It is not impossible that this could be made to work in a manner that will be effective, although necessarily different from that which has flourished for the last few decades. It is unlikely, however, to produce the same kind of intensity of professional relationship that has previously existed between senior and devil,[8] with a single senior being solely responsible for the training and development of each junior.

Expansion of the Office

For very many years it was recognised that the Office was under-staffed, and that the lack of capacity within the Office was one of the main reasons, if not the main reason, why legislation could not be drafted more slowly and with more care. The issue was raised as early as in the course of the *Renton Report*. More recently, a former Minister in charge of Business Management as Leader of the House of Commons, Robin Cook, wrote as follows:

> "Geoffrey Bowman, the new First Parliamentary Counsel, came round to present a very intelligent paper on how we expand the numbers of the Parliamentary Draftsmen. It is an extraordinary, but little known truth, that the real bottleneck on Government legislation is not the Commons, nor even the House of Lords. It is the brute fact that there are fewer than fifty Parliamentary Draftsmen working for the Government. They each have a pos-itively Stakhanovite commitment to their job and in the past Session we got one Bill published in time only by its draftsmen sitting up through the night putting the finishing touches to it. But if we are going to improve the quality of the legislation, and if I am going to succeed in getting Bills published in draft, we

---

[8] The traditional term for the junior in a team, reflecting the fact that most of the early members of the Office came from the Bar, where devil is the colloquial term for a junior working with a senior.

simply have to increase the capacity of the team. We resolved that I will minute the Prime Minister on Geoffrey's proposal to increase its capacity by a quarter over the next three years."[9]

In reality, a program to expand the capacity of the Office had already begun by that time; but it was certainly continued after that point with considerable success. By the early part of 2010 there were 15 "full" Parliamentary Counsel, and a similar number in each of the three junior grades, deputy Parliamentary Counsel, senior assistant, and assistant.

In 2010 however, it was decided to reduce the number of Counsel, and as part of the government's spending cuts, the most senior grade in the Office, of which about fifteen were in post of the beginning of 2010, was reduced to five.

How powerful are Counsel?

In principle, the wording of an Act is entirely a matter for the senior Counsel to whom the Bill has been assigned. And in very many cases this principle adequately expresses the reality. The vast majority of provisions in the vast majority of Bills are not particularly controversial; or even if their substance is controversial, their precise form is not.

Departmental lawyers are taught to instruct Counsel by reference to prose descriptions of what is to be achieved and not by proffering drafts; and by and large Counsel enforce this demarcation of roles very strictly, for good reason. Departmental lawyers should be and generally are experts in the area of law on which they advise, and Counsel should always defer to them on questions of the wider legal picture in that area. Counsel are experts in how legislation works and is applied, and the process of law-making works best when these distinct areas of expertise are mutually respected.

Indeed, apart from technical knowledge about and experience of the operation and application of legislation, the only other added-value

---

[9] Robin Cook, *The Point of Departure* (Simon and Schuster, 2003), pp.210–211.

which Counsel bring to the process is by providing an opportunity for critical analysis of the policy as developed by the time it reaches the stage of instructions to Parliamentary Counsel: very often, this analysis reveals that the policy is less clearly developed than had been imagined, or has undesirable side-effects that had not been noticed. When the process works as it should, a dialogue of analysis and recon-struction ensues that brings the policy gradually to an appropriately sharp focus.

As a general approximation, it is probably fair to say that in the course of this process something over 99 per cent of the language of the statute book is chosen entirely by Parliamentary Counsel. Not even one word in every hundred is likely to be specifically discussed by the Department or any of its Ministers or to be questioned in the course of the Bill's passage; and the number of cases in which the lan-guage will be changed at the instance of anyone other than Counsel will be even fewer. Of course, a considerable number of provisions will be discussed between Counsel and the Department (although often fewer than one might think) or questioned in Parliament; but it is generally the effect of the provision that is questioned, and the choice of language is left to Counsel.[10]

How much influence do Counsel have?

It will be seen from what I say above that the personal influence of the senior drafter on an Act is potentially immense. At the end of the day, almost every word of the Act has been personally chosen by him or her, or by someone working under his or her supervision. Personal preference therefore influences stylistic choices that permeate the final

---

[10] The House of Commons even has a rule that an amendment in Committee that is "merely verbal", in the sense of not changing the legal effect of the pro-vision, will not in general be selected by the Chair for debate; the rule is, how-ever, applied less rigorously nowadays than was once the case, and was never without its exceptions. When it is applied, however, the House Authorities—as to whom see further Ch.9—are unlikely to wish to act except on the advice of Parliamentary Counsel that the effect of the amendment would be nugatory; so once again it is Counsel's word that is likely to be determinative.

product. Although there is inevitably a certain amount of homogeneity in drafting style, the more innovative and extreme exponents of the art leave their mark on each and every Act that they write. One of my former assistants telephoned a few years after he had ceased to work for me to ask me to explain something on an Act that I had drafted a year or two previously: by way of introduction he explained that he had no need to ask the clerks to let him know who had drafted that Act, because he had instantly recognised my peculiarly staccato style.[11]

It is, of course, going to be rare for people to recognise individual drafters' personal style in Acts, and there will be few if any people outside the Office of the Parliamentary Counsel who are in a position to do so. But the fact that there are personal styles, and that they leave a deep imprint on the face of the statute book, perhaps needs to be more widely recognised than it is. In particular, when a judge is invited to wrestle with the potential implications of minor differences between two provisions in two different Acts, perhaps his or her first question ought to be "who wrote each of them, and to what extent do the differences merely reflect different stylistic preferences?" Of course, in extreme cases the judges are already capable of working out for themselves that differences of form reflect differences of style and not differences of substance.[12] But perhaps judges need to be readier to apply a similar reasoning when comparing Acts of the same period; or even when comparing provisions in different parts of the same Act, since it is common practice for different Parts to be assigned to different senior Parliamentary Counsel.

As to how much influence a drafter has on questions of substance

---

[11] To this day, I have carefully refrained from inquiring or considering whether this was intended as a compliment or the reverse.

[12] See, for example, the following observation of Lord Woolf CJ in *R.v V (Attorney General for Northern Ireland's Reference)* [2005] UKHL 35 at [43]: ". . . techniques in drafting of section 3 of the [Terrorism Act 2000] and section 19(3) of the 1973 Act differ. Section 3(1) of the 2000 Act is drafted more succinctly and more clearly than its predecessor. It is in a crisper, more contemporary style. However, there is no reason to think that the difference in style means that it should be interpreted in any different way from its predecessor in the 1973 Act . . .".

and presentation, this depends on a combination of factors: the
Counsel's personality and how much he or she wants to influence
the process; the attitude of the Departmental lawyers and administrators on the particular Bill; and, sometimes, on the willingness of
individual Ministers to listen to advice.[13] Some Counsel are more
naturally self-effacing than others, or more inclined to trust their own
judgment as to how an Act should work; and there are some Acts
where the substance may make even a normally modest drafter feel
that he or she knows as much or more about how the provisions
ought to work as anyone on the Bill team; while there are other Acts
that are so supremely technical and specialist that even a usually self-
confident operator is likely to feel little inclined to dictate on matters
of substance.

Should Counsel be identified?

The fact that in some circumstances Counsel can have a profound
influence on the precise wording of legislation in a way that determines substance and not merely form naturally leads one to wonder
whether judges, practitioners and the public ought to be able to discover for themselves who was the author of each Act that they are
construing. The principal Minister in charge of the Act is a matter of
public record. Any influence exerted on the drafting by back-benchers
through the tabling of successful amendments will also be a matter of
public record.[14] But the person who has exerted the most influence on
the precise shape of the Act is invisible to the public.

There are, of course, reasons of principle behind this invisibility,
and, like most reasons of principle, they are probably rather less compelling in practice than they appear in theory. The anonymity of the
civil service has already been eroded to a significant extent by the
greater willingness of Ministers to seek to evade personal responsibility through the identification of individual officials responsible
for particular decisions. When Ministers attend Select Committees

---

[13] As to which see further Chs 6 and 12.
[14] Although it will not always be publicly recorded who or what encouraged
them to move the amendment—as to which see further Ch.8.

of either House of Parliament they are routinely attended by officials who speak directly in answering questions put to them; and civil servants routinely attend Select Committees and answer questions even when not attended by Ministers. The public are therefore already able to identify which officials are responsible for a range of activities and decisions within government. One wonders whether any harm would be done were the public also able to identify which drafter was responsible for the precise form of a particular Act: there are, after all, few decisions taken by officials alone that can have a greater impact on society.

Many of the objections that might be advanced to this suggestion are in fact points of practicality rather than principle, and could be met by a practical solution. For example, if the aim were to protect individual drafters from being subjected to criticism or interrogation about particular Acts, that could easily be avoided by having the drafter of each Act recorded not by name but by a number assigned within the Parliamentary Counsel Office. That would lead to partial anonymity: judges and practitioners would not be able to attribute a particular Act to a named individual, but they would be assisted in a comparison of different Acts by knowing whether or not they had the same senior drafter.

But for my part I wonder whether any harm would be done by allowing Counsel to be identified with their Acts by name. It already happens to some extent, and appears to cause no harm. When I joined the Parliamentary Counsel Office it was suggested to me by a senior Counsel that as a rule it was better not to tell people outside the Office what Bills one was working on, principally to avoid being questioned on matters of policy that were confidential and to risk saying more than one ought without having meant to. I never heard this formalised as a general rule, however, and I saw it being honoured much more in the breach than in the observance: there was no serious attempt to hide different people's involvement in different Bills, and Counsel with particular functions, such as the drafter in charge of the Finance Bill, would frequently give talks both inside and outside Government about their present role. For my part, I tended to apply the rule when I was involved in Bills of particular political importance or sensitivity, or when I was dealing with classified material, and not otherwise. In any event, this rule is mostly relevant while a Bill is in progress, and except for Bills involving the most continuingly sensitive kinds of material it becomes pretty much irrelevant after Royal Assent.

As to possible abuses of a drafter's being formally identified with his or her work, as one would expect, the courts have resisted invitations to have regard to the drafter's opinions about what his or her work was intended to mean: clearly, that falls on the wrong side of the line between considering useful background material and allowing the Government machine to have a "second bite at the cherry".[15] That need not, however, mean that the court should prevent itself from drawing inferences about construction having identified the drafter of a particular measure, that being a process distinct from giving any special status to the stated intentions of the drafter, except insofar as they can be deduced from the language that he or she chose to use.

Should Counsel be less individualistic?

Identifying Counsel is one possible answer to the potentially misleading result of having different styles employed in the production of the statute book. Another answer is to try to eliminate differences in style and to standardise drafting approaches.

There are two objections to this approach: first, that it is impossible; secondly, that it is undesirable.

By using manuals of drafting, and by frequent diktat from senior members of the Office, one could stamp out a great deal of the innovation which is the lifeblood of legislative drafting. But even having done that, one would probably find that one had eliminated the good, without having eliminated the bad. Drafting is not and cannot be a precise science. As long as human beings are used for the drafting of legislation,[16] their personality will imprint itself. Standardisation

---

[15] See further *Craies on Legislation*, 9th edn, Ch.27.

[16] The use of computers for all or part of the process is regularly proposed: while I was working with the First Parliamentary Counsel in the early 1990s one person in particular with impressive academic and commercial credentials, came to see us with an advanced proposal for a taxonomic-based computer programme that could write laws with consistency and precision. We welcomed him warmly, gave him piles of useful material, invited him to go away

could be achieved at the margins, in relation to common form provisions such as the manner of introducing Schedules, or the manner of providing for the extent of Acts. But differences in style of those provisions are in any event the most unlikely to mislead the reader, or to be the subject of attempts by professional lawyers to argue for substantive differences based on what were in fact mere differences of stylistic preference. As soon as one comes to the more serious and substantive propositions, standardisation of form ceases to be a practicable option, and attempting it will succeed only in producing more stilted, less clear and less easily understood legislation. Drafters are at their best, and therefore produce clearest and simplest law, when their choice of language is constrained only by answering the question "how can I best present the material in front of me?", each in their own way.[17]

In the final analysis, legislative drafting is not a precise science that can be performed by robots or other machines, but a form of technical art that is best performed by people actuated by artistic creativity, and constrained and informed by technical knowledge and an understanding of the purpose of law and the manner of its application. If you destroy or over-discipline the artist in the good legislative drafter, you remove the ability to function effectively.

The nature of Counsel

Much has been written about the nature of and training for the role of Parliamentary Counsel.[18] I am not going to go over old ground and provide a lot of technical information here. I do, however, want to offer a few observations about the nature of Parliamentary Counsel as people, and here seems as good a place as any.

---

and produce anything he liked by way of showing us in his own time what his machine could do, and never heard from him again. I also attended conferences of computer scientists at which the same ideas were discussed, again with intense academic interest and no practical results.

[17] I discuss this issue in greater length in Ch.27.

[18] See, for example, the *Renton Report* and the *Hansard Society Report* (see Ch.2).

Parliamentary Counsel have something of a reputation within Whitehall for individuality and even eccentricity; or, at least, they had such a reputation until recently. This is not a matter of mere chance. The task of writing legislation requires a peculiar combination of skills, and is best performed in a slightly peculiar way. For one thing, it is important to realise that the action of drafting legislation is in reality two separate actions, each of which in some way pulls in a different direction, but which require for reasons of practicality to be performed at one and the same time. The first and most important thing that the legislative drafter is doing, is making the law: the second thing that the legislative drafter is doing is communicating the law that he or she is making. It is very easy to forget that these are two distinct processes, but an understanding of each of them is essential for the making of effective law. So, for example, because we are making the law we have to use technical legal concepts that have a precise technical legal result. On the other hand, however, because we are also communicating the law that we are making, we have so far as possible to use language that the target audience is reasonably likely to be able to understand. It will readily be seen that these two objectives are capable of creating a tension.

In order to achieve these two tasks effectively, and to combine them with as little tension as possible, the legislative drafter has to combine the ability to analyse the policy and determine an effective precise technical legal solution, with the ability to present that solution in a relatively clear and simple form. The result is that the legislative drafter requires to be in essence, as I say above, a technical artist: he or she has to have all the pedantry of a supremely analytical lawyer, combined with the creativity of an artist who is not satisfied until the material has been presented in the most satisfactory way. This is an unusual combination, and results in an unusual kind of personality: so if people are not already somewhat eccentric by the time they reach the Office of the Parliamentary Counsel, they are certainly likely to become so after they have been there for some time, if they have any kind of aptitude for the job.

The appreciation that legislative drafting is actually two jobs rolled into one—law-making and communicating—is important if the drafter is to have a proper respect for both parts of the job. One needs to appreciate that when a Bill becomes an Act of Parliament, the law has been created, with rights and duties that immediately have the potential to affect real people in real ways. Arguably, one cannot overdo the respect one shows to that part of the job which involves making the law. The rule of law, which is the essence of our Parliamentary democracy, depends on everybody treating the law with respect, and nobody thinking that they own the law, or are entitled to play with it, more than anybody else.

The result is that a good Parliamentary drafter is punctilious in the extreme, completely without fear, and totally dedicated to the rule of law.

I can best give an example of the extremes of all three of these matters to which an aptitude for Parliamentary drafting may lead one, by describing an incident which occurred at the outset of my legislative drafting career, while I was still in the Lord Chancellor's Department. After I had been there for a couple of years I was involved in the preparation of an Order which dealt with a relatively trivial and technical matter in the context of civil enforcement. After the Order had gone up to the Lord Chancellor for signature, with an appropriate covering submission, it emerged that there was a small policy mistake reflected in the draft that had been presented. Administrative colleagues were anxious to correct the mistake and instructed me to produce a new draft and to submit it for signature in place of the old. The only problem was that on enquiry it emerged that the Lord Chancellor had already signed the original draft. The draft had, however, not yet left his desk, and everybody seemed to think that the appropriate solution was to ask his private secretary to retrieve it, throw it in the bin, and submit the new draft for signature.

At this point, however, the applied pedantry that showed the latent drafter within me came to the surface and suggested a problem. The Lord Chancellor had power under the relevant Act to make the law by signing a draft: the act of signature was the formality that created the new law, in much the same way as the act of giving Royal Assent to a Bill converts it into actual law. The Lord Chancellor could also revoke an Order, relying on implied powers under the Interpretation Act 1978, by making another Order in due form. He had, however, no power to revoke the law that he had validly and formally made, simply by throwing a piece of paper into the bin. The matter was argued out at considerable length and with the involvement of a number of different administrators and lawyers within the Department: on the one side there was considerable frustration at the apparent pig-headed pedantry that was likely to put everybody to a great deal of trouble that could be avoided simply by discarding a piece of paper that almost nobody knew about; on the other side there was a realisation that exercising delegated power to make law is a rather serious process, that involves and invokes powers that go beyond the individuals involved. Lawyers should never make objections for their own sake, and they should never invoke legal technicality when it runs contrary to common sense: but lawyers and administrators alike should show a profound respect for the law, and recognise that the most convenient and practical option is not always that which is the most lawful.

It was for reasons of this kind that for some time my entry on one of the Government internal websites described me as being responsible for "applied pedantry". Similarly, when it became the fashion for Government notepaper to carry meaningless slogans by way of self-congratulation at the top or bottom, for some time my letters went out with a small footer at the bottom saying "Parliamentary Counsel—we aim to displease". Although I felt compelled to discontinue both of these when a sufficient number of the wrong people discovered them, I still feel that they neatly summarise the original attitude and purpose of Parliamentary Counsel and, to a considerable extent, the civil service as it was intended to operate after the reforms based on the Northcote-Trevelyan report of 1854. Saying "yes" to elected politicians or anybody else is easy and popular but adds nothing to the process: when one starts from the position that "no" is probably the correct answer, and one requires to be persuaded otherwise but is careful to be open to all reasonable persuasion, one brings a genuine added value to the process and enhances the quality and reliability of the result.

Conclusion

Parliamentary Counsel are in one sense the principal influence on and control over the precise wording of Acts of Parliament. Although it is necessarily an unscientific statement, I estimate that well in excess of 99 per cent of the words of the statute book not only are chosen by Counsel but are not seriously questioned or tested by anyone else before enactment. More than that, for a variety of practical reasons it would not be possible to have all the effects and implications of each Counsel's work checked by Ministers or their officials. Although in theory every clause is scrutinised by Parliament, the scrutiny does not in practice extend to every provision in any meaningful way, and is carried out by persons who, and in circumstances which, make it impossible for the technicalities of each provision to be tested against the substantive policy to which it is designed to give effect.

Technically, however, Counsel are mere civil servants, without even policy responsibility within the Departmental structure, let alone the kind of accountable power or responsibility which vests only in Ministers of the elected Government.

This makes Counsel something of an anomaly, to account for or deal with which two approaches are possible.

First, one can appoint only people who are thought to be sufficiently trustworthy to exercise, in effect, a good deal of power and influence, and then train them carefully over a period of several years until each of them is capable of exercising that power and influence in a proper way. That was the traditional approach.

Alternatively, one can seek to constrain the power and influence of each Counsel by an increasingly rigid system of management and control. That appears to be the modern trend; but it is not likely to achieve the purpose of making the minute technicalities of each Counsel's draft more accountable or better scrutinised.

5 DEPARTMENTAL LAWYERS

The role

Put simply, the role of a Departmental lawyer forming part of a Bill team in a Department is to take the policy instructions of Ministers and administrative clients and to turn them into effective instructions to Parliamentary Counsel. That is true both at the pre-introduction stage when the Bill is being drafted, and during the passage of the Bill through Parliament as and when amendments are required.

It is certainly true that instructions to Parliamentary Counsel are produced almost exclusively by Departmental lawyers.[1] But to portray those lawyers as nothing more than go-betweens turning administrative policy into legal instructions would be greatly to understate both the importance of Departmental lawyers in the entire process and their potential contribution to the precise shape of the final product.

Demarcation

In essence, the distinction between the role of Parliamentary Counsel and the role of Departmental lawyers is as follows. Departmental lawyers are meant to be experts in the substantive area of law on which they are responsible for advising their Departmental administrative clients; as well as that, they are taken to have a basic understanding of the way in which legislation works, and in many cases their understanding of that process is a great deal more than basic. Parliamentary Counsel, on the other hand, are meant to be experts in the way in which legislation works as well as experienced in the manner and art of its construction; but they are not to be relied upon as having any

---

[1] The principal exception is in the case of Finance Bills, where (normally excellent) instructions are generally received from officials of Her Majesty's Revenue and Customs or the Treasury, drawing on their lawyers for any support that they may need where technical issues arise.

knowledge at all of the substantive area of law with which they are dealing.

It will readily be seen from this that the process involves a delicate balance of roles and expertise, and it is in practice relatively rare for that balance to be struck absolutely correctly. Indeed many people find it bizarre that the system appears to pride itself on having laws drafted by ignoramuses, that is to say people who are neither expected nor encouraged to become experts in the area of law on which they are operating. It is certainly difficult to justify the process as a matter of theory. In practice, however, at its best it appears to work remarkably well, and Departmental lawyers and others who have had an opportunity to work with some of the more effective Parliamentary Counsel are generally enthusiastic supporters of their role. Equally, with the very occasional exception, where legislation is given out to be drafted by private lawyers who are experts in a particular substantive area but have no specialist expertise or experience in legislative drafting, the result is rarely a notable success, and is very often a complete failure.

Quality

Departmental lawyers vary enormously in quality and aptitude.

At one end of the spectrum, there are many lawyers in the Government Legal Service whose knowledge both of their particular area of law and of public law and legislation in general is superb, and who provide an unbeatable service to their administrative clients.

It is worth noting that the Government Legal Service often gets better than it deserves in the way of recruits, since although it does not try to match the salaries of the City law firms, it is still able to encourage a considerable stream of refugees from the City based on its comparatively favourable attitude towards the work-life balance in general, and family commitments in particular. It is therefore probably not a calumny to observe that a majority of lawyers in the Government Legal Service, and a very strong majority of the really impressive lawyers in the Government Legal Service, are women, who have left the City or a similar environment for the public service on the understanding that they are more likely to be able to combine a successful public service legal career with family responsibilities. But there are, of course, also a large number of men who leave because they wish to work in an environment that they find more congenial than the City.

One might speculate that this ability of the public service to attract higher quality lawyers than it in one sense deserves—or that it at any rate pays for—is already considerably less than it once was, and may be about to diminish further for two reasons. First, in recent years the City and other commercial legal environments have become increasingly sensitive to the need to offer an appropriate work-life balance in order to attract and retain good staff. Of course, some private practice lawyers in highly pressured environments reading this last sentence might be likely to greet it with a hollow groan: but, first, they are a smaller percentage of private practice lawyers than they might have been even ten years ago, and, secondly, they are unlikely to be allowed the leisure to read a book of this kind at all.

The other reason why the refugee rate from the City to Government Legal Service is declining and is likely to decline further is that the civil service no longer offers the security and other attractive working conditions for which it was once famous: in particular, lower salary levels were regularly accepted in the context of extremely attractive pension, insurance and compensation arrangements, which the Government has now altered significantly.[2]

Whether or not the public service will continue to be able to attract high calibre lawyers by virtue of the conditions of service that it offers, it is without doubt true that for many years it has been able to do so, and as a result the Government Legal Service contains some of the most powerful and acute legal minds in the country. On the other hand, unhappily, at the other end of the spectrum it is also true that there are lawyers who are attracted to Government service as a relatively soft option, not because they are particularly interested in or suited to public service law or because they have a particular commitment to public service principles. To put it bluntly, in fact, there have always been a number of lawyers in public service who one suspects were attracted to it purely because they knew they were not up to

---

[2] In particular the Superannuation Act 2010 was enacted to influence negotiations with the civil service trade unions as a result of which wide-ranging changes were made to the compensation scheme.

the rigours of private practice; and there have always been a small number of lawyers who, even if that were not their motivation for joining the public service, have certainly managed to continue despite a level of performance that would not have been tolerated outside.

The result is that Parliamentary Counsel may find themselves at the start of a new Bill project faced with anything between an experienced and extremely able lawyer who really knows how to get the best out of the system, and a less than competent lawyer who is almost immediately out of his or her depth. The importance of the difference for the resulting product cannot be overstated. When the system works at its best, Parliamentary Counsel can feel himself or herself almost like a musical instrument being played upon by an experienced and able Departmental lawyer, who knows how to get the best out of the drafter in the context of the area of law, and policy objectives, in which the Departmental lawyer is an expert. There is a synthesis or synergy which produces legislation at its best, and of which it is enormously enjoyable to be a part. In contrast, Departmental lawyers who know that they are not up to the job become an increasingly frustrated and frustrating barrier to the entire process: although it is sometimes possible to minimise their disruptive influence by dealing with the policy clients direct so far as possible, that technique has its own dangers and limitations.[3]

So although it is Parliamentary Counsel who is ultimately responsible for the final shape of a Bill, it is no exaggeration to say that the quality of the Departmental lawyer instructing him or her makes or breaks the entire enterprise. As I said in the entry for "drafting of legislation" in *The New Oxford Companion to the Law*[4]—

"It is essential, however, for the drafter to be instructed by those with expert knowledge of the precise purpose for which the provisions are required, and to be fully briefed on the political, social and legal context. The drafter can temper the legislation by reference to its purpose and context; but drafting expertise can no more compensate for inherent weakness in the instructions or

---

[3] In particular, one rapidly loses the very objectivity that is Counsel's most valuable asset in analysing and implementing Departmental policy.

[4] Oxford University Press, 2008.

underlying policy than building expertise can remedy inherent faults of design."

The wide variety of skills and aptitudes within the Government Legal Service was less critical to the production of Bills years ago when Bill work was highly prized within Departments, and senior Government lawyers were very careful about both which juniors they allowed to become involved in it, and the degree of responsibility they were allowed to take. When one looks back through files dealing with the preparation of Bills 50 years ago or more, it is immediately apparent that the work of providing instructions to Parliamentary Counsel was not regarded as something that would simply be given to any junior and inexperienced lawyer to handle without significant supervision. It is true that promising juniors might be allowed to prove themselves by instructing on a Bill for the first time: but they would be supervised with a considerable degree of care, and Parliamentary Counsel would be likely to be consulted from time to time about how well they were doing their job. Nowadays, however, particularly on a Bill that is perceived to be of relatively little importance, it is far from uncommon to find oneself being instructed by a junior lawyer who has never run a Bill before, without anything very rigorous in the way of apparent supervision. That need not necessarily be a problem, if the lawyer is extremely fast at learning, willing to learn, and fundamentally able; but that is not always the case.

Despite the creativity at the heart of what Parliamentary Counsel do, ultimately they are to some extent machines, although hopefully intelligent and self-willed machines, that require to be driven by Departmental lawyers. If the driver does not fully understand the capabilities of the engine and how it requires to be handled, it is not possible to produce a creditable result.

It therefore can on occasion happen that the Departmental lawyer responsible for instructing Counsel on a Bill is simply not up to the job. When that unhappy situation arises one of two possibilities follows. The Departmental lawyer may simply throw up his or her hands and abandon the attempt to serve a useful function, becoming a mere post box for transmitting policy instructions from clients to Counsel. It is nowadays less unusual than it once was or than it should be for Counsel to receive the administrative clients' policy instructions simply forwarded to them. The result of that is that it becomes necessary for

Counsel to bridge the gap and become more involved than would normally be the case in, in effect, creating the legal policy out of the social
policy; apart from the fact that Counsel is not adequately equipped
to perform this function, lacking expertise in the relevant substantive
area, it also causes Counsel to lose the objectivity and distance that is
crucial to the successful performance of his or her role.

The alternative approach of the occasional inadequate Departmental
solicitor is to try to bluff their way through it, by pretending to understand more than they do of what is going on. Provided Counsel spots
this early enough this can be tedious but not disastrous. Where, however, the Departmental lawyer is unhelpfully plausible, a good deal
of fundamentally unsound material may make its way into the Bill
before anybody has spotted that it has not been thoroughly checked
as fit for purpose by a substantive legal expert.

Drafting suggestions

Occasionally even highly competent Departmental lawyers will try to
shorten the process by suggesting to Counsel what words he or she
should use, particularly if there is what appears to the lawyer to be
a suitable precedent in a similar context. If Counsel is doing his or
her job effectively, which is not always the case, an attempt of this
kind will serve only to lengthen the process, because the only proper
response to it is to demand fresh instructions.

In the old days it was part of the folklore of Departmental lawyers that in preparing instructions for Parliamentary Counsel one
must remember two things: first, never to offer a draft; and, secondly, always to send two copies of every letter (one for the principal
Counsel and one for his or her devil[5]).

The second rule, which when I joined the civil service in 1988 was
almost the only thing that many Departmental lawyers knew about
Parliamentary Counsel, died with the advent of email. The first rule
is alive and kicking, although it is enforced differently today than was
once the case. An instructing solicitor sending a suggested draft to Sir

---

[5] A term for junior assistant, borrowed from the Bar from which most Counsel
came when the Office was first established, although solicitors now preponderate.

Granville Ram[6] or Harold Chorley[7] would have had the instructions returned with a terse demand for a fresh set, possibly accompanied by some unsolicited personal advice. On the first occasion when I observed this rule being breached I was working for Euan Sutherland, a man who combined rare skill as a Parliamentary draftsman with almost unbelievable patience and consideration for others. Instead of getting angry as others might have done even then, and as his forebears certainly would have done, he replied to the Department in measured but firm terms, to the effect that a draft is rarely an effective method of communicating policy, and in any case if the drafter only has a suggested draft to look at, he or she has no way of testing it for efficacy against a statement of policy intention. As well as being humane, this struck me at the time as being a particularly well-expressed statement of the purpose behind the rule, and I have followed it in my dealings with Departments ever since.

But all these considerations apply only at the formative stage of a draft. Once the policy has been expressed effectively and an initial draft produced, any sensible Counsel will welcome and encourage drafting comments from the instructing Department. Apart from the fact that each additional pair of eyes to check a draft is an additional potential opportunity to discover defects and suggest solutions, it is at this point that the instructing solicitor's special familiarity with the area of law or social policy in which the draft is operating may enable him or her to discover inaccuracies or infelicities, or to suggest particularly desirable approaches.

There are still Parliamentary Counsel who appear to resent drafting suggestions even at this stage in the process as incursions upon their territory.

How much influence do Departmental lawyers have on the shape of the Act?

I have already argued that the quality of the instructing solicitor is an essential factor in determining the quality of the overall result.

---

[6] First Parliamentary Counsel (born 1885; died 1952).

[7] Second Parliamentary Counsel (born 1912; died 1990).

The question now arises of the degree of conscious influence a Departmental lawyer is expected and able to exert over the precise details of the drafting, beyond the kind of suggestions as to style and execution discussed above. To put it a slightly different way, how much power do Departmental lawyers have?

To a large extent the answer is, as much as they want to have. If instructions descend to a very precise level of detail, together with well-argued explanations of the approach that is being suggested, a wise Parliamentary Counsel, having prodded and tested once or twice to check that the quality of the material is sound, will allow himself or herself to follow fairly passively in the direction in which they are being led. So, for example, if in my drafting instructions the instructing solicitor mentioned to me that a particular precedent for what I was being asked to do could be found in a particular earlier Act, I would pay little attention to that observation and might, depending on the other pressures on my time, not even trouble to look at the precedent indicated.[8] But if, in the course of instructions that were generally well put together, I was invited to follow a particular form or approach found elsewhere in the statute book, and a good substantive case was made out in the instructions for the suggested consistency, I would certainly take that suggestion seriously, and would only reject it for a good reason—which might be one of style or substance—which I would certainly point out to, and expect to discuss with, my instructing solicitor if he or she so wished.

From some Departmental lawyers one gets the feeling that they regard themselves as being as much part-authors of the final product as are Parliamentary Counsel, and when in the good hands of a competent instructing solicitor that is a feeling which Parliamentary Counsel should share and respect, and indeed relish. In other cases, one feels that the Departmental lawyer is completely uninterested in how the product turns out, and sees the Bill simply as another file in their in-tray to be got rid of as quickly and as painlessly as possible. Although that attitude is very often likely to be excusable on the grounds that Departmental lawyers are frequently under enormous

---

[8] It being a fundamental principle of good drafting that there is, really, no such thing as a precedent—see further Ch.27.

pressure, with a great number of other matters to occupy their time in addition to any legislative burden, it does not contribute to the quality of legislation.

So to answer the question simply, a good Departmental lawyer both wants to have and does have a considerable degree of influence over the precise shape of legislation; while a bad Departmental lawyer neither has nor aspires to any significant influence at all.

6 MINISTERS

Introduction

Ministers are both more important and less important than they and others often think. This chapter examines different aspects of that assertion as it applies to the preparation and final shape of primary legislation.

The main role

In describing the proper role of Ministers in relation to the preparation of legislation I am reminded of a comment that Sir Humphrey Appleby makes to Jim Hacker in *Yes, Prime Minister* shortly after the latter has been appointed Prime Minister. The new Prime Minister is surprised to find his diary rather less full than he remembers from when he was a mere Departmental Minister, and his new Cabinet Secretary gently explains to him that far from being the busiest job in the world, Prime Minister is potentially one of the least busy jobs in the world. To paraphrase, he explains that while there are one or two things that a Prime Minister *should* do, and any number of things that a Prime Minister *may* do, there is almost nothing that a Prime Minister *must* do.

In a similar vein, the only thing that a Minister *must* do in relation to a Bill for which he or she is responsible, is take the blame.

Even that has become rather less fashionable than it once was. On one Bill for which I was responsible, a new criminal offence was to be created, subject to a number of exceptions. I was specifically asked to frame one of the exceptions so as to exclude an activity for which an exemption had been particularly sought by interested pressure groups. I did as I was instructed and it was consequently impossible to read the exemption as including that group. Politics moved on, however, as they so often do, and by the time the Bill came to be scrutinised in Committee in the House of Commons, the Government's policy was no longer to resist the pressure to have this particular activity included in the exemption. When the provision in question was reached, an amendment was proposed by a back-bencher that would have brought the activity within the exemption, and the proposer asked why the Government had not achieved that themselves. The Minister replied to the effect that nobody ever said that Parliamentary Counsel were perfect! Unhappily for him, I had some loyal friends on the Departmental Bill team who were outraged at this and invited me to look at the *Hansard* record. Having done so, I wrote a formal complaint to the Minister's Private Secretary, reminding him that it was contrary to the rules of the civil service as I had always understood them for Ministers to seek to evade their personal responsibility by blaming individual civil servants; I also referred him to the passage in my instructions which unequivocally required me to achieve the result set out in the Bill. The end of the story was a four-page handwritten letter from the junior Minister concerned, apologising, recognising the fault and thanking me effusively for my work on the Bill.

Although instances of this kind are rare, they do seem to be increasing if anything, not necessarily as regards Bills particularly but certainly as regards piercing the corporate veil of the civil service and seeking to identify and blame individuals. And if a similar incident had arisen towards the end of my time in the civil service, I am far from sure that I would have dared to complain in the same way, or that my complaint would have been treated in the very decent and honourable way that it was.

Despite this, the fundamental role of the Minister in relation to a Bill remains that of front-man or front-woman. The traditional bargain between Ministers and the civil service is that the former are entitled to take all the credit for work which nobody seriously attributes to them, provided that they are also prepared to take blame for mistakes that are equally clearly not really theirs.

Good Ministers continue to take this seriously and apply it rigorously. Relatively recently I was asked to provide briefing for a junior Minister in the House of Lords on an amendment when the Government had, in effect, made up their minds to resist the House of Lords whatever they did, and if necessary to reverse their decision when the Bill returned to the House of Commons. It being a technical matter I drafted the briefing myself, at the request of the

Departmental lawyer. Timing been rather tight, I printed it out myself and brought it down to the House of Lords, and handed a copy to the Minister just as she was about to go in for the sitting at which the amendment would be proposed. She looked at it, and turned to me aghast: "if I read this out, I'll be shot down in flames", she said. "Flames are fine Minister" I said; "in you go!". Rather to the surprise of her civil servants, the Minister simply said "okay", trotted back into the House of Lords, read out the brief, and was promptly defeated by a large majority. That happened to suit the Government on that occasion, there being no substantive compromise that they were prepared to offer, and a straight defeat, followed by reversal in the House of Commons, being the neatest and most honest solution.

On a much earlier occasion soon after I joined the civil service in 1988, I was part of a team briefing one of the Law Officers on a Bill for which they were partly responsible. A particular House of Lords amendment from the Opposition was marked in the Law Officer's brief as "resist". The Law Officer found it difficult to extract from the civil servants briefing him any clear ground for resisting the amendment. On being appealed to, I said that so far as I could see there wasn't one. The Law Officer beamed happily and said that was fine; he had no objection to "batting on a sticky wicket", but he did need to know the way the land lay before he started. He then went happily into bat against the amendment and produced an extraordinarily convincing and authoritative sounding defence of the Government's position, which was so plausibly weighty that the amendment was duly withdrawn.

It therefore remains the fact that the principal role of the Minister is to present the Government's case, and to receive comments, questions, approbation and criticism. The most active part of this role is the function of correspondence, and occasional meetings, with outside voices that wish to be heard on particular aspects of the Bill. As the front-man or front-woman, the Minister is of crucial importance in facilitating dialogue between the Government and outside expertise and interests. When this function is performed well, it seriously enhances the content of the Bill, since instead of simply resisting all attempts to influence the content of the Bill on principle, a process of correspondence and mediation can be used to distil from the objections and criticism any points that can be accommodated without risk to the underlying policy. Without doubt the best performer of this kind of Ministerial function that I came across in my 22 years in the civil service was Lady Ashton, who for a number of years was a junior, and then senior, Minister in the House of Lords, where her unceasing willingness to undertake to hold meetings, write letters, read letters, and generally introduce everybody to everybody else, brought her universal admiration from peers on all sides of the House, greatly improved the quality of Bills on which she worked, and left her civil servants exhausted, sometimes exasperated, but with a general feeling of being competently led (by no means as common a feeling as one would like it to be).

Policy decisions

If one were to ask the average Minister what his or her key role was in connection with the preparation of a Bill, only some of them would reply that their principal function was to serve as front-man or front-woman. The others would assert that their principal function was to determine questions of policy.

It is of course undoubtedly the preserve of politicians to determine policy, and that is as true of Bills before Parliament as it is of any other government operation. However, it deserves a number of qualifications.

First, what amounts to policy? Politicians generally tend to classify issues during the progress of a Bill according to whether they are substantive policy or "technical". To give an example, almost everybody would regard a question of cross-border extent of a Bill about drainage management as being a technical issue; unless it happens to be of particular political sensitivity for some reason, it is the kind of detail that would be left to be determined by Parliamentary Counsel, in consultation with the Departmental lawyer. Provisions or amendments about it would be described by the Minister as "merely technical" and would generally be accepted as such without question by back-benchers in both Houses. But if you are a developer operating close to the border between Scotland and England and planning to lay the foundations for a major construction site, whether or not you are going to be required to comply with new and expensive regulations about sustainable drainage that generally apply only to England is not a boring technicality at all; it may be crucial to the financial viability of the project that you have in mind.

Since the classification of a Bill's provisions into substantive and technical is more or less inevitable, because clearly a Minister cannot look personally at every provision of the Bill and this seems a serviceable method of determining what does and does not need to be looked at, a lawyer or judge looking at a provision of an Act can assume that the more "technical" it appears to be, the less likely it is that its language was chosen with precision by deliberate policy decision of a Minister. Of course, that does not make it any less the authoritative voice of the legislature, and Ministers are bound to defend it both in Parliament and afterwards. But it is a factor perhaps worth bearing in mind during the search for the "legislative intention".

Involvement in the drafting

To what extent do Ministers actually get involved in the drafting of legislation? To listen to some Ministers at the Despatch Box one would think that they were responsible for the entirety of the Bill from start to finish, and that while they might have had some advice from civil servants in general and Parliamentary Counsel in particular, the choice of wording was theirs and theirs alone. Other Ministers give the impression (which may or may not be accurate) that they have only just seen the Bill for the first time and that most of its contents and all of its wording are really nothing to do with them.

Indeed, on occasions it is convenient and proper for Ministers to assert that the choice of language has not been theirs and is not therefore their responsibility.[1] Sometimes Ministers go further than that, and seek to blame the drafter for having made decisions of style that are in fact decisions of policy.[2]

The reality in the case of most Bills falls, as one would expect, somewhere between these two extremes. In a Bill which is mostly of technical interest with perhaps one or two provisions of political sensitivity, it would be normal to expect that the Minister would not see anything

---

[1] See, for example, fn.11 below.
[2] See p.46 above.

of the wording of most of the clauses until a very late stage; and he or she would not normally be expected to take any interest in, or make any comment on, the drafting of the majority of the Bill. There are likely to be, however, one or two provisions in any Bill that reflect a particular political sensitivity, where the precise nature of the wording is likely to determine whether the political objective is achieved satisfactorily or not. That is precisely the kind of case where the drafter with his or her technical expertise is not going to be capable of giving a warranty to the Minister that the political objective has been realised, without some input from political advisers or the Minister himself or herself.

A good example would be the provision in the Flood and Water Management Act 2010 about drainage rates for certain kinds of community buildings. Coming as it does in a Bill that largely reflects technical concerns, that provision seems aimed at particular social issues likely to have been raised with Ministers or back-benchers in correspondence; it would be reasonable to assume, therefore, that Ministers would have taken some significant interest in the precise wording of the provision. Indeed, when one looks at the debate in Public Bill Committee, one finds that the tenor of the Minister's description suggests a considerable personal interest in the phrasing of the clause concerned.

For many courts, the concept of the search for the intention of the legislature is based on a search into the mind of, if not the actual Minister tasked with taking the Bill through Parliament, nevertheless an "objective Minister".[3] That is based on an illusion that Ministers have actually turned their minds to the phrasing of each clause in the Bill. Although courts have become increasingly ready to assume that the drafter of the Bill has made a mistake,[4] they also need to become increasingly aware that very often the choice of words has been not only entirely that of the drafter, but also made by him or her more or less at random and without any particular political or legal consideration. The very search for consistency which led to the establishment of

---

[3] See "The Nature of Legislative Intention and Its Implications for Legislative Drafting", (2006) 27(1) *Statute Law Review* 15–28.

[4] See Ch.28.

a single Office of Parliamentary Counsel means that while the drafter is likely to be an expert in the way in which legislation works, and while he or she may be aiming to achieve a degree of consistency between the provision at hand and other similar provisions appearing to attempt to achieve similar results elsewhere in the statute book, the drafter rarely has very great expertise in the subject matter at hand. So without necessarily needing to invoke the rule against absurdity,[5] where a particular word or expression appears surprising or unexpectedly significant, the court might as a general rule do better to attribute it to infelicity owing to the inexperience of the drafter in that particular subject area, than to deliberate decision on behalf of the notional policy-maker.

The best proof that a Minister has turned his or her mind to whether or not a particular expression should be used will be evidence from *Hansard* that an alternative was suggested by way of opposition amendment, and was rejected. Even here, of course, the rejection may have been based on technical advice from Parliamentary Counsel, or on the legal or policy advice from other civil servants, and may have received only scant attention from the Minister himself or herself.[6] Again, the tenor of *Hansard* itself may give some indication as to the degree to which the Minister has actually focused on the wording in that case. It is arguable that, technical ambiguity aside, this is one respect in which the courts should permit themselves to look at *Hansard*, under a variant of the rule in *Pepper v Hart*, to establish the legislative content behind a particular provision. The more Ministers can be shown to have focused publicly on the wording used and defended it against possible alternatives, the greater significance the courts can reasonably be asked to give to their choice of language: where, however, there is no evidence to suggest that Ministers focused particularly on the choice of words, courts should be mindful of the reality that the choice may have been made by someone who was not particularly well-versed in the legal or social policy underlying the intention of the Bill.

That does not, of course, mean that a purposive construction

---

[5] As to which see *Craies on Legislation,* 9th edn, Ch.19.1.

[6] Or may have been based on political or even personal considerations that had nothing to do with the technical effect of the Bill.

should be allowed to contradict the clear natural meaning of the words used;[7] but it might justify the courts in requiring less weighty evidence to depart from one possible construction of a phrase in favour of another.

Senior and junior Ministers

A surprising number of people, even within Government, fail to appreciate the hierarchy of Ministerial positions. Most Whitehall Departments these days have as many as four or five Ministers, and in some cases even more. The senior Departmental Minister is generally a Secretary of State; the next rank down is that of Minister of State; and the most junior rank is called Parliamentary Under-Secretary.[8]

Discussions between Departmental officials, or between them and

---

[7] For discussion of the myths and realities of literal and purposive construction, see *Craies on Legislation*, 9th edn, Ch.18.

[8] The position of Parliamentary Private Secretary is not a Ministerial office at all. It is an unpaid and entirely unofficial position occupied in the House of Commons by a Member who, in effect, volunteers to assist a Minister in his Parliamentary duties; perhaps to serve an aspiration to a formal Ministerial post in due course. Parliamentary Private Secretaries routinely sit behind the Minister during important debates, and fetch and carry notes to and from the civil servants in the Officials' Box. Whether they are also accorded a share of less menial duties, such as participation in discussions with civil servants over formation of policy, depends on each senior Minister, as well as on circumstances. The media routinely, and possibly deliberately, fail to understand that Parliamentary Private Secretary is not a post in the Government in any formal sense; so resignations of Parliamentary Private Secretaries over points of principle are frequently reported as resignations of Ministers. Although a slightly strange creation, the post can be of particular use in the context of Parliamentary procedure; on one occasion, I was able effectively to circumvent the rule of Parliamentary procedure according to which Ministers may not table an amendment to their own amendment (despite the occasional tactical advantages that this could confer) by having an amendment tabled by a Parliamentary Private Secretary: the House Authorities could not object, since the Parliamentary Private Secretary is not formally part of the Government, but it gave the necessary signal to back-benchers that the amendment to the amendment was in effect being recommended by Government.

others, routinely refer to "the Minister" as if a single Minister were involved in decisions relating to the Bill. In reality, however, for all but the most important Bills, the Minister in charge of the Bill will be a junior Minister within the Department. There may well therefore be decisions which he or she considers to be "above their pay grade" and which require to be referred above. By the same token, an adverse decision of the Minister in charge of the Bill is not necessarily the end of the story: a disappointed outside interest, or even a disappointed Government official, may find a way to have the matter brought to the attention of the senior Minister in charge of the Department, as a result of which the junior Minister's decision may be reversed.

On one occasion, I was asked to draft a provision for a Bill in such a way as to resolve a dispute between two Ministers, one within the Department and one outside. The Departmental Minister very much wanted something to appear in the Bill. The other Minister considered it unnecessary to legislate at all on the matter concerned, and felt that legislation, being unnecessary, was therefore inappropriate.[9] I managed to contrive a legislative proposition that had a semblance of effectiveness, sufficient (just) to make it impossible for the outside Minister to deny that it had any legislative effect. So far so good; but once the draft had been approved by the junior Departmental Minister for whom I was working, it was, as a matter of routine, circulated to her Ministerial colleagues. The senior Minister in charge of the Department saw it and was not happy: we were all, junior Minister, other Ministers, Departmental officials, Departmental lawyers and me, summoned to a meeting with the senior Minister. In the end, the draft was approved, upon my explaining that I considered the senior Departmental Minister to be behaving extremely ungratefully, since I had "managed to turn his meaningless advertising programme into a genuine legislative proposition that not even [the other Minister outside the Department] could object to". While jaws dropped all around the table, the senior Minister concerned simply smiled benignly, denied ingratitude and agreed to proceed with the draft as prepared.

So it is important for outside interests, and indeed civil servants,

---

[9] In which respect that Minister was correct—see further p.55.

when dealing with Ministers to discover what rank of Minister one is dealing with, and therefore what level of decision-making is open to him or her, and what kinds or decision are likely to have to be referred to higher authority.

How much influence do Ministers have on the shape of Acts?

The obvious answer to this question is "as much as they want to have". The result is that sensible Ministers, who know their limitations and responsibilities, will try to avoid interfering with aspects of the Act that are beyond their understanding, but will not shrink from accepting and exercising responsibility for matters which require a political decision.

There are obvious political advantages to Ministers in exercising proper restraint and avoiding the temptation to interfere with matters that are not properly for them. For example, it was well understood for many years that the choice of short titles for Bills was that of the drafter alone, and that, in particular, they should not be used as an opportunity for political propaganda by Governments. That understanding has become considerably eroded over the years.[10] But wherever it is adhered to it provides the Minister with an instant and conclusive defence to any suggestion that the short title is inappropriate and has been chosen for some overtly political reason.[11]

When, however, Ministers are determined to exert their fullest

---

[10] Although they appear to be proliferating, propaganda short titles are by no means a very recent phenomenon. See, for example, the Education Reform Act 1988: the short title Education Act would have been just as descriptive, there being nothing more obviously reforming in the nature of the 1988 Act than there is in any other Act that provides a major new code for a particular area of law.

[11] So, for example, the short title is chosen by the drafter of the Bill: sometimes it is discussed with the Department with principal responsibility for the Bill, and sometimes aspects of it are discussed with the House Authorities. But leaving it to the drafter enabled the Parliamentary Under Secretary in the Home Office to say of the Disqualifications Bill 1999–2000, "The title of the Bill is a matter for Parliamentary draftsmen; Ministers have not been involved in decisions of that kind." *Hansard*, HC Vol.343, col.480 (January 25, 2000).

influence, there is nothing to stop them from doing as they like. If a Minister directs the drafter to exclude particular material, or to phrase things in a particular way, the drafter has ultimately no choice but to comply. He or she can, it is true, attempt to appeal the Minister's decision within Government: in particular, either by attempting to seek a reference to a more senior Minister within the Department, or by referring a matter of legal concern to the Law Officers. But once Ministers have taken a decision as an appropriate exercise of collective responsibility, the drafter has no further resource.

To give an extreme example, it is open to Ministers to insist upon the production of an entire Act that is empty of legislative purpose, and is designed only to serve some function of political advertising. Perhaps the best example of this is the Fiscal Responsibility Act 2010. Not only is that Act entirely pointless, but it even goes to the extraordinary lengths of protesting its pointlessness, and in effect demanding that the courts treat it as a piece of political posturing and not as a piece of law.[12] The entire Act is therefore clearly an inappropriate use of legislation, and one which will make it much more difficult for Ministers to argue against the insertion of other inert and therefore potentially misleading and harmful material into other Acts.[13]

Although there are no theoretical limits on Ministers' powers in

---

[12] See s.4(2), (3): "(2) The only means of securing accountability in relation to—(a) the duties in section 1, and (b) duties imposed by orders under section 2, is that established by the provision made by or under section 3 for the making of progress reports and reports as to compliance and the duty imposed by subsection (1). (3) Accordingly, the fact that—(a) any duty in section 1, or (b) any duty imposed by an order under section 2, has not been, or will or may not be, complied with does not affect the lawfulness of anything done, or omitted to be done, by any person."

[13] It is perhaps not surprising that the other most striking recent example of an entirely pointless Act—the Anti-slavery Day Act 2010—comes in the same Session as the Fiscal Responsibility Act; although Ministers did raise questions about the appropriateness of an Act without any genuine legislative proposition within it, it is not impossible that they felt a little constrained by their own efforts in relation to fiscal responsibility from pushing that argument as strongly in resisting the Bill as they might have done otherwise.

relation to the shape of Acts,[14] since in our jurisdiction the courts do not have any general supervisory function in relation to the content of legislation, practical politics does, or can, intervene to some extent to encourage them to exercise restraint. My general tactic, during my time in the Office of Parliamentary Counsel, when faced with Ministerial interference over, for example, the short title of a Bill, was to respond along the lines that it was of course open to the Minister to instruct me as he or she thought fit, but if the Minister wished to take advantage of the ability to claim that a decision had been taken without political interference then my choice would be. . .! I was surprised by how often that tactic was effective; indeed, it very rarely failed.

On other occasions, an element of negotiation was possible. In one case a Minister took exception to the heading that I had chosen for a particular section of a Bill on the grounds, in effect, that it made its content too explicit. The Minister concerned was anxious to avoid drawing attention to the fact that a particular kind of interference with property could be carried out without a warrant. My chosen heading had included a reference to the absence of a warrant, in order to make clear the contrast with the preceding sections where a warrant was expressly required. I refused on principle to adopt a heading that deliberately concealed the effect of the section. After one or two exchanges on the matter I said that I would give effect to the request, but only on the direct orders of the Law Officers. On that occasion the threat of a reference to the Law Officers was sufficient to encourage the Minister, in effect, to back down: and we negotiated a face-saving compromise that still contained an express reference to the lack of a warrant but was sufficiently different from my original choice to enable the Minister to feel, or perhaps merely to say, that he had not been entirely worsted in the encounter.

On other occasions, however, I was less successful. Over the course of my career in the Parliamentary Counsel Office I would estimate that I referred perhaps an average of two questions to the Law Officers per calendar year, and that my objection was upheld by them in perhaps two-thirds of cases. On one occasion, however, a strong objection of

---

[14] At least subject to the limitations imposed by the Human Rights Act 1998 and the European Communities Act 1972.

mine was upheld by the Law Officers, but even so the senior Minister in charge of the Department concerned, who had a considerable amount of political influence within Cabinet at the time, overruled the combination of me and the Law Officers and elected to proceed with the provision to which we had taken exception.

In order to avoid giving a misleading impression of the process as it works generally, I feel I should add that I have a clear impression of having been more pugnacious as Parliamentary Counsel than many of my colleagues. Indeed, one of the clear and regrettable changes in the civil service generally, from which the Office of the Parliamentary Counsel has not been immune, is that civil servants are encouraged much less than they once were to stand up to Ministers and other politicians, and to fight them on even minor matters of principle. Partly because of the intervention of special advisers,[15] and partly for a range of other reasons, career civil servants are nowadays expected to show a kind of subservience and deference that was neither shown by, nor expected of, the best civil servants when I joined the civil service in 1988.

Briefing notes—who is speaking?

The whole concept of *Pepper v Hart* and the courts' permitted use of *Hansard* is predicated on the notion that when Ministers speak they are giving a considered and authoritative indication of the thinking that the Government is inviting Parliament to endorse by passing the provision concerned.[16] That theory applies both to explanations of the provisions of the Bill as it already stands, offered in the course of debate on those provisions or on non-Government proposed amendments to them, and also to explanations of proposed Government amendments.

The theory is, of course, flawed in a number of ways but, like so much else about our Parliamentary democracy, accepted for the

---

[15] See further Ch.12.

[16] As to the reliability of *Hansard* as a transcript, see further D. Greenberg, "Hansard, the Whole Hansard and Nothing But the Hansard", (2008) 124 LQR 182–185.

kernel of truth within it, because the alternative is to accept a more
practical application to politics of the chaos theory than the average
citizen's stomach can reasonably be expected to stand.

Regardless both of the essential theory and its flaws, however, since
the purpose of this book is to offer practical observations that may
broaden the courts' and other readers' understanding of the reality
behind the theories, I want to offer some thoughts about the different
ways in which Ministers are briefed on Bills, with a view to inviting
conclusions to be drawn about how much weight can be attached to
their words on different occasions and in different respects.

Traditionally, a civil service note for a Minister on a Government
clause in Committee or on a Government amendment at any stage
includes a Background Note and a Speaking Note, the latter designed
to be read out verbatim. The first point to make is that the degree
to which Ministers stick to their Speaking Notes varies according
to the nature of the Minister, the quality of the Speaking Notes and
the predictability of the debate. Broadly speaking, "good" Ministers
recognise that the notes have been carefully written by civil servants who know more than Ministers do about the complexities of
the policy, and have been checked by other civil servants who know
more about the technicalities of legislation than Ministers do, and
Ministers accordingly read the note verbatim into the record, with
such minimal variations only as are suggested by the course of the
debate. Also broadly speaking, "bad" Ministers pride themselves on
how adaptable and flexible they are to the complexities of debate, how
ingeniously they counter arguments raised during debate, how naturally and elegantly they speak for themselves, and how quickly and
thoroughly they are able to master the complexities and technicalities
of their legislation so that they come to know more about it than the
entire Bill team put together; as a result of which they move effort-
lessly from clause to clause, and from amendment to amendment,
commanding the debate with impressively plausible material which
confounds both their political opponents at the time and all readers
who try to make sense of it in the future. Between these two hypotheti-
cal extremes lie varying realities, with some Ministers inclining more
towards one extreme than the other.

In the old days, it was possible to go up to the *Hansard* Office in
either House after the end of the debate, to provide them with the

Minister's Speaking Notes and to persuade them to substitute expressions from the notes for whatever the Minister may actually have said. Quite properly, that is no longer done;[17] it is still routine for the civil servants in the Officials' Box to be asked during the course of a debate to send a copy of the Minister's notes to the *Hansard* Office, but the notes are "checked against delivery" and used only to make it easier to comprehend names and references in the Minister's speeches, rather than to substitute what he or she should have said for what he or she actually said.

That being so, there is perhaps something to be said for a system allowing the Minister's notes to be printed, and there is of course nothing to stop a Department from doing so. But Ministers are for obvious reasons reluctant to emphasise the differences between what they were advised to say and what they did say, so this is unlikely to happen.

At all stages in both Houses, the key civil servants on a Bill[18] have sufficient access to Ministers to enable them to provide additional notes during the course of debate, so as to react to points raised. The precise nature of the access varies from stage to stage and between the Houses. During Committees of the House of Commons, the four or five members of the Bill team most needed for each part of the debate are sitting literally within hand's reach of the Minister, and can therefore brief him or her endlessly and constantly. While Opposition

---

[17] See further D. Greenberg, "Hansard, the Whole Hansard and Nothing But the Hansard", (2008) 124 LQR 182–185.

[18] Including Parliamentary Counsel when he or she turns up; it used to be routine for Counsel to attend all amendable stages of debates on their Bills, but for the last few decades it has become increasingly rare for Counsel to attend Parliamentary debates at all, except on the most sensitive and controversial of Bills. Counsel ought to attend, because one cannot advise about Parliamentary procedure and the likely reception of particular approaches unless one has spent a good deal of time soaking up the feel and atmosphere of the two Chambers on different occasions. It is generally said that the pressures on Counsel's time have made it more and more difficult for them to find the time to attend Parliamentary proceedings on their Bills, but my own impression is that, although that is sometimes true, the reality is that Counsel have simply become decreasingly interested in this aspect of their work and less inclined to make time for sitting in on proceedings.

Members are speaking, the officials are scribbling away, and benevolent front-bench spokesmen and spokeswomen frequently prolong their remarks until they can see that the note responding to their questions has been produced and handed to the Minister. Needless to say, however, this kind of speed and pressure are rarely conducive to the production of the most carefully considered explanations and answers, and a fair amount of tosh is necessarily read into the record with as much gravity and plausibility as if it made sense. Until, however, Members are encouraged and enabled to give notice not merely of their amendments but also of the ideas underpinning them,[19] this unenlightening game will continue to be played with consistently unsatisfactory results. More importantly from the point of view of the courts or other readers looking through *Hansard* for elucidation of the Bill, there is no formal way of distinguishing a carefully constructed passage from the original Speaking Notes from something hastily put together from a handful of bits of paper thrust into the Minister's hand as he or she rose to respond.

In the Chamber of the House of Commons—where Second Reading, Report and Third Reading debates are routinely conducted[20]—the Officials' Box is next to the Speaker's Chair, a little behind the front-bench and extending to the back row. This accommodates as many as eight or nine officials, but whereas in the Committee rooms other officials may be just at the back of the room and therefore within a few seconds' reach if needed, the Gallery places for surplus officials in the Chamber are minutes away up flights of stairs; so there is no real prospect of someone hearing the debate from the Gallery getting downstairs in time to hand a note in to the Minister on an amendment

---

[19] Opposition amendments are very often so inscrutable that it is impossible to prepare any kind of sensible note in reaction to them in advance, and one just has to take a random guess at the point they might be getting at: of course, it would make sense in cases like this to make contact with the Opposition Member and ask their intentions, but although I have seen this done occasionally, and even done it myself once or twice, Ministers seem as a rule surprisingly disinclined to take this method of clarifying the subject of the debate in advance.

[20] And Committee of the Whole House for all or part of the most important or controversial Bills.

or in response to an intervention. The officials in the Box have more of a chance—but even here, they have to write the note and then catch the eye of an obliging Member who will take it to the Minister at the Despatch Box.[21]

In the House of Lords Chamber, the Box holds about six officials, depending upon girth, and there are four "Whips' chairs" a little further away from which officials can hear the proceedings, although they can see little. The attendants are[22] permitted to pass messages to peers, so the officials as they scribble away will try to catch the nearest attendant's eye and have him take the note to the Minister in time for use in reply to the speech during which it was written.[23] Sometimes the Minister will send a colleague to the Officials' Box to request a note on a point and carry it away for delivery to the Minister.

The result of all this is that the wisest and most experienced Ministers actually discourage the passing of notes during the debate. They take the view that briefing notes produced by way of frantic scribble against the clock are rarely worth very much, and that it is more profitable for everybody if the Minister simply replies on the points on which he or she has been properly briefed, and leaves other matters to be dealt with at a later stage. While I have impliedly criticised Ministers who think they know better than their Speaking Notes, it is also a sign of lack of self-confidence or sense when one sees Ministers, normally but not solely junior and inexperienced ones, continually signalling to the Officials' Box for note after note on points being raised in the debate. By far the better attitude is for the Minister to sit and take the debate on the chin and think about the points being raised: wherever the answer is obvious based on the briefing that the

---

[21] The most senior Ministers have Parliamentary Private Secretaries who are in attendance at most debates and one of whose functions is to carry notes from the Box to the Minister, and vice versa.

[22] Unlike in the Commons—but then the House of Lords has always been the more democratic Chamber.

[23] Sometimes the door attendant goes for a little walk into the Prince's Chamber, and officials are left waggling bits of paper over the front of the Box unable to attract another attendant's eye or the eye of any peer who wishes to admit to having seen them; it is, of course, wrong that the accuracy of the record on a particular point should depend to this extent on this kind of possibility.

Minister has already received, he or she can safely give it; and wherever the answer is not obvious he or she will do better to wait for a full and considered briefing later on. This is, however, a counsel of perfection; and the chaotic scramble continues to be the norm.

Conditions in Committee Rooms in the House of Lords are similar for these purposes to those in Commons Committee Rooms.[24]

I conclude these observations on conditions for briefing Ministers with the following thought. The courts and others when reading *Hansard*, whether under the rule in *Pepper v Hart* or otherwise, routinely say "The Minister said . . ." as if there were one process of the Minister speaking, and equal weight should be given to all pronouncements. Of course, it is difficult to see how the courts in particular could do anything else: it is hard to imagine it ever being appropriate for a judge to say:

> "The Minister said X, but I bet it wasn't in her Speaking Notes: it sounds like a hash made up at the last minute, so I will ignore it".

One of the problems of Ministerial pronouncements is that as well as being less important than some of them like to think in some respects, in other respects Ministers are more important than they realise—when they speak in a Parliamentary debate, however inconsequential or lightweight they believe and expect their remarks to be, they are taken for purposes that may affect people's lives to be speaking in a considered way on behalf of the Government, and to at least a limited extent reflecting the intention of Parliament.

My reprise of these issues therefore causes me to make two suggestions.

First, that the courts should at least permit themselves to remember that "the Minister said" may mean anything from (a) a considered statement by an expert civil servant who really knew what they were writing about, to (b) a hopeless guess made up by the Minister on the hoof because the questioner sat down before the note from

---

[24] Most Committee stages in the Lords take place as a Committee of the Whole House in the Chamber; some Bills, however, may be sent to a Committee Room—normally the Moses Room just outside the Chamber.

the Officials' Box could reach him or her, or (c) a statement mis-read by way of frantic garble from a crushed handful of last-minute scribble.

Secondly, that Ministers and civil servants should reflect on this particularly bizarre part of the legislative process with a view to helping the *Hansard* record to deserve the authority that the courts are bound to give it. On the whole, the fewer notes that are passed up to Ministers in the flow of debate the better for all concerned;[25] most matters that are not already covered in careful briefing are best left to be addressed at a later stage.

Letters to Members and peers

Which brings me to my final point on Ministerial communications: letters to Members and peers. It is already common, and I have argued that it should become more common, for Ministers to respond to points in debates at early stages by saying that they do not have the necessary information to hand but that they will write to the Member or peer. That is generally sufficient to cause Members or peers to withdraw any amendment that they have moved to probe the Government on the point, and to agree to await the Minister's reply before deciding whether to re-table the amendment at a later stage.

The principal problem with that approach is one of publicity. The question, and perhaps the Minister's first unsatisfactory attempts at a reply, will form part of the *Hansard* record of the proceedings for the Bill, and will be relied on under *Pepper v Hart* and in other ways as authoritative pronouncements. The eventual letter, however, which will probably contain the most authoritative and informative

---

[25] That would not include, or at least not to anything like the same extent, notes prepared in response to points made during a Second Reading debate, which are collected together while back-benchers make their speeches and are used by the Minister who winds up the debate; because there is generally a few hours to prepare most of these notes, they can be properly informed and reasonably carefully composed. But the nature of Second Reading compared to Committee means that these notes relatively rarely illuminate points of fine technical detail.

statement on the subject, is delivered off the radar of *Hansard* and forms no part of the official record.

It is common—although it does not always happen—for Ministers when promising to write on a point to undertake to have a copy of the letter placed in the Library of the House in which they are speaking, or sometimes in both Libraries. And irrespective of that it is normal practice for a letter on a particular point to be copied to Members or peers who have shown interest in the same point, perhaps by speaking on the amendment that raised it. In Commons Committee, moreover, it is normal for letters from the Minister to one Member in response to a point raised to be copied to all other Members of the Committee.

So arrangements are in place for giving adequate publicity to these letters for Parliamentarians. But this is yet another aspect of the legislative process that tends to forget that Parliamentarians are neither the most important nor the most permanent of the groups who need effective access to legislation and anything that affects its application and interpretation. The most important and permanent class of users of legislation is that of citizens and their advisers. At present, a citizen can ask a friendly politician to forward a promised letter from the Minister, and the request may or may not be granted. But something as capricious as that is not acceptable when dealing with what are in effect Ministerial pronouncements that may have some kind of legal effect.

What is therefore needed is some method of publicising any letter sent by a Minister in pursuance of an undertaking given in the course of a debate on a Bill, together with a method of making a formal link between the relevant passage of *Hansard* in which the undertaking was given and the letter itself. In these days of technological brilliance it should be neither expensive nor difficult to arrange for a system of this kind, and until it is provided there will remain a significant flaw in one of the most important processes that Parliament carries out.

Conclusion

Ministers are one of the oddest aspects of our (and most countries') political process. You take someone who has never been within 50 yards of a cow, and suddenly they are Secretary of State for Agriculture, making decisions that affect and control the activities of thousands of farmers. This oddity—about which one can probably say, like democracy, that it is the worst possible system except for all the alternatives—is felt perhaps most keenly in the matter of legislation. Men and women who have never exchanged a civil word with a section of an Act in their lives are suddenly responsible for proposing legislation, explaining it, giving undertakings about it, and determining its content and effect.

When Ministers acknowledge that by training and temperament they are basically ill-suited to this function, they generally end up performing it superbly. Their advisers are generally well-suited to supporting and guiding inexperienced legislators and helping them to achieve a good result, while leaving them as much freedom as they require to make the fundamental policy decisions for which they were elected.[26] It is only when Ministers begin to feel that they have acquired an expertise in the technicalities of legislation that they are prone to do more harm than good.

---

[26] Or at least for which they were appointed by others who were elected.

7 PRIVATE LAWYERS

Introduction

A glance at the website of a number of barristers in private practice or large firms of solicitors will often reveal the claim that they have been involved in the drafting of one or more pieces of legislation. These claims are often somewhat exaggerated. There are, however, occasions on which private lawyers can significantly influence the shape of legislation; and it would probably be to everyone's advantage if they were used for that purpose more often than they actually are.

Privatisation of drafting

The Government never employs non-Government lawyers to draft Acts of Parliament. From time to time suggestions are made that this would be a more efficient and effective way of having legislation drafted. The last major privatisation exercise took place in 1996, and centred around inviting non-Government barristers and solicitors to draft small parts of the annual Finance Bill. There were obvious advantages to making the experiment in the context of tax legislation: first, the annual Finance Bill is easily divided into a great many small pieces, each of which is more or less entirely discrete; secondly, the effectiveness of fiscal legislating depends possibly less than in any other context on understanding the technicalities of how legislation works, and much more on an ability to comprehend and describe complexities of fiscal policy and the accounting and other business practices to which it is to be applied. So if a privatisation exercise were going to work at all, it should have been this one: but it was a flop.[1]

---

[1] See Sir Geoffrey Bowman KCB, "Why is there a Parliamentary Counsel Office?", (2005) 26(2) *Statute Law Review*, p.81: "The real proof, however, that nobody considered the exercise a success, was that there has been no attempt to repeat it". (See also Terence Daintith and Alan Page, *The Executive and the*

68 Private lawyers

Existing opportunities for involvement

The fact that the Government does not, and should not, put its draft-ing of Bills as a general rule into the hands of private lawyers, does not mean, however, that all claims by private lawyers to have been involved in drafting an Act are necessarily untrue.

For one thing, a number of private Members' Bills are drafted by private lawyers instructed by pressure groups seeking to change the law, and although most of those fail for lack of support and time, a small number do succeed. The Government is likely to offer Parliamentary Counsel's services to "clean up" a private Member's Bill that looks likely to become an Act: but that does not always happen, and even where it does happen a considerable portion of the original drafter's efforts may well remain.

Private Members' Bills apart, there are other ways in which private lawyers may become critically involved in the drafting of a provision. On a Bill of technical complexity where points of contention arise between the Government and lawyers representing outside interests, a wise Minister is likely to invite those lawyers and their clients to hold direct talks with Departmental lawyers; or even with Parliamentary Counsel direct.

Meetings between private lawyers and Parliamentary Counsel

Meetings between private lawyers and Parliamentary Counsel are relatively rare. Rightly so, because if every Bill of significance were to be drafted in a committee of government and non-government lawyers, the structural and linguistic coherence of our Acts would be significantly diminished. On the right occasion, however, it is the only effective method of discovering exactly what it is that private interests object to about the Government's proposed provision; and once one has discovered what the objections are, more often than not it is possible to do something towards meeting them without disturb-

Constitution (Oxford: Oxford University Press, 1999. p.251.) Doubtless, as memories fade, another exercise will be mounted in due course.

ing the Government's underlying policy.[2] Although both practical considerations and reasons of principle dictate that meetings of this kind will be relatively rare, I always found them helpful and I suspect that they could profitably be used more often than they are.

That this is so can be seen from the context of Legislative Reform Orders and other subordinate legislation where a high degree of consensus is required if the project is to be successful. The procedure under which Legislative Reform Orders are enacted[3] is designed to ensure a high degree of consultation; and the political realities are such that without a high degree of consensus emerging as a result of consultation, a Legislative Reform Order is unlikely to be passed. In an exercise of that kind, therefore, the close engagement of lawyers and others with expertise in the field is going to be a practical necessity.[4] The reality is, moreover, that their involvement is not

---

[2] A good example of this would be the discussions between City of London lawyers and the Treasury on particularly technical provisions of the Bill for the Banking Act 2009, dealing with the impact on termination rights of orders under the Bill. At Third Reading of the Bill in the House of Lords, Lord Myners, Financial Services Secretary to the Treasury, said as follows: "Government Amendments 7 and 13 seek to respond to concerns which have been raised by interested parties, including at a meeting arranged between Treasury officials, Parliamentary Counsel and the City of London Law Society, which was attended by the noble Baroness, Lady Noakes. A further meeting has since taken place between tripartite officials and the City of London Law Society." *Hansard*, HL Vol.707, col.964 (February 9, 2009).

[3] See the Legislative and Regulatory Reform Act 2006.

[4] See, for example, the following passage from the Department for Business, Enterprise and Regulatory Reform's commentary on the Legislative Reform (Limited Partnerships) Order 2009: "29. We sought to contact all 33 respondents. Annex D is the basic text used for writing to them, and as a basis for speaking to them. We had five meetings involving nine respondents, as follows: Mark Blackett-Ord (Chancery Bar Association) on 26 March; BVCA on 27 March; Roderick I'Anson Banks and Simon Jelf (Partnership Counsel) on 7 April; The Scottish Rural Property Business Association, the Scottish Estates Business Group, and the Scottish Government on 21 April; Tod's Murray and Brodies, also on 21 April. We also had subsequent correspondence, by email and phone, with a number of these respondents. 30. We discussed by telephone with three respondents: the Law Society, Berwin Leighton Paisner, and

merely a tedious charade to be gone through as a condition of being allowed to exercise or influence the exercise of considerable legislative power by secondary legislation. If the consultation is approached as a genuine partnership, then what amounts to a process of negotiation with interested and knowledgeable parties, although considerably burdensome for the Department, significantly increases the quality of the resulting legislation. If that is true for secondary legislation, there is no reason in principle why it should not be true for primary legislation.

So why does the Government routinely involve private lawyers in the development of complex and technical primary legislation much less than is the case with a Legislative Reform Order? At least part of the answer is simply that they can get away with it. To a large extent, primary legislation is taken through both Houses on the basis of a Parliamentary majority, and a presumption even in the House of Lords that by and large the Government is entitled to complete its business. Although on occasions detailed negotiation may become a practical necessity, as in the case of the Banking Act 2009 discussed above, on the whole, Parliamentary tactics alone will suffice to ensure the passage of legislation. There is therefore little incentive for the Government to engage with interested parties except at a level of policy, and even then the level of engagement is sometimes cursory. Having experienced the benefits of having knowledgeable outside lawyers involved in technical issues, both on the Banking Act and in relation to other earlier measures, I would hope that the Government will become increasingly open to, in effect, sharing the process of constructing legislation.

Gillespie Macandrew. A further four respondents responded by email: Elspeth Berry, Nabarro, Osborne Clark and the Association of Pension Lawyers. 31. We are very grateful to all of those who responded to our questions in such a short timescale. As well as informing our decision that it would be worth proceeding with a limited Order this year, they provided valuable inputs into the way in which this draft Order should be framed, and helpful comments towards our consideration of the way in which we should pursue the remaining reforms." http://www.bis.gov.uk/files/file51586.pdf [accessed November 9, 2010].

Need for openness

If the Government needs to learn to be more open to the idea of
sharing the process of developing the shape and form of the law,
rather than merely consulting on underlying policy, private lawyers
also need to be capable of altering their behaviour to some extent if
they are to be a useful part of the process.

The basic problem insofar as it emerges from my experience of
dealing with private lawyers in the preparation of Bills from time to
time, is that lawyers often appear to find it difficult to explain clearly
and simply what they actually want and, more importantly, why they
actually want it. There can appear to be an obsession with the tactical
advantage of revealing no more of one's thoughts than is essential;
and if one can achieve one's desired results without actually explaining anything about the true reason for wanting it, one has scored a
particular success. This may be an approach which is effective in, and
possibly necessary for, commercial negotiations. But it is not designed
to produce clear, simple and effective law.

Even when they are not arguing the case for a particular client,
when lawyers try to influence proposals for legislation they may be
doing so either formally or informally on behalf of a group of clients
for whom they habitually act, or to further their own interests directly
or indirectly. When that is the case, they tend to behave as though
they were negotiating, rather than co-operating. Nor is this by any
means a characteristic of solicitors alone: on some occasions on which
I was involved in discussions with barristers about proposed changes
to the law, I found them just as opaque, and I sometimes thought
I could guess reasons for their opacity that had more to do with
the protection of their professional interests than with furthering the
interests of the law and the citizen.

This was not, however, by any means the inevitable position. One
instance that stands out strongly in my memory was the involvement of city lawyers and expert barristers in the preparation of the
Legislative Reform (Limited Partnerships) Order 2009. A large
number of lawyers in England and Scotland gave very generously
of their time in that process, and, so far as I could judge, in a spirit
of genuine co-operation and helpfulness. That does not mean that
none of them stood to gain by the resolution of the law; but my

general perception was that their personal professional interests were not driving or shaping their involvement as much as a public-spirited desire for clarity in a particularly complicated area. To a considerable extent, this reflects the more consensual environment of the Legislative Reform Order. But it also shows what can be done by way of co-operation between the private and public sectors in the shaping of legislation, when the will is there on both sides.

Conclusion: how much influence do private lawyers have on the shape of Acts?

In essence, the message is this: private lawyers are not experts in the drafting of legislation, and when they think they can do it entirely themselves they are generally wrong. But they certainly have a great deal to offer in the preparation of legislation, and it would be better for everybody if they were allowed to have more influence when they want to.

8 OUTSIDE INTERESTS

Whose law is it anyway?

The most important thing to note about the involvement of outside interests in the preparation of legislation, is that there is no such thing as outside interests. The expression, and equivalent expressions, are frequently used by Ministers, Departmental lawyers, Parliamentarians, Parliamentary Counsel and administrators to designate that not inconsiderable portion of the population that falls into none of those classes. They are "outside the game" that is being played out on the stage of Parliament.

But it is not a game, however much it is treated like one and sometimes appears like one. It is the process of making the law, which will always—if it be genuine law—affect people who are not in any of those classes a great deal more than it affects those who are. Law belongs to the citizens, who are therefore very much the "inside interests" to be considered during its construction.

The problem

If it is private citizens and those people who represent their interests who are to be primarily affected by legislation, one might think that they were entitled to a significant role in its construction. Although in one sense, of course, private citizens are represented in Parliament through their Members of Parliament, few people who observe practical politics in Westminster will deny that politicians enmeshed in playing the party-political game become, at least to some extent, handicapped in their ability to comprehend and represent the interests of "ordinary people". So direct involvement of some kind may be the only way to ensure that those interests are adequately represented.

There are two reasons, however, why much in the way of actual involvement is impossible or undesirable. First, simple practicalities make it impossible for individuals, or even representative groups, to be given much opportunity to influence proceedings. Secondly, and more importantly, however much one may dislike a view of the state as a benign patriarch who knows what is best for the children, there are inevitably aspects of legislation that are so complex and technical that many individuals will be unable or unwilling to play a useful part in shaping it or influencing it, however critically it may affect them personally after enactment.

The solution

For the most part this conundrum is solved by the simple but sad expedient of ignoring private individuals, and their representative interest groups, in the construction of legislation. Despite the enormous increase in the use by Government of consultation papers in recent years, and despite the emergence of a pre-legislative scrutiny procedure,[1] many important Bills pass each year without those who are going to be affected by them having much of an opportunity to influence the process.

Of course, in recent years there have been some procedural changes that give, or at least appear to give, "outside interests" a distinct role in fashioning legislation. Apart from pre-legislative scrutiny, the best example is the replacement of Standing Committees in the House of Commons, as the routine method for examining the detail of Bills, with Public Bill Committees, whose proceedings open with a number of sessions dedicated to the reception of oral evidence, including evidence submitted directly by interest groups. Other evidence can be submitted to Public Bill Committees in writing, and it is by no means unknown for oral and written evidence from outside groups to be referred to and relied upon when members of the Committee are moving or responding to amendments. The Conservative Party's manifesto for the 2010 General Election also included suggestions that there might be some kind of public session built into the proceedings for examination of Bills in Parliament; public in the sense of inviting participation by the public and not merely allowing them to listen, as presently happens.

---

[1] As to which, see Ch.15.

One must not, however, overestimate the influence that these opportunities have or are likely to have on the construction of legislation itself. By the time a Bill gets into Committee, its fundamental structure is generally more or less set in stone; and it will take something fairly devastating by way of input from outside the key political players even to persuade the Government to accept or provide for a change of wording on a relatively minor point. Even pre-legislative scrutiny takes place in the context of a completed draft Bill, where similar considerations apply, although to a slightly lesser extent.

If "outside interests" are to be able seriously to participate in the eventual shape and tone of legislation, they need to make the impression before the Bill is introduced into Parliament, and preferably before a formal draft Bill is submitted to a Parliamentary Committee for pre-legislative scrutiny. At present, whether they are given that opportunity depends entirely upon the attitude of the Departmental Bill team and the Departmental Bill Minister. In some instances Parliamentary Counsel is introduced at a very early stage in the Bill's preparation to the concept of the "stakeholders", and left in no doubt that their views are to be elicited and reflected so far as appropriate. In other cases, the Bill is put together without even anything serious in the way of consultation.

When one looks at the Cabinet Office's Guide to Legislative Procedures, one is struck by the fact that although there are references from time to time to outside interests and methods of "handling" them, despite the considerable complexity of the procedures laid out in that guide, no formal and standard structures are put in place for ensuring that outside interests have an opportunity to influence the precise form of the legislation, and not merely the underlying policy; or for ensuring that their opportunity for influence comes at a time before the structure and wording of the legislation has firmed up too much to make it reasonably easy to change it. At present, the Guide leaves this open to be taken care of according to the taste of the Departmental Bill team. That is fine when the Bill team happens to be good and sensitive to outside interests; but it is important to have best practice in this respect properly codified in the Guide so that all Bill teams will recognise the importance of implementing it.

The blackboard clause

It might, of course, be argued that it is neither necessary nor indeed
desirable for outside interests to have a say in the precise wording
of legislation. It could be argued that their role should be restricted
to being consulted on the policy; but that once the policy has been
determined by Government, the expert technicians, in the shape of
Departmental lawyers and Parliamentary Counsel, should be left to
get on with the job as they think best.

There is, of course, an element of truth in this. As I have already
said, the success of the legislative process as a whole depends on each
player recognising the strengths and weaknesses both of themselves
and of all the other players. Most individuals and most interest and
pressure groups are not experts in the construction of legislation,
and one could ask whether they are therefore likely to have anything
useful to offer to the drafting process as it develops.

The answer, however, is that they frequently will have a greater
sensitivity for the context, both legal and social, within which the
legislation will fall to be construed; and they will therefore be able to
advise on expressions that will or will not hit the right note. This can
sometimes lead to their requesting, or even insisting on, the insertion
of particular words or phrases that they believe will give the right
signals to citizens and the courts, and without which the legislation
will be perceived as lacking in some way, irrespective of the legal force
of that perception. Since all law falls to be construed within its own
context,[2] if the text of the law itself can give the right flavour and context, without readers being sent to explanatory material, the certainty
of the law is thereby enhanced.

Take, for example, s.3 of the Equality Act 2006,[3] which reads as
follows:

"The Commission shall exercise its functions under this Part
with a view to encouraging and supporting the development of
a society in which—

---

[2] See "All Trains Stop at Crewe: The Rise and Rise of Contextual
Drafting", (2005) 7 *European Journal of Law Reform* 31–46.

[3] Now overtaken by the Equality Act 2010.

(a) people's ability to achieve their potential is not limited by prejudice or discrimination,
(b) there is respect for and protection of each individual's human rights,
(c) there is respect for the dignity and worth of each individual,
(d) each individual has an equal opportunity to participate in society, and
(e) there is mutual respect between groups based on understanding and valuing of diversity and on shared respect for equality and human rights."

The wording of that section seems rather out of place in an Act of Parliament, even in the somewhat looser context of what is essentially a purpose clause.[4] It rather has the air of having been constructed by a committee, each member of which had a particular component that he or she wanted to throw into the pot. And that is pretty much how it was indeed constructed: as the Minister for Women and Equality (Meg Munn MP) said in speaking to the clause that became s.3 during the course of proceedings in Standing Committee in the House of Commons:

"As the hon. Member for Epping Forest said, clause 3 is the outcome of a full consultative policy development and significant discussion in the other place. It was shaped and developed in partnership with key equality and human rights interest groups in businesses and trade unions, and it sets out the context in which the Commission for Equality and Human Rights must exercise its duty. It does not give the Commission any powers; rather, it places its role in context. . . . The clause also gives coherence to the duties that are set out in clauses 8 and 10(1), as the hon. Member for Hornchurch said, by describing the outcomes that the Commission must encourage and support. Those outcomes will help to shape the Commission's three principal duties—equality, human rights and good relations—so that they work together and in the same direction. The

---

[4] As to which, see further Ch.29.

Commission should exercise its powers with a view to encouraging and supporting the development of a society in which prejudice or discrimination do not limit people's ability to achieve their potential. In that way, it will fulfil its remit on equality of opportunity and anti-discrimination. The Commission will be required to encourage and support a society in which all people are valued. In ensuring that everyone has an equal opportunity to participate in society, the Commission goes beyond the traditional understanding of equality and fair treatment. That links with the requirement to support good relations between groups."[5]

The section is therefore deliberately designed to satisfy the needs of different interest groups to see phrases that resonate for them in a particular way set out clearly on the face of the statute book. It does so expressly without creating separate legal rights and duties that would be barely justiciable because of the inherent vagueness of the concepts that these interest groups required to see reflected in law. Nevertheless, the fact that these concepts are referred to in the Act and not merely in explanatory material, is of enormous presentational importance to the interest groups involved, and, of course, it does have a distinct effect in law. When construing the general rights and duties under the Act the courts would be likely to give weight to the section as setting the context within which the other provisions are to be construed. The material has therefore been separated from more "black-letter" parts of the Act so as to render it harmless on account of its less than precise nature, without depriving it altogether of legal effect. (Hence the expression "blackboard clause", which derives from analogy with a teacher who provides students with their own blackboard on which they can indulge in necessary forms of self-expression, while agreeing to leave the "real" blackboard for the teacher alone!)

---

[5] *Hansard*, HC Deb Standing Committee A, col.35 (November 29, 2005).

Private Members' Bills

Outside interests have a special role to play in relation to private Members' Bills. It is rare for private Members to come up with either the subject or substance of a private Member's Bill for themselves: as a general rule, they are supplied both with the idea and the execution by one or more interest groups who are trying to have the law changed, and with whom the Member may have had a long-standing previous relationship. When this happens, the outside interest group, or more often a coalition of outside interest groups, stand in relation to the Bill and the Member in Charge of it very much as the civil service stands in relation to Government Bills. The legal and other advisers of the special interest group become the Member in Charge's Bill team. A great deal could be said about how an interest group can perform that task most effectively, but this is probably not the occasion for saying it.

How much influence do outside interests have on the shape of Acts?

As for private lawyers, often less than they think they have, or claim to have had; but also often less than they could usefully have, if the right mechanisms were in place for utilising their expertise.

On a number of occasions I found myself dealing directly with interested parties of various kinds on Bills, from pressure groups and charities to representative groups of lawyers acting for particular industries. When these were pure lobbying exercises they were rarely effective, and mostly counter-productive. My natural reaction to being persuaded to move in one textual direction without an adequate explanation of precisely what it would achieve and why, was to move either not at all or in precisely the opposite direction. It is the nature of lobbying as understood and undertaken by many people that they should reveal as little as possible of their own or their clients' actual motives, aiming to achieve as much of their desired result as they can without revealing why they want it. It is clearly the duty of Government servants to resist pressure of that kind.

On some occasions, however, the approach of the outside interests was to disclose their aims and the reasons for them and, in effect, not to attempt to dictate either text or policy, but to place their expertise and understanding at the disposal of the Government in general and the drafter in particular, in order to achieve an appropriate result that would give effect to the Government's policy without harming private interests unnecessarily or unintentionally.

I always appreciated collaboration of that kind, and I believe it is greatly under-utilised. Despite the modern mania for consultation, there is still often an apparently adversarial relationship between Government Departments and commercial or other interests on Bills. Direct involvement is not as a rule either encouraged or facilitated, and the Bills which are well-known to have been the product of close collaboration are the exceptions which by their very fame prove the rule.

I would like to see a formal liaison function of every Bill team established to facilitate a degree of co-operation going beyond the present system of consultation, so that those who have expertise or information to contribute can be sure that they are used properly at the appropriate stage of the preparation of the Bill.

In particular, it is undesirable to leave outside interests to the Committee Stage of one of the Houses before they have any real opportunity to influence the drafting of a Bill.

At one stage it was becoming increasingly common for Bills to be published in draft and considered by a Joint Committee or by a Commons Departmental Select Committee.[6] That salutary trend in theory gave a formal opportunity for outside interests to comment on the drafting and precise language of a Bill before its final introduction: but what was designed to become the norm rather than the exception has quickly relapsed back into its former exceptional state; and even when it does happen, there are often so many policy developments between the pre-legislative scrutiny stage and the introduction of the final Bill that comments on precise language during the former have ceased to be of much relevance to the latter.

Ideally, therefore, Bills would be published in draft before introduction, as a stage distinct from the earlier policy consultation process, and outside interests would be encouraged to make their drafting suggestions at a time when they could be absorbed or reflected without either the Parliamentary difficulties or the structural disturbance of a post-introduction amendment.

---

[6] See *Craies on Legislation*, 9th edn, para.5.2.4.

While this may be a counsel of perfection that would not be feasible in all cases, it might be worth trying. My guess is that where successful it would so greatly ease the passage of the legislation through the two Houses that it would pay for itself in terms of time and Government resources. Apart from the confidence that it would give the Government in resisting further amendments to the Bill having considered the technical offerings of outside interests, the process would be likely, based on my occasional experience of effective collaboration with industry or other experts, significantly to improve the quality of the legislation as introduced and therefore as passed into law.

Accountability

The identity of a Member of Parliament or peer who moves an amendment to a Bill during its Parliamentary proceedings is a matter of public record. Unless the Member or peer chooses to disclose it, however, there is no formal method of establishing on whose behalf, or at whose instigation, they are acting.[7] Very often they will want to mention on the record[8] who inspired an amendment they are moving, as a way of gaining authority for the amendment and encouraging other non-Government Members to support them, or to induce the Government to accept either the amendment or the principle behind it. But if they choose not to mention who has briefed them or drafted the amendment for them, there is nothing to oblige them to do so.

It could be argued that it would be beneficial in various ways, including for the courts and other readers construing provisions after their enactment, to know the identity of the influences behind them. Provisions that encapsulate Government policy will be construed in the context of any consultation papers or other policy documents produced in connection with the Bill. An amendment produced or inspired by an outside interest could benefit from construction in

---

[7] Each House of Parliament has a system for the declaration of registrable interests, but it is primarily concerned with financial interests and even in respect of those it is not, for various reasons, necessarily comprehensive.

[8] That is to say, in a speech in the House or in Committee which is then recorded in *Hansard*.

the light of the policy documents produced by that interest group. Although in various ways it is already possible for a back-bencher in either House to make some reference in *Hansard* to the briefing or other policy paper that underpins their amendment, there is no formal system for the registration of papers of that kind, and their recording and retrieval in connection with amendments reflecting them. It could be that this would be worth instituting, if not as something that Members and peers are obliged to do, at least as a facility for those who wish to do it; so that those who see themselves as willing spokesmen and spokeswomen for worthy organisations are able to record a formal connection between amendments that they move and the policy papers from which they arose.

A system of this kind would be a natural development of the recent innovation mentioned above, when Standing Committees in the House of Commons gave way to Public Bill Committees in 2006, one of the most important aspects of the innovation being the ability to take oral evidence on the Bill from outside bodies and to receive and publish written evidence from interested parties. It would be possible to build on that system so as to make it easier and more common for Members to refer to specific passages of the evidence in support of their amendments, or for the evidence to include draft amendments which when tabled and moved by Members would then readily be associated with the relevant passages of the accompanying evidence, which could be used for contextual construction in the same way as Government papers and statements are used for the construction of those parts of the Bill that are the responsibility of the Government alone.

Conclusion

There are considerable opportunities for outside interests to influence the precise shape of legislation. In some respects it would be preferable for these opportunities to be restricted, at least insofar as the influence is not openly recorded. On the other hand, there is an argument for opening the text of legislation to much greater collaboration with outside interests, in a formally controlled and recorded, and therefore accountable, way.

9 HOUSE AUTHORITIES

Introduction

Many lawyers have never so much as heard of the Clerks of Public Bills or the other Parliamentary authorities involved in the passage of legislation. Even if they have heard of the figures known collectively as the "House Authorities", most lawyers will have only a very shadowy conception of what it is they do. And yet almost every piece of legislation goes to the House Authorities in draft form; they are consulted on a number of different aspects of the shape of legislation and its accompanying documents; and through the medium of Parliamentary procedure—without having or claiming any right to be involved in the policy or substance—they can end up exercising significant influence over the final shape of the legislative product.

It is therefore probably a good thing for lawyers in general, and judges in particular, to have a more detailed understanding of the role of the House Authorities: and that is the purpose of this chapter.

This chapter mentions a number of aspects of Parliamentary procedure which are described in great detail in *Erskine May*,[1] and which are therefore touched upon in this book simply insofar as they are relevant to the eventual shape of legislation. The reader will be assumed either to have already consulted *Erskine May* as to the nature of these procedural stages, or to be able to do so if in any doubt as to what they amount to.

Who are the House Authorities?

The first thing to note is that Clerks in the House of Commons and the House of Lords are not civil servants. They are employed, on terms very similar to those of the civil service, not even by Parliament as an institution but by each House separately. They are generally career

---

[1] See Ch.2 above.

Parliamentary officials in the same way as most of the civil servants involved in the legislative process will be career civil servants. They are therefore to a very considerable extent independent of Ministers, and they are certainly completely independent of individual Departmental pressures and concerns. Their loyalties are generally to Parliament as an institution and, specifically, to the House to whose service they have been appointed.

In the House of Commons it is the Speaker from time to time who is the nominal head of the entire institution and therefore holds a similar position to that of the senior Departmental Minister in charge of a Government Department. He or she comes and goes, and is therefore in one sense of less permanent importance to the career Clerk than is the Clerk of the House of Commons, who fulfils a role similar to that of the Permanent Secretary of a Government Department. Having said which, of course, in recent years at least Speakers have tended to come and go with less frequency than senior Departmental Ministers, and a Speaker who wished to place his or her stamp on individual subdivisions of the permanent administration would certainly have considerable opportunity to do so.

In the House of Lords, since the reorganisation of the Office of Lord Chancellor there is a Lord Speaker who, at least for administrative purposes, exercises a not dissimilar function to that of the Speaker in the House of Commons. The Clerk of the Parliaments is the senior Clerk in that House, with the role equivalent to that of Clerk of the House of Commons in the other House (with a nominal superiority implied by the title of the Office that reflects only the historical superiority of the House of Lords over the House of Commons, contrasting increasingly with the practical precedence of the House of Commons over the House of Lords).

The nature of the work required of Clerks in the two Houses is unlike any other job that one can imagine. At any one time the majority of them are consigned to the black hole known forbiddingly as the "Committee Office", from which place they may be expected to emerge at any moment with a draft report dealing with the complexities of climate change, the Government of Pakistan, the effect of speculation on the strength of sterling, badger-culling as a method of combating tuberculosis, or any one of many hundreds of other topics on which any of the Parliamentary committees may suddenly wish to opine. So they are, to put it mildly, expected to be and to wish to be generalists. The other significant thing about their employment is that although at times their routines can be enormously demanding, particularly if required to service all night sittings, the length of their holidays has traditionally made the career of schoolteacher look unpleasantly constraining. These two factors have combined to attract people who are both by nature scholars, and interested in having the time and resources to conduct scholarly research. I have the impression that it was at one time more or less compulsory for a young Clerk in either House to be pursuing researches for a doctorate or at least for the purpose of producing a scholarly work on a matter as recondite as possible. That has changed to a considerable extent, and the two Houses are by no means immune from the pressures and trends of modern public service management. It remains the case, however, that for the most part the Clerks who deal with legislation are men and women of an original turn of mind, with an active and enquiring intelligence that they bring to bear, sometimes with ruthless efficiency and powerful results, on each of the varied tasks that fall to them in the course of the legislative process. It also remains the case that they are to a very large extent indeed fully independent of the Government of the day,[2] an independence which becomes all the more critical and valuable as it diminishes within the civil service.

---

[2] The principal qualification on this proposition relates to the position of the Leader of the House of Commons and the Leader of the House of Lords. While these are Ministerial appointments, and generally senior political appointments, they inevitably have an element of responsibility to the House as distinct from responsibility to the Government, and the incumbent of each office from time to time is therefore brought into contact with the House Officials and expected to "bat for their side" at least to some extent. This is particularly the case in the House of Lords where the traditional absence of a Speaker with disciplinary powers as in the House of Commons meant that the Leader of the House was required to take an independent stance in relation to, for example, disputed questions on the scope of amendments. In recognition of that, the Private Secretaries to the Leader of the House of Lords and to the Chief Whip in the House of Lords have for many years been members of the Clerks' Department in the House of Lords seconded to civil service for that specific role; in contrast to the Private Secretaries to the Leader of the House

The most important member of the House Authorities in each House in the context of the passage of a Bill is the Clerk of Public Bills. It is he or she who is likely in practice to take any significant procedural decision in relation to the Bill, even if technically the decision is by way of advice to a more senior official, who in turn officially advises the Speaker of either House. Every Bill is, however, assigned to a more junior Clerk in the House of Commons Public Bill Office, with whom Parliamentary Counsel and Departmental administrators will have a considerable amount of contact during the passage of the Bill, including routine discussions about selection and grouping of amendments and administrative matters relating to documents for the Committee. The House of Lords Public Bill Office has rather fewer junior Clerks, who also become significantly involved in procedural and administrative matters. The Clerk of the Parliaments and the Clerk of the House of Commons are not routinely involved in specific issues relating to particular Bills; but they, or their Assistants, may become involved in the case of particularly important decisions on particularly sensitive matters or Bills.

What do the Clerks do?

By simply giving a list of all the different functions that the Clerks of the two Houses are required to exercise in relation to legislation, it will be possible for the reader to get an inkling of the various ways in which they may come to exercise influence over the final product.

To begin with, before a Bill is introduced in either House there are various matters as to which it is necessary or desirable for the Government and the House Authorities to be in agreement. Shortly before a Bill is introduced, therefore, Parliamentary Counsel writes to the House Authorities, generally making a guess as to the House in which the Bill is most likely to be introduced, pointing out a number of different matters. In particular, the letter will advert to: the short title and long title of the Bill; whether or not there are financial provisions in it that will require the cover of a Money Resolution or a

---

of Commons and the Chief Whip in the House of Commons who have been career civil servants.

Ways and Means Resolution; whether Queen's Consent is likely to be required; and whether any issue of hybridity apparently arises. All these are matters that fall squarely within the competence of the House Authorities and as to which it will, at least, be necessary for Counsel and Clerks to have reached agreement before the Bill is introduced. Where a matter of particular difficulty or complexity arises, therefore, it will be routine for correspondence to have begun some weeks or even months before the draft Bill is ready for introduction.

In recent years, the Government have undertaken to produce a set of Explanatory Notes to accompany the Bill as introduced into its first House of Parliament and as transferred from the first House to the second. Because these Notes are printed as House documents and at that House's expense, it falls to the Clerks to be satisfied that their content complies with the House rules. The most important of these is that as House documents their permitted purpose is to assist Members generally in understanding the effect of the draft legislation; they are not permitted to cross the line into political propaganda, justifying why the legislation seeks to do what it does. Of course, there is sometimes a fine line to be drawn between referring to relevant social or political background in the context of which the provisions of a Bill require to be understood, and justifying the policy. A great deal therefore depends on the individual judgment of the Clerk of Public Bills in each House, which in turn varies according to the nature of the holder of the Office from time to time. Some have tended to appear to give a relatively cursory glance to the Notes to check for any obvious cases of attempted extreme propaganda; while others appear to have gone through the Notes with a fine-tooth comb, excising anything that could be regarded as justification and even frequently making other suggestions of style. Although it is technically open to Departments to debate questions of the content of the Notes, the reality is that they are generally finalised very close to the introduction of the Bill, and since the Department would be likely to be criticised if they were not printed simultaneously with or very soon after the printing of the Bill itself, it is easier to accede to suggestions of the Clerks than to attempt to open a discussion.[3]

---

[3] When the Explanatory Notes are reprinted after Royal Assent, they are printed not as a House document but as a Government document printed at

During the passage of a Bill, the House Authorities have a key role in relation to amendments. First, and most importantly, they advise the Chair as to whether a proposed amendment is or is not within the scope of the Bill. If it is not within the scope of the Bill, then as a matter of order it cannot be considered. This is a rule that is very strictly applied in the House of Commons, but in practice much less so in the House of Lords. Technically speaking, the Clerks' function is limited to advising the Chair. But this is very similar to what happens when a junior official in a Government Department is said to advise the Secretary of State on the contents of a letter, replying, for example, to an application in connection with planning law. The theory is that the official advises a Minister who turns his or her mind to the content of the advice and makes a political judgment: the reality is that in 99 cases out of 100 it is in the official's mind that the exercise of the discretion starts and stops. So too here, the reality is that most decisions on scope are taken at official level, and many are taken at a significantly junior official level. Particularly if Parliamentary Counsel and the junior Clerk who is first looking at a selection list are of the same mind as to the selectability of a particular proposed amendment, that is likely to be the end of the matter. If Parliamentary Counsel take a different view, however, the matter is likely to be referred to higher authority. Only in matters of the highest political sensitivity, however, is it likely that the Chair of a Committee or, for Report, the Speaker, would be asked to bring his or her mind to any significant extent to bear on the question of whether or not the amendment were within scope.

On questions of money, Consent, and hybridity, it is also generally the case that the Clerks' decision is likely to be the final word. An important exception to this principle occurred recently in the

---

Government expense by The Stationery Office. House rules therefore at that point cease to apply, and it would be open to a Department to seek to restore or introduce at that stage a considerable amount of argumentative material. The reality, however, is that there is rarely time or appetite for an exercise of this kind, and the Notes are generally reprinted after Royal Assent with minimal alteration to reflect amendments made to the Bill at a late stage during its progress through the Houses.

House of Lords, although to a large extent it is one of those exceptions that proves the rule. On the Local Government Bill 2010 the Clerk of Public Bills in the House of Lords had in accordance with normal practice considered a Bill in draft, concluded that it was not hybrid and gave rise to no issues of hybridity, and stated his opinion to that effect to the Minister in charge of the Bill prior to introduction: as a result, when the House of Lords on a vote took a contrary view and decided that a prima facie issue of hybridity arose that required to be referred to the Examiners, the Clerk of Public Bills in the Lords who would normally have been one of those Examiners was regarded as being "conflicted out" and took no part in those proceedings.[4]

Relationship between the House Authorities and Government

The most important part of the relationship between the House Authorities and the Government in relation to Bills centres on the relationship between the Clerks in the Public Bill Offices of each House and Parliamentary Counsel. That relationship has traditionally been one of strong mutual support, and of considerable mutual confidence. In particular, it was always understood that the Clerks could come to Parliamentary Counsel for advice or an opinion on a matter of Parliamentary procedure and receive, not merely advocacy on behalf of the Government, but a truthful and experienced view which, whether or not it coincided with the approach that most suited the Government's particular convenience at the time, would be expressed openly and honestly.

This independence of role was generally understood by Ministers and appreciated by them, since the resulting degree of confidence and respect between Counsel and the House Authorities was frequently of enormous service to Government. When I assured the Clerks

---

[4] See the first footnote to the Examiners' Statement of Reasons—HL Paper 12; this is an exception that proves the rule, because if it was at all common for decisions as to hybridity to progress further than the opinion of the Clerk of Public Bills, it would not be regarded as convenient for that office to be held together with the office of Examiner of Private Bills.

in either House, for example, that in my opinion a matter that the Government wished to insert into the Bill was rendered within the scope of the Bill by matters lying under the surface that would not appear to the lay reader at first glance but were nevertheless real and significant, I expected that opinion to be given considerable weight, and generally found it so; but I knew that it was treated in that way only because the Clerks knew that if I thought that the proposed amendment was not within the scope of the Bill I would certainly say so, even if it were extremely inconvenient for the Government. I have over the years reminded Ministers on numerous occasions that on matters of selection and grouping I was an adviser of the House and not merely the Government's mouthpiece: and on each occasion on which I expressed that view it was recognised and respected. There are signs, however, that this is no longer regarded everywhere within Government as acceptable or appropriate, and it could be that the relationship between Counsel and Clerks in the two Houses may become more distant, and therefore less useful, as a result.

However that may be, in respect of most procedural matters that arise on a Bill the political consequences are trivial either way, and there should be no obstacle to the Clerks and Counsel working together without conflict. As always, there are different degrees to which this relationship is valued and used, depending on the particular Parliamentary Counsel and Clerk involved.

For example, some Clerks rely more than others on the experience and advice of Parliamentary Counsel on matters of selection and grouping of amendments, and the extent to which they do so is frequently determined either by their own experience or lack of experience, or by the experience or lack of experience of the particular Parliamentary Counsel with whom they are dealing. Most Parliamentary Counsel delegate "housekeeping" matters such as grouping and selection to their junior, and if insufficient training and supervision is given to the junior in this task, their lack of experience and authority may rapidly become felt, in which case the Clerks may come to rely on them less. Again, some members of the Parliamentary Counsel Office have made a greater study of the rules of Parliamentary procedure than others, so even among the senior Counsel there are some whose views are likely to be regarded as carrying more weight than those of others.

At its best, the relationship between Parliamentary Counsel and the Clerks in the Public Bill Office in either House is a wonderful example of the effective combination of complementary experience and understanding. None of the Clerks is a qualified lawyer, and even if one of the Clerks had a legal background he or she would not be serving as a lawyer and would not acquire or maintain understanding of legislation: the result is that, for example, when it comes to understanding the potential effect of a highly technical amendment, and therefore being able to rule whether or not it is within the scope of the Bill, the Clerks are often dependent on the advice that they receive from Parliamentary Counsel. Of course, there are lawyers in the service of the House, forming a legal services Department under the headship of the Counsel to the Speaker in the House of Commons, and under the Counsel to the Chairman of Committees in the House of Lords, and it would be possible for Clerks to consult them on the question of potential effect of amendments. However, even they would be at a comparative disadvantage in construing the effect of amendments compared to the drafter of the Bill. So to have quick and easy access to the drafter of the Bill is an enormously useful resource for the Clerks.

For their part, the Clerks have unparalleled experience and expertise in practice and precedent in relation to the passage of Bills through either House. Even though sometimes an experienced drafter can find that he or she has been responsible for the passage of many more Bills than the relatively junior Clerk to whom the Bill is assigned in either House, that junior Clerk has immediate and complete access to the combined collective memory and authority of all the Clerks in that House, a combination which is put effectively at the disposal of Parliamentary Counsel, and therefore the Government, through the relationship between the drafter of the Bill or his or her junior and the assigned Clerk. Collective memory is of particular importance because decisions on procedure in both Houses are to a very considerable extent precedent-driven: although many matters of procedure are based on principle and it should therefore be possible to argue the case, for example, for requiring or not requiring a Money Resolution for a particular Bill based on first principles, the reality is that if a close precedent can be found pointing in either direction, that will be the end of the argument in 99 per cent of cases. Put the other way around, even where principle and common sense indicate that a

particular result is the better one, the existence of any clear and relatively recent precedent the other way will determine the issue, and it is
therefore enormously helpful for Parliamentary Counsel, and therefore the Government, to have ready and early access to the Houses'
collective precedent memory.

The enormous benefits that are therefore available to both sides
from a close and symbiotic relationship mean that it is achieved to a
remarkable extent in many cases. Mutual confidence between Clerks
and Parliamentary Counsel can grow so strong that, for example,
individual Clerks feel able to call upon individual Parliamentary
Counsel with whom they have had a close working relationship
for help in matters such as the drafting of private Members' Bills
or amendments. A slight sensitivity can arise here. Ministers very
often find it convenient to be able to object to a private Member's
amendment or Bill on the grounds of significant technical defects. If
Parliamentary Counsel has advised on the preparation of the Bill or
amendment then, hopefully, it will be relatively technically secure;
moreover, of course, if it were known that Counsel had assisted it
would become difficult or embarrassing for the Minister to argue that
the Bill or amendment was wholly defective. Whenever I helped one
of the Clerks in either House in preparing or commenting on a draft
private Member's Bill or amendment—and it was relatively rare that I
was asked to do so—I understood that I was doing so informally and
unattributably; and that my doing so was helpful to the Government,
and tacitly endorsed by them, because of the advantages to be gained
by the close mutual confidence between me and the Clerks.

Despite this, there are undoubtedly occasions on which the different responsibilities and accountabilities of Clerks and Counsel
make it necessary for each to act with restraint and circumspection.
Ultimately, Parliamentary Counsel advise Ministers and are bound
by their decisions; the House Authorities advise the two Houses and
are bound by their decisions. If a Minister wishes to conceal his or
her objective in a particular matter for tactical procedural reasons,
Parliamentary Counsel would have to respect that and conduct negotiations with the House Authorities accordingly, avoiding dishonesty
but falling short of complete openness, in the same way as any other
professional legal adviser. And doubtless similar considerations arise
on the other side too.

On rare occasions, also, Counsel and Clerks can come into open and sharp conflict. In my 20 years as Parliamentary Counsel I can only think of three important instances of this, but each of them illustrates the potential for conflict of a serious political nature.

The first case concerned the application of the "stalemate" rule at the to and fro stage of the Parliamentary proceedings on a particularly sensitive Bill.[5] In simple terms, the Government had a political objective of ensuring that it was the House of Lords which was seen to defeat the Bill by a straight rejection, while there were many members of the House of Lords who wanted it to be perceived as the Commons' intransigent refusal to compromise that was responsible for the death of the Bill. This turned into a procedural issue, because my assurance to Ministers was that I could keep the dispute between the two Houses alive by an adroit use of the "packaging" of amendments, as a result of which the House of Lords would never be asked to reject precisely the same set of amendments on two occasions, and stalemate in its technical sense would therefore be avoided. I was accused by the Lords Authorities of abusing the concept of packaging of amendments to try to keep alive an issue that had in reality reached stalemate. But the Clerks in the House of Commons were in agreement with me, and Ministers were very urgent in their insistence that the matter should be seen to return to the House of Lords. In the absence of any further procedural arguments I pointed out to the Lords Authorities that it would not appear well to the public to be told that unelected officials had refused to allow the House of Lords to consider a message sent to them in good faith by the House of Commons. Twenty minutes later the matter was listed on the House of Lords' Order Paper. This illustrates the degree of conflict that can very occasionally arise on politically sensitive issues; and it also raises an issue about the constitutional status of the House Authorities to which I return below.

The second and third serious conflicts that I can remember with the House Authorities each concerned how many decisions could be wrapped up into a single motion for the purposes of the Standing Orders. Without descending into too much tedious technicality, in each case there were significant procedural advantages to the

---

[5] See further Ch.19.

Government in going rather beyond existing precedent in incorporating a number of questions into a single motion. On the first occasion that I tried to do this, again on a Bill of considerable political sensitivity, I was told that if I insisted on the motion in that form it would lose the protection of the particular Standing Order under which it was proposed: I advised the Private Secretary to the Chief Whip in the House of Commons to take the political temperature on the issue and, he having done so, we advised the Chief Whip to "call the House Authorities' bluff", by proceeding without the protection of the Standing Order and relying on the political reality that the Speaker would be more or less bound to grant a Closure within a reasonable period of time; which is what happened. The final instance of conflict was very similar, although in an even more politically charged environment; faced with my refusal to follow precedent or advice from the Clerks, but to insist on the method of proceeding that I thought to be most in accordance with Ministers' wishes and aims, a very senior Clerk took it upon himself to tell me that I was "trampling roughshod over democracy"; while appreciating the compliment, I felt it necessary to remind him that neither of us was entitled to regard himself as in any sense an accountable representative of democracy, neither of us having been elected or being directly accountable.

These three incidents stand out in my recollection simply because they were particularly unusual disruptions in what was generally a strong and enjoyable relationship of mutual confidence with many members of each Public Bill Office during my time as Parliamentary Counsel.

As to the relationship between the House Authorities and civil servants apart from Parliamentary Counsel, much less requires to be said, principally because it is a well-understood rule that in matters relating to a particular Bill the Government should approach the House Authorities only through Parliamentary Counsel. Like the rule against instructing Parliamentary Counsel in the form of a draft, this rule has its origins not in the protection of the dignity of Parliamentary Counsel but in important practicality. As I always used to explain to Bill teams in my first meeting with them in advance of preparing a Bill, when approaching the House Authorities to ask a question about Parliamentary procedure, an enormous amount depends upon the way in which the question is asked. In determining whether a proposed Bill may be hybrid, for example, one needs to be able to present all the relevant information required to determine subordinate questions such as the relevant defining factors of the different commercial classes in the case concerned; failure to identify these aptly could very easily lead to an initial conclusion that was not supported by the totality of the evidence and might be significantly contrary to the Government's wishes. Once an initial view has been formed, however, it is inevitably a complicated and lengthy process to return to first principles and start again; indeed, sometimes it is impossible entirely to eradicate preliminary false impressions. Incautious members of a Departmental Bill team may think that they are merely passing the time of day with a Clerk and discussing certain aspects of the likely effects of the Bill in an informal way, suddenly to discover that they have actually planted doubts in the Clerks' mind about hybridity, money, Queen's Consent or any of the other procedural technicalities that could significantly obstruct orderly achievement of the Government's legislative business.

It is therefore good practice for all significant business, and when in doubt insignificant business, to be channelled through Parliamentary Counsel. Inevitably, however, and particularly during the Committee Stage in the House of Commons, a good working relationship needs to be established between administrative members of the Bill team and the Clerks. An enormous amount of correspondence passes between the Government and Members of a Public Bill Committee, in particular, and papers have to be produced and presented to the Committee either by way of general background or in response to specific requests by Members or undertakings of Ministers. For that and other administrative reasons, there is a considerable amount of practical business that does need to be transacted directly between the Clerks' and the Departments, and a good working relationship is both normal and essential to the smooth progress of the Bill.

In every Government Department there is at least one person designated as Parliamentary Clerk, who handles Parliamentary business including answering Parliamentary Questions and handling the administrative aspects of secondary legislation. The Parliamentary Clerk may have acquired general expertise in relation to certain matters of Parliamentary procedure, and frequently advises the

Departmental Bill team on relatively complicated technical issues. At its best, the Office of Parliamentary Clerk is an enormously useful and responsible administrative function which when carried out efficiently significantly enhances the flow of Departmental business. At its worst, the Office is filled by those whose proximity to the legislative process makes them dissatisfied with their administrative role and turns them into frustrated would-be Parliamentary lawyers, as a result of which they neither fulfil their own role effectively nor help anybody else to fulfil theirs.

Finally on the issue of the relationship between the Government and the House Authorities, it is necessary to explain that in general there neither is nor should be any contact between Ministers or their political advisers and the House Authorities on matters of Parliamentary procedure (although, as with administrators in the Departmental Bill team and papers for committee, there are timings or other practical issues on which Ministers, particularly Whips, routinely liaise with the Clerks). But again, the proper practice occasionally gives way to personal frustration, sometimes with significantly undesirable results. On matters of considerable political importance, it is not unknown for Ministers to respond to firm advice from Parliamentary Counsel that a particular proceeding has been definitely ruled out by the House Authorities with an urbane "Oh, I'll have a word with the Speaker about it . . .". Although they can sometimes be persuaded out of this, Ministers who think that the collective experience and wisdom of 30 or 40 civil servants and House Authorities combined can easily be overridden by a word to the Speaker are rarely the kind of Ministers who are readily persuadable. This kind of situation generally arises on particularly sensitive or fraught Bills, and what generally happens as a result is that the Minister may buttonhole the Speaker at some suitably inappropriate occasion, the Minister and the Speaker have a hurried conversation at cross-purposes, a garbled message returns to the Departmental Bill team on the one part and the Public Bill Office on the other, and the civil servants and the House Authorities clear up the mess between them, generally by reverting to the position they had agreed before. These situations are, however, mercifully rare and for the most part Ministers are only too happy to leave Parliamentary procedure to be operated and determined by those whose job it is to understand it.

How much influence do House officials have on the shape of Acts?

The discussion above about the nature of the House Authorities' job makes it fairly obvious what the answer to this question is: briefly, it is no part of the House Authorities' role to exercise direct influence on the substance of legislation, but their indirect influence on the final product, whether or not exercised intentionally, can be considerable.

To expand the first part of this proposition first, it is axiomatic that the House Authorities are there to guide and facilitate the procedures of the House, and they have no role in determining or advising about the substance or policy of legislation before the House. In the same way that civil servants are the servants of Ministers, the House Authorities are the servants of the two Houses; both sets of officials are there to achieve in an efficient and effective way the policy goals set by their masters.

When I was a very junior Parliamentary Counsel I was once telephoned by one of the most senior House Authorities in response to a letter I had sent enclosing a draft Bill, of a trivial nature, that was about to be introduced into his House. For some reason or another our attention was diverted to a Schedule to the Bill which was headed Consequential Amendments. We were discussing whether a particular paragraph was within the scope of the Bill, and we quickly agreed that it was; but the Clerk went on to question whether it was strictly speaking a consequence of the clause which introduced it, and suggested that the Schedule could more properly be headed "Minor and Consequential Amendments". Even at that stage in my training, and despite the diffidence I felt in the face of such seniority, my instincts kicked in and I responded, hesitantly but firmly, that it seemed to me that he had now left the question of Parliamentary procedure and was raising an issue of substance of the Bill, which presumably, I said, was not something on which he had intended to express an opinion; to my considerable relief, he backed off very fast and the matter rested there.

My reflexes on this point were probably particularly sharp as a result of an early introduction in my time in the Office to a note written by a former First Parliamentary Counsel to his colleagues, in effect rebuking them for having entered into discussions with the

House Authorities about whether or not they could draft a Bill in a way that referred to the provisions of another Bill, and insisting that it was no business of the House Authorities to intervene in this matter at all, and that it was open to us to "legislate by reference to the Ordinances of the Man in the Moon" if we so chose.

So as a matter of simple theory, policy and substance are questions for the Government while practice and procedure are questions for the House. But in the same way that Governments influence practice and procedure in various ways, both directly and indirectly and both intentionally and unintentionally, so too the House Authorities have a considerable influence on the substance of legislation in various ways.

It will be obvious from the picture of the House Authorities' role set out above that the most important and direct influence that they have on the content of legislation is not on what is included in the final product but what is excluded from it. This arises through their determinative influence on questions of scope, which in theory are determined by the Speaker in the House of Commons and by the House itself in the case of the House of Lords, but which in 99 per cent of cases are determined by the Clerks' themselves for all practical purposes. This is not merely a theoretical issue, but one of considerable practical importance. On almost every Bill of any size a number of the amendments tabled in the House of Commons will be ruled ineligible for selection in Committee or on Report on grounds of scope. In the House of Lords it is much more rare for an amendment once tabled to be ruled irrelevant to the Bill:[6] on the rare occasions when the issue does arise, what has happened traditionally is that the Clerks brief the Leader of the House to advise the House before the amendment is moved that it would not be relevant to the subject matter of the Bill, the Leader of the House then does so, and the peer who tabled the amendment then rises and explains that in deference to the will of the House he or she does not intend to move the amendment that has been ruled out of order, and goes on to explain at some length what he

---

[6] In the House of Lords "relevance" is the technical equivalent to scope in the House of Commons, although one commonly hears people using the term "scope" in relation to both Houses.

or she would have said about it had he or she been permitted to move it! But the reason why this is a very rare event in the House of Lords, is that the Clerks in that House exert their influence at an earlier stage than the Clerks in the House of Commons: in the House of Commons any Member can table any amendments to any Bill, and they are scrutinised only when it comes to questions of grouping and selection; in the House of Lords, on the other hand, proposed amendments are considered in substance by the Clerks before being tabled, who will generally advise peers not to table amendments that appear to be irrelevant to the subject matter of the Bill. Only on rare occasions of particular political importance, or particular personal stubbornness, is their advice disregarded.

So the principal influence that the Clerks exercise in relation to the substance of the Bill is by acting as gatekeepers, preventing a Bill from being boarded by irrelevant material. Of course, in one sense this is only relevant after introduction. Before the Bill has been introduced, it is open to the Government to pile any clauses they like into it, and the scope of the Bill will be determined by the content of the Bill upon introduction. In reality, however, that is far from the whole picture. Even on a Bill of relatively limited political significance, Ministers and, in particular, those Ministers responsible for Business Management, need to know long before introduction something about the likely the effect of the rules of scope once the Bill is introduced. That is one of the matters on which Parliamentary Counsel routinely correspond with the House Authorities shortly before introduction, and it is frequently a matter of discussion and correspondence weeks or months before introduction.

For example, imagine that a lengthy Bill about various aspects of planning law is in preparation at a time when a controversy arises about the environmental effects of offshore drilling for oil, as a result of which Ministers wish to introduce a new consent regime for offshore drilling. The question arises at an inter-departmental level whether the proposed planning Bill presents a suitable legislative opportunity for the new proposals for consent. At one level, because this is before introduction of the Planning Bill, there is no issue of scope at all: the Government can add the clauses about offshore drilling consents to the present clauses of the Planning Bill and introduce it, at which point its scope will become whatever scope is produced by the combination of the provisions chosen by the Government. In reality, however, the inter-departmental decision of Ministers whether or not to allow the Planning Bill to be used for the new proposals on off-shore drilling will be partly influenced by the likely effect of the inclusion on the scope of the Planning Bill. If the advice of Parliamentary Counsel, having consulted the House Authorities, is that the inclusion of these proposals would bring general issues about offshore drilling within the scope of the Planning Bill, both the Departmental Ministers responsible for planning, and the Chief Whip and other Ministers responsible for Business Management in both Houses, are likely to resist the inclusion of the material on the grounds that it will make the Planning Bill itself more difficult to get through the two Houses, or that it will prolong the process undesirably. That is then one of the factors that would have to be taken into consideration when Ministers of the relevant Departments, or possibly Ministers at a general Cabinet level of collective responsibility, make a decision. It is at this point, therefore, that the decision of the House Authorities is partly, although indirectly, determinative of the eventual content of the Act of Parliament that results from the Planning Bill. Although in many cases their decision will be a formality, since the merits of the situation are obvious to all, in many other cases the issue will be finely balanced, and their personal attitudes and exercise of discretion will play a very significant part in the outcome.

All the other procedural decisions that fall to the House Authorities to advise on, including hybridity and Consents, may clearly have a similar kind of influence over the content of Acts of Parliament, in the sense that they can influence Departmental decisions about what to include, and, more importantly, what to exclude, when preparing Bills. The mere threat of an issue of hybridity arising, for example, may be enough to persuade Ministers to drop a provision altogether from a draft Bill, or radically to alter its shape.[7]

There is one other relatively direct way in which the House Authorities may come to influence the content of legislation. Although they are not responsible for policy or substance, they do have a function of assisting non-Government members of each House in

---

[7] See further Ch.18.

preparing amendments to Bills;[8] and they sometimes even draft whole Bills for non-Government members to propose as private Members' Bills. It would be very unusual for a private Member's Bill that was likely to be accepted and to become law to be drafted entirely by one of the Clerks in one of the Public Bill Offices: but it could happen in theory, and for all I know it has on occasion happened. For amendments too, the front bench opposition spokespersons will have their legal and other advisers who will prepare amendments for them, as will back-benchers who are being briefed or assisted by significant outside interests. So the most politically critical amendments, and the ones most likely to end up becoming law, are unlikely to have been drafted by the House Authorities alone. And almost all amendments, whoever drafted them initially, are likely to receive the attention of Parliamentary Counsel in one way or another before actually passing into law. But for all this it remains true that the House Authorities do on occasion draft or assist in the drafting of amendments, and that they could thereby influence the shape of the resulting Act; in practice, however, for the reasons I have given this is rare.

There are other matters on which it is impossible to say whether the House Authorities have any formal influence or not, and on which the extent of their informal influence therefore depends on the robustness of the civil servants with whom they are dealing and on the political stakes.

The best example of this in the context of legislation is probably the short title of Bills. Each Bill has a short title which becomes the title of the Act after Royal Assent, by which handle the Act is known and referred to by all the lawyers and other readers who deal with it from day to day. The short title is therefore of considerable practical importance,[9] and one might be excused for thinking that questions relating to it should be determined by the convenience of the ultimate

---

[8] Front-bench Opposition spokespersons will have drafting resources at their disposal for amendments, as will Members who are being briefed or supported by outside organisations; but genuinely "private" Private Members are likely to look to the Public Bill Office for drafting assistance.

[9] Although, unlike the long title, it is of no legal significance—see *Craies on Legislation*, 9th edn, Ch.2.

readers who will use and refer to the Act for possibly many years, rather than the convenience of the relatively few Parliamentarians who will have to refer to it for a relatively short period of time. The main issue that arises as a matter of controversy over short titles concerns their use for political propaganda by the Government. The title "Education Bill" is short and expressive, and probably cannot be improved upon for a Bill that contains a miscellaneous variety of provisions relating to education. But it sounds boring. Call it the "Education Reform Bill" or "Education Modernisation Bill", and it suddenly sounds more exciting, and more worth staying up until two o'clock in the morning to vote for. But once you start to categorise particular Bills as being reforming or modernising, you start a trend that Ministers will neither be able nor want to resist, and there will be pressure for every single Bill to include one or other of the words. This is a matter on which the House Authorities have expressed views from time to time, sometimes trenchantly; but it is far from clear whether even the Speaker has the power to intervene formally to prevent a short title of which he or she disapproves on the grounds of propaganda.

The issue therefore generally becomes one of brinkmanship, with the question of who backs down first—Ministers or the House Authorities—depending on the characters of the individuals from time to time involved, and on the amount at stake politically on each occasion. Whenever I heard the phrase "I think the Speaker would rather deprecate . . ." or something along those lines, I understood it, and interpreted it to Ministers, as meaning "we recognise that we have no real business interfering in this matter, but we're going to have a shot anyway".

Editorial responsibility

On the issue of the extent to which the House Authorities influence the content of legislation there is one particular matter which deserves to be mentioned separately. The Clerks in each House serve as editors of Bills in that House; and the Clerks in the Public Bill Office in the House of Lords serve as editors of the Royal Assent copy of the Bill, which becomes the definitive and authoritative text of the resultant Act of Parliament.

As part of their role as editor, it falls to the House Authorities to determine what corrections of a typographical or printing nature can be effected without formal amendment. This is worthy of comment for two reasons: first, because although it has been recorded elsewhere from time to time, it still comes as a surprise to judges, lawyers and others to learn that the text of a Bill or Act can be amended at all in this informal and technically unaccountable way; secondly, because this is undoubtedly one issue of importance on which the personal preference of particular Clerks, and personal understanding of their role, shapes changing policy over the years.

In the 20 years during which I served as Parliamentary Counsel, attitudes as to what kinds of correction could and could not be made as mere matters of printing varied from Clerk to Clerk and from time to time, with something of a pendulum effect being observable. Being for the most part reasonable, sensible and helpful people, one felt that most Clerks started with a desire to assist everybody by remedying obvious mistakes, without wasting public time and money by requiring a formal amendment to no good purpose (or, perhaps, in circumstances where the Bill had gone beyond its last amendable stage anyway). Then something would happen as a result of which a Clerk, or one of their colleagues, would wonder whether they had perhaps been induced to go a little too far in the direction of helpfulness, and the pendulum would for a while swing back in the other direction.

Despite having been a major beneficiary of Clerical kindness in the matter of printing corrections over the years, on looking back over my time in the Office and considering the matter from the point of view of an outsider, I am strongly of the view that the entire practice of editorial corrections without formal trace should be halted. In the same way that the text of an Act of Parliament can be corrected in a typographical matter after Royal Assent, but only by the issue of a Correction Slip which leaves a formal trace, I would institute a similar procedure for Bills and prevent the Clerks from changing so much as a comma or a space without issuing a formal notice attesting to their having done so. That way, it would still be possible for important editorial corrections to made without troubling the House to correct them by way of amendment, which takes up debating time; but the process would leave a clear audit trail which would enable people quickly and easily to see precisely what had been done, and which would ensure that when the Clerks were making editorial corrections, or Parliamentary Counsel were inviting them to do so, they would know that their actions would be subject to ready scrutiny by readers.

In many ways, this issue is similar to the controversy that arose over the making of editorial corrections to *Hansard*. After a few significant problems over the years, and a pendular process similar to that described above, it was decided to institute a process of formal corrections, which would be printed separately, thereby enabling Ministers to have the record corrected quickly and clearly, without the editor of *Hansard* having to appear to submit to political pressure.[10]

Relationship between the two Houses

I want to add some brief comments about the relationship between the House of Commons and the House of Lords at an official level, mostly because this is something that is unlikely to be discussed in many other publications.

The administrations of the two Houses are entirely separate theoretically, and almost entirely separate practically. The idea that efficiencies of economy and scale might be produced by having the administrations of the two Houses partially conflated was apparently so radical that it required an Act of Parliament to permit it, a radical step that was not actually taken until the passing of the Parliament (Joint Departments) Act 2007. The history of the development of each House, and the political nature of their relationship, makes it hardly surprising that each House should feel the need for a body of servants who owe allegiance to that House alone. Certainly, as one walks through the Palace of Westminster and the colour of the carpet changes from green to red or vice versa, one is left in no doubt that one has entered a new administrative regime, with separate traditions and practices.

This can be frustrating for members of Government or the public who have to deal with the two Houses, and therefore have to keep in mind two entirely separate sets of rules. For example, in the context of legislation, the rules for the formatting and laying out of amendments

---

[10] See further D. Greenberg, "Hansard, the Whole Hansard and Nothing But the Hansard", (2008) 124 LQR 182–185.

to be tabled are precise and exacting, with just sufficient similarity between the two Houses to make it difficult and frustrating to remember the precise differences. Whether inserted text ends with a single inverted comma or with double inverted commas depends on which House you are in; and while all amendments in the Commons end with a full stop, in the Lords none ever do. So far so quaint and, one might think, so unimportant: but there undoubtedly are inefficiencies inflicted on the public service in general, and therefore paid for by taxpayers, which are wholly attributable to differences of procedure and practice in the two Houses. Sheer cost apart, in times when Parliamentarians are generally thought to be working to re-establish trust between the electorate and Parliament, there is surely much to be said for anything that shows that the two Houses are trying to modernise and streamline their processes, and restricting practical differences arising out of historical factors to those which continue to have genuine modern relevance. In particular, coordination of minor matters of procedure might facilitate the electronic handling and use by commercial editors of amendment papers and other documents relating to legislation in progress

In the meantime, Parliamentary Counsel and others simply have to learn two sets of rules and comply with them.

In more substantive areas, there is some feeling among the Clerks that the two Houses should at least be seen to be co-operating and working together, particularly in areas of procedure where different approaches would cause considerable problems. It is, in particular, generally recognised that once one of the two Houses has ruled as to the need or lack of need for Queen's Consent in respect of a particular Bill, its decision will be respected by the other House in accordance with the principle of comity. A similar principle may apply, to a greater or lesser extent, in early discussions on hybridity or scope. The result of this is that it is generally necessary to engage both Houses at the same time in questions relating to the more substantial procedural issues; so even if one is fairly sure that a Bill is likely to start in the House of Commons, a letter concerning hybridity, scope or Queen's Consent would be likely to be copied to the authorities in the House of Lords as well.

Overall, it would be fair to describe my impression of the working relationships between officials in the two Houses as fragile and mostly serviceable, rather than cordial and robust. Of course, there are instances of close friendships between officers of the different Houses; there are, however, also deep antipathies which undoubtedly contribute on occasion to making it more difficult to solve procedural issues.

Accountability

The issue of accountability of the House Authorities could possibly best be introduced by the question "is it right that the House Authorities have as much influence over the final shape of legislation as they undoubtedly do as a result of their procedural responsibilities?".

One is tempted to answer no out of hand, based simply on the fact that the House Authorities are neither elected nor appointed in accordance with a system that is publicly transparent; nor are they generally answerable in public for their individual decisions.

The same is, however, true of civil servants in Government Departments, who both formally and informally make or influence hundreds of decisions every day for which their political masters and not they are technically responsible and practically answerable. The public tolerates this system simply because it works and because, despite the occasional faults and abuses that are inevitable with any system, it is a great deal preferable to any alternative system that can be thought of. And that very much applies to the nature of the House Authorities too. If any House official were thought to be abusing his or her authority, or exercising it in an arbitrary or corrupt manner, there are in practice many ways by which this could be brought to the attention either of his or her senior colleagues, or of senior members of either House, and one would expect serious and effective consequences to follow.

On balance, therefore, although it seems right that the courts and others should be aware of the extent of the potential influence of the House Authorities on the shape and substance of legislation, there is nothing wrong with the present system in that respect, or at any rate nothing that one would not make worse by attempting to improve.

10 BACK-BENCHERS

Introduction

This chapter explores the question of how much influence on the shape of legislation is and can be exercised by individual Members of Parliament or Members of the House of Lords who are not members of the Government from time to time.

The issue does, of course, require to be divided into two parts: private Members' Bills, and the influence of back-benchers on the content of Government Bills (which form, of course, the vast majority of those Bills which pass into law)

How much influence should back-benchers have?

In considering this question, it may be appropriate to begin by saying something about how much influence back-benchers ought to have. I recently gave a talk to the Administrative Law Bar Association immediately after the first speaker who was a former Member of Parliament and who devoted his speech to complaining, in effect, about how few opportunities back-bench Members of Parliament have to control the content of legislation. I began my speech by suggesting that in reality there is no reason why back-bench Members Parliament should be allowed any particularly strong influence over the technical content of laws; they are elected to participate in debates about, and to participate in the making of decisions about, general social policy, and not as an expression of confidence in their technical ability in the matter of the drafting and application of legislation. So it seems only honest to the reader to begin my discussion of the question of how much influence back-benchers actually have by stating my opinion of the limited extent to which back-benchers should be allowed to exert influence over the precise content of legislation.

By way of justification of this opinion, I invite the reader to begin by considering exactly what Members of Parliament are and are not. Most Members of Parliament are not lawyers by training or practice:

even those who are, rarely have any expertise in applying and construing legislation. Immediately on their election to Parliament, however, they find themselves very close to the process of legislating, so close that they can easily be tempted to begin to consider themselves experts.

In a way, the situation is very similar to the governors of schools. Few of them have direct experience of delivering education before they are appointed as governors. Within a few weeks, however, they may find themselves so close to the process of education that they imagine themselves to be experts in how teachers should teach. If they are not very careful, instead of learning how to become useful and effective lay-managers of schools, they may become ineffective and disruptive back-seat drivers.

If back-bench Members of Parliament approach the experience knowing themselves to have been elected to exercise responsibility for setting social and legal policy, but needing expert help from a number of sources in order to translate that policy into effective law, they will rapidly become useful and effective Parliamentarians. Those who, however, mistake proximity to the legislative process with the acquisition of expertise by osmosis, rapidly become back-seat drivers of the worst and most dangerous kind.

Put another way, being elected to Parliament gives one the right to propose legislative and other improvements: it does not make one an immediate expert in how that should be done.

How much influence do back-benchers have on the precise shape of Acts?

In order to answer this question accurately one needs to begin by distinguishing between power and influence.

Back-bench members of either House have virtually no power individually in relation to the content of Acts of Parliament; even collectively, they have power only in relation to those very few provisions or Acts which are made the subject of a free vote and on which there is a sufficiently large consensus one way or the other to enable them to pass into law.

There are two reasons for this virtually complete lack of power.

First, almost everything that happens in either House of Parliament

is subject to a tight Whipping system. Everybody who knows anything at all about politics knows about the operation of the party
Whips. Surprisingly few people, however, realise just how tight and
all-embracing the Whipping system actually is. For example, in
every Public Bill Committee in the House of Commons, however ill-
attended by "real members", one of the two constant attendants on
the Government side is a member of the Government Whips Office,
who is there principally to ensure that every single vote is won by
the Government. Since every Public Bill Committee is composed of
Members representing the balance of power in the House as a whole,
provided the Government has an overall majority in the House of
Commons, the only way a vote can be won against the Government
in Public Bill Committee is if a free vote is declared on the particular
issue; and this happens only extremely rarely.[1]

Even on the most technical or trivial of matters, therefore, the
control of the party Whips is absolute and inflexible, and there are
few politicians who are brave enough to wish to defy the party Whip
even on matters of considerable importance; defying the party Whip,
and thereby incurring serious disciplinary proceedings, on a matter
of merely technical legal importance would be regarded as an act of
derangement. The result is that on the technical details of all Bills
which form part of the Government's legislative programme, or which
the Government has added to its programme, or which it has decided
to adopt or support, back-benchers have no power whatsoever.

Secondly, opportunities for Parliament to pass legislation outside the Government's programme and without the support of
Government time, are very few.[2] And even if time is found to debate a
matter of importance to back-benchers in connection with legislation,
if there becomes a significant prospect of the legislation passing into
law, the Government will, quite properly, assert that whatever the
merits of the matter it becomes a Government responsibility to ensure

---

[1] To be absolutely accurate, a vote can also be won, in effect, against the
Government if the Whip dozes off, miscounts or makes a mistake about which
way his or her side are meant to be voting; rare events, but not quite as rare as
one might wish.

[2] See further p.114.

that if it passes into law it does so in an effective form; the technicalities will therefore revert to being a matter of party discipline under Whipped votes.[3]

In the House of Lords, on this matter as on others back-benchers are able to exercise a greater degree of power. For one thing, there is much more often a lack of an overall Government majority in the House of Lords than in the House of Commons.[4] And the Whipping system is much less effective in the House of Lords than in the House of Commons, principally because while the House of Commons is composed largely either of those who wish to keep office or those who aspire to attain it, the House of Lords has a large number of members who have nothing left to lose in the matter of their personal political careers. The result is that comparing the effectiveness of the Whipping regimes in the House of Commons and the House of Lords is like comparing the four-times winner of the all-Wales working-dog trials with the efforts of an untrained collie dog suddenly let loose in a field of sheep.

Despite this, however, because all legislation has to pass through the House of Commons before it becomes law, the greater power of back-benchers in the House of Lords does not translate into much in the way of a collective power to force through, or affect the content of, legislation.

---

[3] At the time of writing, the House of Commons has just taken the novel step of establishing and appointing a Back-bench Business Committee: depending on how that Committee views its work, and on how successful it is in establishing and maintaining its influence, the picture of back-bench power in relation to legislation could change significantly; but this remains to be seen.

[4] It used to be the case that a Labour Government had to operate without a majority in the House of Lords, with the inbuilt Conservative majority exercising a self-denying restraint (for motives of ultimate self-preservation) in accordance with the Salisbury doctrine and other related practices, while Conservative Governments would enjoy an enormous majority, principally composed of the hereditary peers. With the passing of the House of Lords Act 1998 in particular, and as a result of various other developments, the situation is now rather more complicated, and this is not the place to attempt a thorough analysis of the new balances of power: it remains the case, however, that for almost all practical purposes, no Government can be confident of commanding a majority in the House of Lords on relatively technical or trivial issues.

So the simple answer to the question of how much power back-benchers have in relation to the precise content of legislation is, virtually none: which takes one to the next, and much more important, question of how much influence they do have, despite their lack of power.

As to that question, therefore, the simple answer is that back-benchers in both Houses are able to exert very considerable influence on the shape and precise content of legislation, including Government legislation. There are two principal ways in which this is frequently done.

First, although the party discipline is more or less absolute in the House of Commons and a back-bencher is therefore unable to force through an amendment to a Bill against the wishes of Ministers, the relationship between the party Whips and individual back-benchers is a complex one, and there may be many reasons why Departmental Ministers and the Whips together will wish to show flexibility and helpfulness to a particular back-bench member in relation to a particular technical matter. For example, the back-bencher may be a relatively senior Member at a relatively advanced stage of his or her career, with therefore relatively little to lose by a run-in with the party machine, and potentially much to be gained at a personal political level from being seen to stand up for a particular interest group. Or the back-bencher may be a relatively junior Member of Parliament whom Ministers and Whips simply wish to encourage to take an intelligent interest in Committee proceedings. Or the issue may be one on which the back-bencher can convince Departmental Ministers that there is significant constituency advantage to be obtained by making an amendment contrary to the advice of Departmental lawyers, without inflicting any significant damage on the Government's underlying policy for the Bill. For any of these reasons, or for any of a wide range of other possible reasons, Ministers may decide that they want to accept the principle behind a particular back-bench amendment, in which case they will either accept the amendment itself[5] or they will agree to consider the principle of the amendment, to take it away and

---

[5] Which they ought not to do except with the consent of Parliamentary Counsel—see Ch.4.

to return at a later stage with a Government amendment to the same effect.

Secondly, although as we have said the House of Lords has very little power to force an amendment through against the wishes of the House of Commons, many amendments will be of insufficient importance to the political policy of a Bill for the House of Commons to wish to defy the Lords and resist or reverse it.

Indeed, on a Bill which starts life in the House of Lords, any amendment voted into the Bill in defiance of the Government in the House of Lords, will form part of the Bill as it first appears when printed for the House of Commons: in order to reverse the effect of the amendment the House of Commons will therefore have to pass its own amendment to the Bill removing the effect of the Lords' amendment, and return the Bill to the Lords to have the Commons' amendment agreed to. While the Government will certainly be able to do this, Ministers will think twice before expending that amount of political energy on a matter which is of merely technical importance. To put it another way, Parliamentary Counsel and the Departmental legal advisers are likely to have to come up with a very solid argument indeed as to why the Bill would not achieve its policy objectives if the Lords' amendment were allowed to remain, in order to persuade Ministers to table an amendment in the Commons and insist upon it at the to and fro stage between the House of Lords and the House of Commons. Of course, as with everything else the precise nature of this balance will depend upon all the circumstances of the case, including the personalities of Ministerial and other players, and the surrounding political context.[6]

---

[6] So, for example, at an early stage in a Parliamentary Session on a Bill of relatively little political controversy, Ministers are likely to require less persuading to insist upon a matter against the wishes of the House of Lords; while, at the other extreme, in the wash-up proceedings immediately before a General Election nothing short of a convincing argument that allowing the Lords' amendment to remain will completely defeat the purpose of the Bill or provision concerned is likely to suffice to persuade Ministers to put the matter high enough up on their wish list to insist that it be dealt with as one of the remaining matters of business before Dissolution.

Why would back-benchers want to influence the technicalities of the law?

It is fairly rare for back-bench Members of either House to spot something in a Government Bill that they think needs amending. The majority of amendments to Bills are tabled either by the Government itself or by front bench officials of one of the opposition parties.

Of the relatively small number that are tabled by back-benchers themselves, a proportion that is greater in the House of Lords than in the House of Commons for reasons of party discipline already discussed, the vast majority of these are inspired by an outside group or body that has the ear of the back-bench Member of Parliament or peer concerned. This could be a constituency issue that has been raised with a particular Member of Parliament by one or more members of his or her constituency, and which he or she may have come to feel sufficiently strongly about to wish to express in an amendment. If the point is a good one, and the potential constituency interest significant, then a Government back-bencher may receive a sympathetic response from Ministers on the front bench; even a non-Government back-bencher who raises a point of constituency interest may receive a sympathetic response if the Minister does not wish to be castigated in the local press as having opposed the particular reform suggested.

More usually, however, a back-bench amendment is inspired not by one or more individuals but by an established pressure group or trade or other single-interest organisation. Large trade bodies or charities, in particular, will routinely issue a briefing pack on significant Bills relating to their area of interest, which is likely to include a list of proposed amendments and which will be sent possibly to all Members of Parliament, and certainly to all members of the Public Bill Committee. Members of Parliament may have particular reasons for wishing to further the interests of one or other of the organisations briefing on a particular Bill: they may have a significant constituency interest in a particular trade, for example, or they may have some present or former professional connection that makes them particularly sensitive to the interests of a particular body. For example, the Law Society routinely briefs Members of Parliament on Bills of significant interest to the legal profession, and a present or former solicitor Member of Parliament may well be impressed by their briefing to the point of, in effect, tabling amendments on their behalf. This practice is very well known, although the degree of openness with which Members of Parliament are prepared to acknowledge it varies. On some Bills, a back-bench member of the Public Bill Committee may be entirely open about the fact that he or she has, in effect, turned themselves into the political mouthpiece of a particular charitable or other organisation; its officers and staff may turn up routinely to the Committee and sit together in the public gallery, where the Member in question will join them from time to time for hurried consultations. On other occasions, however, a Member of Parliament will table a series of amendments without acknowledging their source, and will speak to them without apparent prompting from outside, leaving the unseen guiding hand of some person or organisation to be inferred from the improbability of the Member having thought it all up for himself or herself.

Private Members' Bills

In each calendar year as many as 60 Bills will become Acts of Parliament, occasionally even more. Of these, it would not be unusual for five or six to have started out as private Members' Bills. Twenty Bills are brought in by the 20 back-bench Members of Parliament successful in the Ballot held at the beginning of each Session; for various procedural reasons, the top three each Session have a very good chance of becoming law provided that they are not sufficiently controversial to attract serious opposition. Other Ballot Bills, and even some Bills brought in by Members who did not win a place in the Ballot, will be able to proceed to enactment if they have no significant opposition at all, whether from the Government or from other back-benchers. Bills starting in the House of Lords—technically known as private peers' Bills—have a significantly less good chance of becoming enacted, but even so in any given year it is not uncommon for one or two of them to become law.

What not everybody outside Parliament (or even everybody inside Parliament) realises, is that there are two classes of private Members' Bills, which could loosely be categorised as the genuine and the bogus. The genuine class, are those Bills that are genuinely brought forward by Members themselves, to meet a real interest that they have held for some time or which they have newly acquired having perused the several hundred briefings routinely sent to anyone who is successful in the private Members' Ballot. Of these, some are actually drafted by the private Member, who knows that his or her Bill is unlikely to pass into law and therefore minds little or not at all whether it is technically effective and would make good law, provided that it effectively advertises the defect in the present law, or the proposed reform of social policy, that the Member has chosen to give an airing in Parliament and the media.[7] These genuine Bills may, however, sometimes be drafted in reasonably competent, or at least plausible, form, perhaps by lawyers hired for the purpose by the interest group whose cause the private Member has taken up. In all other cases, private Members or private peers will have had to make their own arrangements to receive drafting assistance, which vary enormously according to the particular circumstances of the private Member or private peer concerned, and the precise nature of the Bill.

The second class I designate as bogus because, although nominally presented and steered through the House by a private Member or peer, they are actually Government Bills, albeit Bills that are too trivial to be thought worthy of a place in the acknowledged legislative programme. The Government regularly hand out to private Members or private peers Bills that do not have a sufficiently high priority in policy terms to merit a place in the legislative programme for a particular Session, but which a Department would like to see enacted if it were possible. The private Member or private peer gains brownie points for helping out the Government, which might be useful if he or she has ambitions to be appointed to some kind of Ministerial service or to achieve something else in the gift of Government, while the Government gains a small piece of additional legislation without cost in terms of the legislative programme.

---

[7] It is notable that many Private Members' Bills advancing policy on behalf of a particular interest group achieve success only after a certain number of doomed Bills and other methods of attracting attention—including Parliamentary Questions and Westminster Hall debates—have been strung together as a campaign over a number of years. A certain number of doomed Bills lends a lobbying campaign a certain momentum and plausibility.

Handout Bills will have been drafted by Parliamentary Counsel in the same way as other Government Bills.

The amount and nature of other assistance that the private Member nominally in charge of the Bill receives depends on the circumstances.

As a rule, a Bill is only considered suitable for handout if it is both relatively short and relatively straightforward. Anything more than about three or four pages is likely to present too much flank for amendment in Committee to have much chance of success as a private Member's Bill, whether under the Ballot or not; and if the subject of a Bill is so technical or complicated that the private Member without previous experience of the area cannot be expected to become thoroughly familiar with it, he or she is unlikely to be able to provide convincing answers to probing questions or amendments at Second Reading or in Committee, and the result is likely to be to arouse suspicion among even initially well-disposed colleagues, who may well then effectively block the Bill on the grounds that their reasonable questions (which may have been prompted by briefings from people with interest in the Bill) have not been answered. Nothing is served for a Department by having a non-controversial and technical proposal turned into a long-running bone of contention by an ill-judged attempt to have it slipped through Parliament under cover of a handout Bill, with the Member in Charge being unable to handle it authoritatively; even if the wait for a suitable Departmental Bill to carry the proposal takes a few years, that is in the long run likely to prove the quickest method of making progress.[8]

So the Member in Charge of a handout Bill should not need an enormous amount of briefing and support, because the Bill ought to be relatively simple and clear. There will certainly be one or more oral

---

[8] For a "real" Private Member's Bill, a few failed attempts can generate a helpful long-term momentum and support a final successful push; in contrast, once a Government proposal has been identified as controversial, even where the controversy arises solely from a lack of understanding of what is really intended, it can be close to impossible to shake off the bad reputation, so that even when it is finally slipped into the middle of a larger Government Bill it can end up causing more handling trouble than it is worth as a matter of policy.

briefings by the civil servants responsible for the policy of the Bill, and there is likely to be at least some presence of the Bill team during the Parliamentary stages, ready to provide hastily scribbled answers to questions or objections raised during debate.[9]

Apart from Ballot Bills, not everybody realises that any Member of Parliament can present a Bill without requiring permission at any time.[10] A Bill can be presented simply by being handed in.[11] Of course, it is unlikely to make any further progress, and is therefore unlikely to attract any significant publicity, unless one of two possibilities emerges.

First, if the subject of the Bill is so important and so completely devoid of potential for political or other controversy, that everyone on all sides of the Chamber wants it to proceed, the Bill may be allowed through all its stages without debate and therefore without

---

[9] At one time there were some attempts both by Private Members and civil servants to conceal the fact that a particular Bill was a handout, the motives being that the Private Members wanted to receive the credit for the work and to avoid being perceived as Government stooges, while the Government wished to avoid criticism for in effect using handout Bills as a way of extending the already enormous amount of Government time by swallowing up some of the meagre allowance intended for "real" Private Members' business. After some unhappy incidents, however, it is now understood by all that there is more to be lost than gained by attempting to conceal the true nature of the exercise.

[10] Many people—including some Members of Parliament—assume that permission is required for a non-ballot Bill, because they know about the procedure known as the Ten-Minute Rule Bill, which centres on a short debate on a motion for leave to bring in the Bill. In fact, the use of this procedure is in effect optional, and it is used only because it provides the tactical advantage of allowing a short speech by the Member in Charge of the Bill, at a time of day when there are usually still a few journalists in the press gallery; for a Bill which has no real hope of gaining time for any of its stages in any other way, this may be the best way of ensuring a little bit of publicity for the issue that it is trying to air.

[11] This kind of Bill is sometimes referred to as a "Back of the Chair" Bill, because it was originally presented by being slipped into a large bag hanging immediately behind the Speaker's Chair.

requiring an allocation of Parliamentary time.[12] Secondly, if the Bill is a handout Bill, or starts as a genuine private Member's initiative but attracts Government attention and sympathy during its passage, Government time may be made available to enable it to complete its Commons stages, even in the face of a moderate amount of opposition or scepticism.

The result of this is that a handout Bill could proceed either as a Ballot Bill or as a "back of the chair" Bill. At the beginning of each Session the Chief Whips' officials in the House of Commons conduct a trawl of Departments and produce a list of legislative proposals that would be suitable for implementation through a private Member's handout Bill. They will then approach those successful in the Ballot and invite them to take up one of the proposed handouts. It is not very likely that someone with a high place in the Ballot will pick up a handout Bill, since they are rarely glamorous enough to satisfy someone whose success in the Ballot is such as to give them a serious chance of immortalisation in the statute book. But someone around the middle of the Ballot or lower may well reckon that their chances of pushing through, or even getting debating time for, anything very exciting are so small that they may as well do the Government a favour by picking up a boring but worthy handout Bill, which has a chance of proceeding "on the nod".

---

[12] There is a process known as "call-over" which is extremely important to understanding how Private Member's Bills make progress. When the time for debate at the end of each sitting comes to an end, it is still possible to proceed with unopposed business; what happens is that the Clerk "calls over" all the remaining business, consisting of any motion down on the Order Paper as to be taken at that sitting. The Speaker will put the question on any motion moved and, if it is agreed to without a single objection, it is passed; if even a single Member calls "Object", the matter falls for the time being. It is theoretically possible for a Bill to pass through all its Commons stages at a single Sitting without a word of debate or a single vote, if each stage is called over and agreed to unanimously. A list of examples of Bills that have made significant progress "on the nod" in this way is given in *Craies on Legislation*, 9th edn, para.5.2.55; in the House of Lords there is no equivalent of call-over, but the lesser pressure on debating time means that it is not required—time will always be found for debating a Bill that has any significant back-bench support, whether it has come from the Commons or started in the Lords.

Private peers' Bills are more rarely successful than private Members' Bills. It is, in fact, a great deal easier to get a Bill through the House of Lords than through the House of Commons, primarily because the allocation of time in the Lords is handled by consensus and much more time is made available for non-Government business. But, of course, every Bill has to pass through both Houses if it is to become law: a private Member whose Bill has made its way through the Commons is unlikely to find it difficult to find a friendly peer prepared to take it through the House of Lords, and so long as it is back unamended before the end of the Session its place on the statute book is assured. In contrast, a Bill that has passed through the Lords as its first House finds itself well at the back of the queue for private Members' time in the House of Commons, so even if it is picked up by a friendly Member of Parliament it is most unlikely to make any further progress and it will simply die at the end of the Session. The only exceptions are handouts or other Bills that are allotted Government time, or Bills that are so unexceptionable that they will pass all their stages "on the nod". The result is that very few Acts of Parliament have started life as private peers' Bills, although it does occasionally happen.[13]

Taken overall, how much influence can private Members and peers be said to have as a result of the private Members' and peers' Bill procedure? All in all, a little over 700 Bills have become law under these procedures since they first became available in 1948. One might argue that this represents a considerable degree of influence. But when one puts it into the context of about 600 Members of Parliament each Session and at least as many reasonably active peers, as a 60-year total it perhaps becomes less impressive; and when one makes some deduction to reflect handout Bills that would have been enacted by the Government in their own legislation sooner or later, the degree of influence is further deflated by an unquantifiable amount.

---

[13] Factsheet L3 in the Legislation Series produced by the House of Commons Information Office gives a complete list of successful back-bench Bills, from which it will be seen that the number of successful Private peer's Bills varies from none in some Sessions to as many as seven in 1996–97.

Conclusion

At the outset of this section of the book I spoke about the unwar-
ranted assertions of part-ownership sometimes made in relation to
many Acts of Parliament by people who claim to have been heavily
involved in their production and whose contribution was in fact non-
existent or insignificant. Back-bench Members of Parliament are a
particularly strong example of this kind of claim; and they are commonly believed simply because many people whose knowledge of the
Parliamentary process is rudimentary or largely theoretical assume
that a Member of Parliament, or a peer, is so close to the centre of
legislative power that it is inconceivable that they would not be able
to exert considerable influence. The reality is that almost all provisions of almost all Acts of Parliament are constructed entirely by
Government officials and taken through without real involvement at
a technical level of anybody outside the Government machine.

That is not to belittle or underestimate the role of a back-bench
Member of Parliament. For one thing, their most important function
lies in the raising of constituency and other issues through questioning and debate, in any of the many ways in which back-benchers can
hold the Executive to account. A conscientious back-bench member
of either House can exert political and social influence in a large
number of important and effective ways, and thereby do a great deal
to improve the lives of his or her constituents or of citizens in general.
But the central and natural functions of the back-bencher do not
include contributing at a technical level to the effectiveness of legislation, which is ultimately the job of Government Ministers and their
expert advisers. Impassioned speeches about the general principle of
a Bill or of particular provisions of a Bill at Second Reading in either
House may make headlines in the daily newspapers, but they are
likely to have little or no influence on the precise content of the Act
which emerges at the end of the process, which will depend entirely on
Whipped votes being used to rubber-stamp material produced by the
Government and presented to Parliament. As has been seen, there are
exceptions, some of which may be important: but for the most part,
honest Parliamentarians upon retiring from Parliament will admit
that, time spent in Government office apart, their contribution to the
shape of Acts of Parliament has been minimal; unless they have been

one of the few Parliamentarians to have successfully piloted a private Member's Bill through Parliament, and have been one of the even smaller class who have had genuine knowledge and expertise in the subject matter of that private Member's Bill, they will acknowledge that their role did not involve even understanding, much less affecting, the fine or technical points of the Bills for which they were voting. Wise back-benchers will, however, be able to reflect that instead of pointlessly expending their energy on matters for which they were not trained and in which they were not particularly useful, they concentrated on exerting political influence at the appropriate level to serve their constituents or citizens in general by helping to determine the social policy underlying Government administration, of which the passing of legislation forms just one small part.[14]

---

[14] And, indeed, a part that should be treated as less important, or at least less necessarily useful or appropriate for all circumstances. See further "Nothing Will Come From Nothing, Daniel Greenberg laments the introduction of nonsense legislation", (2010) *New Law Journal*, July 30, p.1084.

11 JUDGES

Introduction

In times gone by it was assumed that the officers who would be tasked with applying and construing legislation should be heavily involved in writing it. The earliest statutes were composed by committees of judges, politicians and officials who were presented with a petition or bill requiring a remedy to be drawn up by the Sovereign in Council.

Nowadays there is no automatic assumption that judges will wish to or be allowed to have anything to do with the drafting of legislation in the ordinary course of events. But that proposition is subject to one or two qualifications which while relatively minor are not entirely without significance, and it is the purpose of this chapter to explore them.

The Law Lords

Until the recent establishment of the Supreme Court, the House of Lords was the senior Court of the United Kingdom, thus exercising a constitutionally interesting dual role of legislature and interpreter of legislation. Business in the Chamber would begin on a number of days with the formal delivery of judgments in cases before the Lords, and then, after a short interval at the end of the completion of judicial business, the House would reassemble for the conduct of its Parliamentary business.

Clearly there was something of a potential conflict of interest presented by that duality or, at least, there was a serious risk of a lack of objectivity if those who expressed a particular point of view during the passage and shaping of legislation were also those who were called upon to pronounce authoritatively on its meaning after the event. As a result, the Law Lords generally operated a self-denying ordinance in accordance with which they did not take part in general debates, including in particular debates on Bills.[1] But they were still as a group able to influence proceedings in a number of ways; first, there was always a strong body of Law Lords who were retired from judicial business but whose recent experience of it would be brought to bear on proceedings, and whose pronouncements on all matters, but particularly on matters with a legal flavour, were generally listened to with profound respect. It is probably fair to say that as a cross-bench group, former Law Lords were one of the most influential groups on matters not controlled by the party Whips, and even sometimes one of the most powerful forces for persuading people to disobey the Whip. In addition to the direct participation in debate of former Law Lords, both former and serving Law Lords were available to offer informal advice to those of their colleagues who sought it.

The future position remains to be seen: although one may guess that the establishment of the Supreme Court itself is likely to make little difference in the long run, since most or all of the Bench will be ennobled and therefore able to participate in the Lords after retirement, the issue of the final stages of Lords reform is still up in the air, and whether serving or former judges have a strong influence in the Lords will of course depend on the eventual shape of that House. On some models, their role may be the same as at present, or even more pervasive; under other models, the role of appointed peers of all kinds would be diminished or even abolished altogether. So we must wait and see; one suspects, however, that one way or another both serving and former senior judges will find ways of influencing proceedings on Bills with a particularly legal flavour, directly or indirectly, and that their views will still be sought informally and, where appropriate, prayed in aid of their colleagues' arguments.

---

[1] See, for example, "Rightly or wrongly, I have taken the view that I ought not to take part in general debates while I was a serving Law Lord, or eligible to sit as a Law Lord after my retirement from judicial office." Lord Steyn, *Hansard*, HL Vol.703, col.686 (July 8, 2008).

Law Commission Chairman

The Law Commission is already a significant source of new legislation, and it is likely to become more so over the next few years.[2] The
Chairman of the Law Commission has to be a senior judge[3] who
inevitably and properly will have a very considerable influence on the
workings of the Commission as a whole. The result is that the Law
Commission is an opportunity for the judiciary to have a significant
involvement in the making of legislation and, in particular, the remedying of anomalies and technical defects in "lawyers' law"; matters
that are not socially or politically controversial but which may be
important for the rule and operation of law as a whole.

The judiciary of the United Kingdom are traditionally very
reluctant to fill in gaps in legislation in a manner that amounts to
judicial legislation, being neither elected nor accountable; but in
reaching unattractive decisions as a necessary result of defective
or infelicitous legislation, judges frequently deplore the state of the
legislation and invite Parliament to correct it. In reality, however,
it is rare for judicial comments of this kind to translate into action;
partly because of the lack of a formal mechanism for converting
judicial deprecation into formal political recommendations, but
more because of the constraints on the legislative programme and
the reluctance of Ministers to be diverted from their political programme into less headline-grabbing, although possibly more useful,
legislative reform.

The Law Commission therefore presents a significant opportunity
for the judiciary to influence legislation and initiate attempts to repair
anomalies or remedy defects, although it is only likely to be effective
for matters that are politically uncontroversial.

---

[2] The passing of the Law Commission Act 2009 is designed to increase the
flow of Bills emanating from the Law Commission that make it into law, and
both Houses have made procedural arrangements to the same effect; and early
signs are that the Act will be successful at least to some extent.

[3] Law Commissions Act 1965 s.1(1A).

Ad hoc involvement

Although it is by no means usual for judges to be involved in the draft-ing of a Bill, their obvious expertise in the practical application of Acts, and the importance of ensuring that they are likely to construe and apply an Act in accordance with the legislative intention, make it obviously sensible to involve them in particular legislative projects from time to time.

One of the best relatively recent examples is the involvement of Lord Justice Saville[4] in the Arbitration Act 1996; the Bill for the Act was preceded by a Departmental committee which the judge chaired, and the drafting exercise was unusually closely linked to the policy development.

But other instances can arise almost by accident. On one Bill that I drafted that included relatively technical legal (although by no means trivial) matters, a member of the judiciary wrote to the instructing Department questioning the efficacy of a particular provision and proposing an alternative draft. As is only to be expected, the draft was not without its points of difficulty; but the issues raised were real and deserved careful analysis and response. I decided to invite the judge to come to meet me and the Bill team, which he did; having rapidly agreed that his proposed draft did not quite meet the needs of the case, we went on to engage in a most harmonious and constructive collaboration, as a result of which the Bill was certainly made a great deal more likely to achieve its intended effect than would otherwise have been the case.

Is judicial involvement in legislative drafting improper?

It could be argued that it is actually improper or at least undesirable for judges to be involved in drafting legislation, on the grounds that their involvement is likely to give them preconceptions about what it is intended to mean, which would prevent them from listening dispas-sionately in due course to arguments from opposing Counsel about what it actually does mean.

---

[4] Now Lord Saville of Newdigate.

Of course, one might reply that surely anyone who can tell one from certain first- hand knowledge what was intended when the legislation was drafted is closer to divining the legislative intention than anyone can be merely as a result of listening to opposing arguments; but that would be to mistake the meaning of the enterprise of discovering the legislative intention. The idea is not to try to find out what any particular individual or group of individuals wanted the statute to mean, but to determine as an objective exercise what a notional legislature must be taken to have meant given the words used and their social, political and legal context.[5]

There is, however, certainly a strong notion in our jurisprudence that it is for Parliament to legislate and for the judges to apply and interpret the result of Parliament's efforts. So it would be possible to argue that judges ought to avoid putting themselves in a position where they will be influenced in considering the construction of legislation by personal involvement in the process of its preparation. This argument, which could also be applied to the writing of books about particular legislation by members of the serving judiciary, does not seem to have been regarded as a serious deterrent, at least by some judges; and it is certainly possible to argue that involvement in the drafting would be no more a potential distracting factor than any of the many and various other ways in which judges can come to be, or seem to be, identified with particular attitudes to the construction of specific legislation.

Conclusion

Judicial involvement in the making of legislation is marginal in our jurisdiction in modern times, and occurs only in the relatively constrained range of cases discussed above. As a body the judges are not a major influence on the shape of legislation; and many of them, and no doubt many others, perhaps think that the statute book would be in better shape if their involvement were more regular and pronounced.

---

[5] See further D. Greenberg, "The Nature of Legislative Intention and Its Implications for Legislative Drafting", (2006) 27(1) *Statute Law Review* 15–28.

12 SPECIAL ADVISERS

Introduction

I have deliberately left special advisers until the end of section 2 of this book. If I had my way, they would be left out of both this book and the machinery of Government altogether. They are, in my personal opinion, one of the most serious flaws in the way Government operates today.

The nature, role and justification of special advisers are discussed in considerable detail in a number of other places, and I do not rehearse them here. In summary, they are political appointees who, when their party succeeds to Government, are permitted to be paid as, and are to a great extent treated as, civil servants.

In a few years we have gone from the situation immortalised in Sir Humphrey Appleby's treatment of Frank Wiesel in *Yes Minister* to a situation where special advisers, with neither the accountability of politicians nor the training of civil servants, frequently wield more power than either. This is strongly to be deplored. Those who wish to inflict their personal political allegiances and ambitions upon the public should do so by presenting themselves for election; while those who are appointed to public service should carry it out without showing allegiance to any particular party. There is no justification for requiring the public to accept in positions of power, and pay for, people who owe loyalty to a particular party but have not been elected in a democratic and accountable manner.

In making these observations I am referring only to those career-politicians who are brought into the civil service in reliance on the special adviser rules which allow them to retain their party loyalties; I am not referring to substantive experts brought within the Government or Parliamentary sphere in any capacity to provide information or opinions based on valuable practical experience gained in the private sector.

Influence on legislation

In the context of legislation, special advisers have no particular formal role to play in the process. Their presence, however, can be felt permeating the Departmental aspects of the process from the beginning; in particular, if the Bill is of considerable political importance, special advisers are likely to attend any significant meeting on the Bill.

In my early days in the Parliamentary Counsel Office I attended one meeting on a Bill of enormous political significance where special advisers were present: a superb civil service lawyer of the old school objected to their presence, and at one point refused to continue unless they were asked to leave. He won, and the meeting continued without them. Today, I doubt if many civil service lawyers or administrators could still be found who appreciate, and care about, the theoretical limitations on the role of special advisers sufficiently to insist upon their leaving a meeting in similar circumstances; and I know of even fewer Ministers who would be likely to feel willing, or even able, to agree to a request to ask them to leave.

A number of special advisers whom I met during my time in the civil service were worryingly dictatorial. I was sometimes able to detect the hand of special advisers from the way things were going, even when it was not openly disclosed.

For example, on one occasion I had proposed what I thought was a perfectly serviceable short title for a Bill, but was told at a fairly late stage in the process, shortly before introduction, that "the Minister" was insisting upon a very different short title. My main objection to the Minister's suggested short title was that it was anything but short. After a certain amount of inconclusive correspondence I suggested that perhaps I should come to see the Minister to discuss the issue. At that point it emerged, as I had already suspected, that the Minister himself neither knew nor cared anything about it. What had happened, however, was that one of the Minister's special political advisers had put up a submission explaining to the Minister that if my shorter short title was used the scope of the Bill would be potentially enormous, with opportunities for back-benchers to attempt to insert material that the Department would not wish to debate on this occasion; while the special adviser's own suggested longer short title would result in a much narrower scope of the Bill. Leaving aside the question of whether it is proper to manipulate the Parliamentary rules about scope for the purpose of excluding material that back-benchers might legitimately think connected with the subject matter of the Bill, the special adviser's submission was based on ignorance of the rules of Parliamentary procedure. The question of scope has never been determined by the short title (although at some points in Parliamentary history the long title has to some extent been persuasive). When I corrected the misunderstanding and insisted upon my suggested title being re-submitted to the Minister, it was accepted without further discussion.

There is no reason to believe that this was an isolated instance of a special adviser being prepared to wield very considerable power within the Department, based on insufficient understanding of the context within which they were trying to wield it.

The problem and the solution

It is generally accepted that the *Yes Minister* programmes were uncomfortably accurate in a number of respects. In particular, it is true to say that the classic relationship between Ministers and the permanent civil service was characterised by the feeling on the part of the civil servants that they generally knew better than Ministers about most things, and a feeling of impotence and frustration on the part of Ministers that they could not mobilise the machinery which was nominally there to serve them. But where the programme was profoundly misleading, was in suggesting that this relationship inevitably led to mutual distrust. The reality is that the good civil servant, at the same time as feeling that he or she knew more about public administration than Ministers, respected the right of Ministers to govern in accordance with their elected mandate, admired a number of important qualities in many politicians, and regarded it as a matter of professional self-respect to help them to bring these qualities most effectively to bear on their political agenda. Similarly, despite a feeling of frustration, good Ministers acknowledged and respected the expertise of many civil servants, and rapidly came to appreciate how the combination of the vision, ambition and accountable power of good elected politicians together with the expertise and experience-based cynicism of good civil servants, could produce beneficial results for the country that neither of them could achieve as a class on their own. There was certainly mistrust sometimes: but the best Ministers and the best civil servants, even when they fought each other with little restraint, trusted each other implicitly, respected each other's territory, and recognised that they were ultimately moving in the same direction, albeit frequently at different paces.

I experienced precisely this kind of relationship on a number of occasions with Ministers with whom I came into close contact. Indeed, I recognised those that I regarded as the best Ministers as those who would, once they saw that I was prepared to tell them precisely what I thought, test out their ideas by provoking me into disagreeing with them.

The rise of the special adviser is the single factor to which I attribute the breakdown in this important relationship between civil servants and Ministers. The issue is principally one of access, and it rapidly becomes one of perspective. The *Yes Minister* programme made a joke of how effectively civil servants managed to keep special advisers away from Ministers. That joke was certainly cutting right to the heart of the problem. At some point, or over some period, the balance of power in this particular battle shifted, and special advisers came to control access to Ministers; career civil servants were excluded from direct access to Ministers more and more, and were almost never allowed to deal with Ministers directly on important matters of policy unless special advisers were present to guard them. My perception was that this arose as a result of a lack of trust between the party hierarchies and Ministers: special advisers were there as much to guard Ministers from themselves as to guard them from civil servants.

So all important policy meetings came to be conducted either in the presence of special advisers or, increasingly, by special advisers as delegates acting on behalf of their Ministers. Career civil servants became increasingly frightened of special advisers, who as their power grew showed an increasing willingness to use it, to impose what they saw as discipline over what had previously been a notably unruly civil service. If discipline is applied sufficiently brutally it tends to work effectively, and fast, to prevent the expression of dissent; it does not, of course, eliminate dissent, or persuade anybody of the argument.

During my 20 years as Parliamentary Counsel the ease of gaining direct access to Ministers decreased, the decrease accelerating significantly in recent years. And it became almost impossible to have direct access to Ministers without the presence of special advisers. Within the last year or two of my time as Parliamentary Counsel by virtue of a freak of timetabling I found myself sitting outside a Committee room in the House of Commons with a senior Minister and nobody else apart from my assistant; we talked openly and frankly and he appeared anxious to hear what I thought about a number of things, and I realised as I spoke that this was a conversation of a kind that would have been relatively normal in my early years as Parliamentary Counsel and had become so rare that I could not remember the last occasion on which it had happened.

This is not about Ministers being made to do what civil servants think: Ministers are elected and accountable and it is their decisions on all matters of policy and administration that count. But it is about ensuring that Ministers have access to the full range of views on what they propose to do, including the views of people who are fundamentally opposed to the project. While Ministers are cocooned by a cadre of professional would-be politicians whose only job is to pursue a political agenda set by party officials, often in a wholly unaccountable way, they are being denied access to the full and frank views of those who have the most experience of good administration.

There is no simple solution. Even simply abolishing the post of special adviser—which is never going to happen—would not in itself be the answer. The process has gone so far that many civil servants have either become unaccustomed to thinking freely and expressing their views trenchantly, or have grown up in a civil service world in which the old lack of constraint plays no part. There is a whole generation of civil servants who have been schooled to think that saying yes to Ministers and their close advisers is the only safe method of career progression.

As a result I write this particular chapter more in sorrow for the past than hope for the future. I genuinely believe that special advisers have done much damage to the quality of legislation, as to other aspects of the public service; but I also genuinely believe that it is almost inconceivable that the damage will be reversed, or that the traditional and precious relationship between civil servants and Ministers will ever be restored.

SECTION 3
PROCESS AND PROCEDURE

13 INTRODUCTION

Purpose of this section

An outline of the entire process of preparing and passing an Act of Parliament from a machinery of Government perspective can be found by reading the Cabinet Office's Guide to Legislative Procedures.[1] And *Erskine May*[2] provides a thorough overview of the procedural steps from the Parliamentary perspective. Since those are detailed and generally accurate accounts, I do not intend to replicate them here. In any event, anyone reading this book is likely to be familiar with the basic outline of Parliamentary procedure according to which Bills are considered.

This section of the book concentrates on identifying certain aspects of the process or procedure that could benefit from specific analysis, or from more detailed description than will be found elsewhere, for the practical benefit of those who have to apply and construe legislation. This chapter offers a few preliminary remarks to set what follows in context.

The increasing pace of the legislative process

By way of opening observation, looking back on some 22 years' involvement in the preparation of legislation my main impression is that the process was already taken less seriously and more hurriedly than had been the case in previous decades; and the pace has become faster, and the process therefore necessarily more superficial, all the time.

When one looks at files on the preparation of legislation 50 years ago or more, one is struck both by the degree of seriousness with which the process was taken, and by the amount of time and energy

---

[1] See Ch.2 above.
[2] See Ch.2 above.

that people were prepared to spend on considering points of complexity, even if they were substantively trivial. Within Departments, both for lawyers and administrators, to be assigned to work on a Bill was a mark of confidence, and people took it correspondingly seriously. Relatively senior lawyers were responsible for preparing instructions to Parliamentary Counsel, and they were by and large given the time and resources necessary for the purpose.

Nowadays, legislation is routinely prepared at a much lower level within Departments, and at a much faster pace. Partly, this is simply a reflection of the greater burdens placed on resources within the Government Legal Service. Whereas a Bill might once have been considered suitable for allocation as a lawyer's only or main occupation for all or most of its passage, nowadays it is not uncommon for Departmental instructing lawyers to be combining their Bill work with a continuing caseload of advisory work for administrative clients, two or three judicial reviews, drafting responsibility for one or more statutory instruments, and perhaps a human rights case or two in Strasbourg. Senior lawyers in Departments are fewer and farther between than they once were, and the burdens on them are enormous; so it is inevitable that they will delegate Bill work further down the line than would once have been the case. Particularly so, given the greater number of Bills that Departments are nowadays required to prepare.

Technology

The increased speed and superficiality of the preparation of legislation is also, in part, significantly attributable to technological advances, which, as so often, might better be described as technological retreats. Examination of the files on a piece of legislation in the early twentieth century might show that after receipt of instructions Parliamentary Counsel might send out the first clause or two to initiate discussion after maybe two or three weeks, in the case of a fairly urgent Bill; the letter covering the draft clauses would be likely to pose a number of questions, to which the Departmental lawyer might reply by letter, having had time to think properly, within a week or two; after another interval of a couple of weeks, a revised draft might emerge with a renewed set of questions.

Nowadays, instead of lengthy letters that have taken a considerable time to prepare, have been proof-read before being sent out, and which deal with a number of issues, the norm is to receive short and sharp emails, sent with such rapidity that it is impossible that the questions to which they reply can possibly have been fully appreciated, let alone a careful answer prepared. The same speed is expected to be shown by Parliamentary Counsel in responding to correspondence from the Department. Increasingly, instructions for provisions in Bills or for amendments to Bills are sent at the last possible minute, or even after the last possible sensible minute at which they could reasonably be expected to be converted into workable drafts.

Does it matter?

At one point it was common for Parliamentary Counsel to protest that if instructions were not delivered by a particular date the Department could not expect to receive the Bill or amendment requested. These protests became taken less and less seriously, however, because one way or another we were always able to pull the stops out and deliver the goods. The fact that the goods may have been in poorer shape than the drafters felt would have been appropriate did not make much of an impact; so far as Departments are concerned, if they receive their Bill or amendment in time, that shows that they must have allowed enough time for its preparation, and the increasingly routine complaints and warnings of Counsel could therefore safely be ignored. It is of little or no use to tell Ministers that the provisions they have received are less good than would have been the case if adequate time had been given for their drafting and consideration, if Ministers are not seriously concerned about the quality of the legislation.

It is difficult to quantify the risks associated with legislation that has been superficially thought out. Put bluntly, the problem is that legislative drafting is very much like brick-laying or teaching.[3] Everybody

---

[3] As I put it in *The New Oxford Companion to the Law*, (Oxford: Oxford University Press, 2008), under the entry "Drafting of Legislation", "Legislative drafting is like brick-laying in that it seems to the casual observer to be such an easy and simple process as not to demand any special knowledge or skill; and

secretly, or sometimes not very secretly, thinks that they could do either of these professions just as well as those who are trained for it, and that the trained professionals make a great deal of unnecessary fuss about performing their job. Worse than that, up to a point, we are all correct. I could have a shot at brick-laying, and the chances are that having finished, my wall would look, if not quite as straight, neat or tidy as a wall built by a professional, fundamentally serviceable: and given favourable conditions, my wall might last several years. On the other hand, the first winter that provided a series of rapid freezes and thaws would be likely to test my mortar-distribution skills to destruction, and my wall would begin to disintegrate, or completely collapse.

Most law created at speed and with only superficial intellectual foundations will look superficially just as plausible as a more considered product. Like the amateurly constructed wall, even if it shows some signs of having been constructed in haste, it will probably serve its fundamental purpose, until it comes to be seriously tested. That may not happen at all, and it is certainly reasonably unlikely to happen during the tenure of the Minister in Charge of the Bill. Indeed, primary legislation is generally designed to be much more temporary than was once the case: in many areas of the law one major codification follows another at a distance of just a year or two, very often before the first one has been fully commenced or implemented. In these circumstances, it is perhaps not surprising that Departments and Ministers are content to have law drafted as quickly as possible, without being overly concerned about its quality or durability.

Perhaps this is the age of disposability, and it is simply pointless to expect people to demand or appreciate quality in legislation, when they have ceased to expect or appreciate it in so many other things. At the end of the day, one could probably not expect Ministers to listen

---

the more expertly it is performed, the more likely it is to give that impression. Indeed, the product of the inexperienced practitioner may be superficially serviceable, but it will not withstand the rigours of analysis routinely applied by those with an interest in challenging, circumventing or undermining the law. An expert insolvency practitioner is no more likely to be competent to draft a new lawyer about bankruptcy than is a teacher to build a school."

to demands to return to a slower and more thorough process without being able to demonstrate in some quantifiable way the cost to the public of having the present fast and superficial system. Certainly, the courts appear to be constantly confronted with legislation that they and others find difficult to understand. The kind of ambiguity with which the case of *Pepper v Hart* was concerned,[4] and as a result of which the courts permitted themselves to have recourse to *Hansard*, appears to be more and more common. And the courts appear to be increasingly prepared to avoid an absurd or improbable result by simply assuming that the drafter has made a mistake.[5] But these are mere impressions; it would take a considerable amount of empirical evidence that poor-quality legislation has ended up costing the public service money to persuade Ministers to provide more time and thought, both costly commodities, for the preparation of legislation. Indeed, Ministers have just taken the decision to reduce the resources available for the drafting of legislation[6]; so, if anything, the trend is the other way, and perhaps that is only to be expected.

It is also worth pointing out that in bricklaying, if the key objective is to achieve a durable product in as short a period of time as possible, one option may be to opt for a thicker wall that requires less expertise in the matter of its pointing and measurements in order to be reliably sturdy (or which can afford to lose a few bricks to crumbling or disintegration while still leaving a serviceable wall). Drafting is the same: the less time I have to prepare a draft, the more likely I am to have to legislate in broad terms, and to take wide powers, which may go further than is required by the essential policy aims, but which can be guaranteed to achieve those aims and more, without the subtleties and complexities that would be required to achieve those aims alone. The result is legislation that is more intrusive upon the citizen than is necessary, in order to ensure that at least the minimum intrusion has been achieved but without the sophistication required to achieve only the minimum.

---

[4] See further Ch.30.
[5] See further Ch.28.
[6] See further Ch.4.

Who is the system designed for?

If I have one other general observation to make at the outset of
this section, it is this: perhaps understandably, the entire legislative
system revolves around the convenience of the Government, up to the
point of introducing a Bill, and around the combined conveniences
of the Government and Parliamentarians from that point until Royal
Assent.

For example, there is considerable controversy about the method
of legislating known as referential legislation, according to which an
Act takes the form of notional directions to a fictional editor of the
statute book to make specified amendments to earlier Acts, rather
than simply repealing and replacing the earlier Act with a new and
complete code. When Parliamentarians discuss this they generally
focus on how difficult it is for them to pick up the Bill and work out
precisely what its intended effect is to be, given that few if any of them
are likely to be well versed in the previous law. But that should not
be the main question, or even a question of particular importance.
Parliamentarians will be required to look at and understand the Bill
over a period of a few weeks: after Royal Assent, the Bill becomes the
property of those at whom its law is aimed, and it is their convenience,
over the period of possibly decades during which that law will have
force, that ought to be the primary consideration.[7]

In other words, too much of the legislative system is designed for
the convenience of those involved in the legislative system, rather than
of its "clients" or victims. Worse still, a significant amount of what
happens in the course of the legislative process is not about legislation
at all, but about party politics, or other kinds of political in-fighting.

For example, take the case of a Department that has produced a
small and non-controversial Bill, useful law but insufficiently important to the political process to gain a slot in the Government's legislative programme, which they have successfully managed to hand out
to a back-bench Member who has drawn a respectable but relatively
low place in that year's Ballot for private Members' Bills. The private Member secures the Number 2 slot for one of the early Second

---

[7] As to which there are arguments either way.

Reading Fridays, and the Department approaches that event in reasonably complacent mood; the Bill appears to have general support within Parliament, and all the relevant "stakeholders" have been consulted and are content; so it seems likely to be fairly plain sailing. The first Bill on the particular Second Reading Friday is discussed for about an hour and a half, leaving three and a half hours for the other two Bills set down for that day. That should be sufficient to allow the passage of both: the Department are expecting no more than one hour's Second Reading debate on their non-controversial handout Bill. The Chamber, however, appears unaccountably well-populated for that time on a Friday and, in particular, six or seven members of one of the opposition parties appear to have turned up with forbiddingly large stacks of paper that might represent planned Second Reading speeches. The Department do not recognise any of these back-benchers, and have no record of any of them having shown any previous interest in the subject matter of the Bill. And yet, once the private Member successful in the Ballot has introduced the handout Bill, all of these opposition back-benchers rise in their places, indicating to the Speaker that they are hoping to be allowed to make a Second Reading speech; and the first of them gets underway, showing clearly that he or she intends to make a long speech, padded out with frequent interventions from colleagues which he or she graciously allows and responds to.

A little bit baffling, but still hopefully not disastrous. If there are only six or seven Members wishing to, in effect, speak against the Bill, it still has a comfortable chance of getting to the end of the Second Reading debate before the 14:30 cut-off point; and the Department have sensibly warned the private Member to have a large number of colleagues sitting in their Westminster offices catching up on constituency work, ready to come in and vote if necessary at the end of the Second Reading debate. But after the first three or four back-benchers have spoken, a further complication arises. Another four or five Members, again people whom the Department have not heard of in connection with the handout Bill and who could have no conceivable interest in objecting to it, come into the Chamber and join the little group that stand up at the end of every speech to indicate to the Speaker that they are waiting for their turn. It now looks as though there is a real possibility of the handout Bill, non-controversial as it appeared to be, failing to receive a Second Reading, not because of an adverse vote, but simply by virtue of being "talked out".

What is going on? The answer is very simple, and entirely understandable to those who are prepared to see law-making as simply part of the wider game of politics; but possibly not to citizens who feel that the process of making the law should concentrate on whether or not it is good law. What has happened is this: Bill Number 3 for that Second Reading Friday has a number of political opponents on one of the opposition benches who are determined to ensure that it does not proceed. There are not enough of them to be sure of overturning it if it comes to a vote, and they are aware that the Bill has sufficient supporters to ensure that the minimum number of votes that have to be cast for a Second Reading of a private Member's Bill on a Friday, are present and waiting in their offices. Their only chance of blocking the Bill is therefore to "talk it out". There are enough of them for that purpose if the time allowed for Second Reading is, say, only about one hour; but they do not have sufficient support to fill more than that time reliably.[8] So they start with Bill Number 2. By taking entirely spurious objections to Bill Number 2, and while purporting to be broadly sympathetic to its underlying purpose, claiming to have a number of issues of principle or detail that require to be ventilated before it is allowed to proceed, they can cut down the amount of time available for Bill Number 3 to the sort of time that they can comfortably rely upon exceeding. So they or their researchers have written what are in effect entirely bogus speeches on Bill Number 2, purely for the purpose of facilitating their opposition to Bill Number 3. The proposers of Bill Number 3 have watched this happening with growing rage and have determined that if their Bill is going to be talked out then nobody else's Bill is going to be allowed through either. Hence their sudden interest in Bill Number 2, designed to talk it out and to make the point that if they are going down they are going to take at least one, rather random, prisoner with them.

Incidents of this kind are not the regular course of Parliamentary

---

[8] And they would perhaps be vulnerable to a Closure motion if they tried to filibuster the third Bill alone.

procedure, even on private Members' Fridays. But they do happen, and when they happen all those involved simply shrug their shoulders and say something along the lines of "well, that's politics for you". But the citizen may be inclined to feel that this is not how politics should be conducted or, at least, that it is certainly not how law-making should be conducted.

The solution

From time to time attempts are made to ensure that Parliamentary procedure is fit for purpose. In particular, the Modernisation Select Committee of the House of Commons, established in 1997, tried to update procedure in a number of ways, and even carried out a specific study of the legislative process in the course of its activities.[9] The problem is, however, that most studies and reports of the legislative process are carried out from the point of view of politicians, having regard primarily to their convenience and to the legislative process insofar as it forms part of the wider political and Parliamentary process. What is now needed is an official re-run of the 1975 *Renton Report*, considering the efficacy of the Parliamentary process as part of the wider law-making enterprise, and not the other way around.

In similar vein, when discussions ensue about the appropriate short title for a Bill, the drafter is likely to remind the Department that shorter titles are inherently preferable to longer ones. The main reason why this is important is that professionals and private individuals who have to refer to the Act during its lifetime are going to want something that is relatively easy to write, pronounce, and remember. Although Departments will never tell one in words that this is of less importance to them than finding a title which presents the Bill in as politically favourable a light as possible, one frequently gets the strong impression that this is the case. All too often, politicians and civil servants alike forget that the project on which they are working is not the production of a Bill, but the production of an incipient Act of Parliament:

---

[9] See First Report Session 1997–98, *The Legislative Process*, HC 190 (July 29, 1997).

and what matters is, therefore, not that it should have a triumphal passage through Parliament bringing Ministers a blaze of favourable publicity, but that it should emerge from the Parliamentary process as fit for purpose as sound law as possible.

14 THE LEGISLATIVE PROGRAMME

What is "the programme"?

Within Government, Bills are divided into "programme Bills" and others. A programme Bill is one that has been allocated a slot in the Government's legislative programme for a particular Session.

Inclusion in the Queen's Speech at the State Opening of Parliament is a related concept; but although there is considerable overlap, the classes are not entirely the same. The Queen's Speech routinely contains a phrase along the lines of "other measures will be laid before you". That is designed to refer to Bills that are added into the programme during the Session to meet crises or other changing circumstances; but it also reflects the fact that the Queen's Speech highlights only the most important of the Bills that the Government already intends to introduce. The legislative programme settled by Cabinet before the Queen's Speech will include a number of Bills that the Cabinet does not wish to announce expressly in the Queen's Speech, perhaps because they are thought to be too trivial to mention expressly or perhaps because they are not expected to be particularly popular.

Who settles the programme?

Notionally, the legislative programme is agreed by the full Cabinet. There is, however, a Cabinet Committee one of the tasks of which is to draw up a draft legislative programme for Cabinet approval.[1] The name of this committee varies from Government to Government, although it normally has "legislation" somewhere in its title. At the moment, the committee is known as the Parliamentary Business and Legislation Committee, and its terms of reference are "to consider the Government's Parliamentary business and implementation of its legislative programme". The key members of this committee are

---

[1] The other principal task is to approve each Bill before introduction.

the Business Managers (that is to say, the Leader of the House of Commons, the Leader of the House of Lords, and the Chief Whip in each House) and the Law Officers.

The legislative programme is settled before the Queen's Speech; but it is, of course, susceptible to variation during the Session.

Significance of the programme

Some time before the legislative programme for each new Session, each Department is invited to prepare one or more bids for a Bill in the programme. The likelihood of success of any particular bid is, of course, determined by a multiplicity of factors. Perceived political pressure in respect of the matters which the Bill will address, and the comparative weight within Cabinet of the senior Minister in charge of the Department, are probably the two most important factors as a general rule.

Winning a place in the legislative programme is more or less a guarantee of having the relevant Bill introduced in that Session of Parliament. If a Department is unsuccessful in respect of a particular bid, that does not necessarily mean that it will fail to have the proposed legislation enacted in that Session. If the Bill is small and non-controversial, it may be possible to hand it out to a back-bencher in either House, to be taken through as a private Member's Bill or private peer's Bill. Alternatively, it may be possible to have some or all of the planned content of the Bill included as provisions in another Bill sponsored by the same Department, or even by a different Department.[2]

Finally, there may be ways in which the Department can achieve the change in the law that it desires without using a Bill. There may be an appropriate power to legislate by secondary legislation, perhaps by instrument implementing a European Union obligation under s. 2(2) of the European Communities Act 1972 or by Legislative Reform Order. Or it could be that administrative action, or amending quasi-legislation such as a code of conduct or guidance, will achieve the required result. One might, of course, consider that these options

---

[2] See further Ch.17.

should be thoroughly explored before it is proposed to introduce a Bill. The reality is, however, that Ministers and Departments are often anxious for purely political reasons to have a Bill, whether or not it is strictly necessary.[3]

Once a place in the legislative programme has been allocated to a Bill, it can still be lost if the Bill is not prepared and brought to the Legislation Committee in time to be introduced in accordance with a central timetable of introductions settled by the Government's Business Management Ministers. Although it is rare for that Committee to refuse a Bill permission to be introduced on grounds of unreadiness, it is not unheard of; and the result could be to delay introduction or to prevent it altogether. It is, however, extremely unlikely that this would be allowed to happen in the case of a Bill that had been announced as part of the Queen's Speech.

Clearance

Before a Bill can be introduced, the policy to which it gives effect must be cleared at a number of levels within Government. This is in addition to any consultation with outside interests that is thought necessary or desirable in order to ensure the legislation a trouble-free passage.

Most policy is likely to originate within a particular branch of a large Department, where it will be developed and refined to satisfy the concerns of that branch. Even if the policy has originated at Ministerial level, it is likely to have whistled down through the various levels of the Department to an appropriate branch, and to stay there for some time being prepared for action. So the Department will have its own mechanisms for enabling the branch concerned to communicate the proposed policy to other branches of the Department, and to invite them to contribute to the development of a policy that achieves as many Departmental aims as possible without obstructing other Departmental initiatives.

---

[3] Ministers want headlines in newspapers; and newspapers are more likely to report Parliamentary proceedings of Bills than the issuing of new administrative guidance to officials.

Once the intra-Departmental clearance process is complete, the policy of the proposed Bill has to be cleared with other Departments around Whitehall, and often with the devolved Administrations as well; to say nothing of a longer or shorter, and more or less formal, process of public consultation.

The effect of the process on legislation

There are a few practical implications of the immensely lengthy and cumbersome process that has to be gone through before a Bill can be introduced into Parliament.

First, judges and other readers are always looking for possible answers to the question "Why on earth would the drafter have expressed the point in the terms of section X, if what he or she was really after was result Y?". There are always innumerable possible answers, including that the drafter may not have been very good; but it may be helpful to add to the list of possibilities a realisation that the constraints on the process of what the drafter can and cannot do in practice start much earlier than many people realise.

For example, although I have said in an earlier Chapter[4] that the vast majority of the words of each Act are not only chosen by Parliamentary Counsel but never seriously considered by anyone else, it is certainly true that a number of words and phrases in a particular Act may be of particular political or presentational importance and may therefore be subjected to scrutiny in various ways. If the word or phrase is of importance to outside interests, it could be that it will be, in effect, negotiated at the stage of public consultation; or, at least, that having exposed the draft legislation to public view in one particular form, the departmental officials will not think it appropriate to change it later on before introduction, in case they are accused of having carried out the process of consultation in bad faith. In the meantime, however, it may have become clear that for any one of a hundred possible reasons the word or phrase is no longer entirely apt for the technical job that it is required to do, perhaps because the surrounding context within the developing Bill has changed. Of course,

---

[4] See Ch.4.

if the deficiency is so pronounced that Counsel can declare that the provision no longer works, then it will have to be changed, and the Bill team will have to undertake any additional consultation that they think necessary. But far more often the infelicity is too slight to allow Counsel to make an unequivocal statement of that kind, but still sufficient to contain the seeds of doubt and puzzlement, and therefore legal uncertainty, when the courts and other readers come to unravel the provision after enactment and ask themselves "but why would the drafter put it quite like that?".

To give another example, in the process of inter-Departmental clearance Department A may insist upon a change to Department B's Bill, to reflect a policy of Department A which subsequently changes, at a point in the process when it is too late to change the Bill. If the point is important, the Bill will be amended; but if it is insufficiently important to justify an amendment, then it will again remain as a mere oddity in the Bill, for people to puzzle over after enactment.

Departmental tensions may also account for oddities of expression or application. In the case of European Union legislation, everyone knows and accepts that it is produced on the back of a process of multi-State negotiation, and political compromise often results in some very strange-looking provisions, including expressions that are deliberately ambiguous or vague because clarity would require coming down on one side or another of a politically intractable argument. It is less well known that precisely the same process can occur, although less routinely, in domestic legislation, with the interests and concerns of different Departments and their Ministers taking the place of different States.

15 THE DRAFTING PROCESS

How does one draft a Bill?

Again, a large amount of technical detail will be found in other places and I am not going to repeat it here.[1] At the expense of a few lines of text, however, it seems worth giving my principal personal impressions of how the job is done.

Some of what I say about Parliamentary Counsel in Ch.4 is also relevant here.

Ignorance, scepticism and pedantry

When the instructions to draft the Bill arrive, the most important thing is to approach them with the assumption that every single word of what they say is based on a misconception. The most useful assets that the drafter brings to the legislative process are scepticism, ignorance and pedantry. The scepticism leads one to assume that everything anybody says is wrong unless and until proven right[2]; the ignorance causes one to ask penetrating questions that go all the way back to the foundations of the proposals, ignoring, and therefore frequently successfully challenging, assumptions of law or policy that have become generally accepted in the process; and the pedantry leads one to analyse each concept to destruction, and to insist upon starting to build only with blocks of such simplicity and accuracy that their

---

[1] See, in particular, the *Renton Report*, the *Hansard Society Report* and *Craies on Legislation*.

[2] The only thing which saves the drafter from arrogance, therefore, is the consciousness that he or she is no more immune than anybody else from the propensity for getting things wrong. One tests one's colleague's drafts to destruction on the assumption that they are wrong from beginning to end; but one treats one's own work of the year before, or even the day before, in the same way and with the same result.

meaning is, ideally, apparent to everyone, whether or not they are already "in the secret" of what is intended and assumed.

Is your journey really necessary?

The most important and useful destructive analysis that the drafter brings to the process is in questioning whether anything is required by way of legislation at all. It always used to be generally accepted within Government that legislation is to be used only to change the law, and not for advertising or other purposes of political propaganda.[3]

If drafters can reduce a proposal for what the Department expects to be 50 pages of legislation to a single basic proposition with a handful of qualifications, they have scored a considerable success: they have saved Parliamentary time, but more importantly they have reduced, and made simpler and clearer, the amount of law with which professionals and others will have to grapple in due course.[4] If a pro-

---

[3] This is no longer accepted to anything like the same extent—see further "Nothing Will Come From Nothing, Daniel Greenberg laments the introduction of nonsense legislation", (2010) *New Law Journal*, July 30, p.1084; but it still holds good for the analysis of technical aspects of legislation that is intended to have substantive effect.

[4] The idea that the more words one uses and the more detailed one's legislation, the more one has enhanced the clarity of the law, is fundamentally misconceived. The pitfall of false accuracy is just as dangerous for the drafter, if not more so, then the possibility of being less detailed than is appropriate. See, for example, the Gambling Act 2005, s.42: it would have been possible, and many would have preferred, to attempt to set out in great detail the circumstances that did and did not amount to cheating. The attempt would, however, have been bound to fail, and the plethora of words used would simply have given opportunities for lawyers to make work for themselves. By using a concept of the natural world which is well understood within most circumstances, and has no greater margin of unclarity than attempted detail would also have left, the Act has left it for magistrates and juries to decide what amounts to cheating in any particular set of circumstances, a process that would have been unavoidable irrespective of the shape of the legislation. It has, however, avoided constraining the courts in reaching a decision by reference to an attempt to imagine every conceivable set of circumstances and to prescribe for it.

posed Bill can be seen off altogether as unnecessary, perhaps because alternative methods of legislation or regulation already exist, drafters are really earning their money. Far from being paid for productivity, therefore, drafters really ought to be paid for non-productivity.[5]

Initial approaches

Eventually, one admits that something in the instructions before one does require legislation, and one begins to draft. There are, broadly speaking, two extremes in how one goes about this. One approach is to start by thinking through the instructions until one has a broad but complete grasp of what it is one is trying to achieve and then, and only then, to write something down. The other extreme approach is to start drafting, or at least sketching, from the first moment that one starts to read the instructions, constantly adapting and revisiting the draft as one goes. There are actually a few people who follow one or other of these two extremes. Most people, however, go for something between the two on most occasions, nearer to one extreme or the other depending on how one's mind works and on the nature of the particular set of instructions.

One of my most influential teachers of the art of drafting, who was one of the most powerful and effective drafters of relatively recent times, intensely disliked writing anything down until he had a very clear picture of the overall scenery. The result was that on occasion he could spend some weeks contemplating a set of instructions and then reduce them to a very short series of legislative propositions, at which nobody who favours the "rush in and scramble" approach could have arrived, even after considerable rounds of refinement. Sometimes, however, adhering to the "think before you leap" approach makes it difficult to start at all, or at least within the short time that is sometimes all that is available for producing a first draft.

---

[5] I always thought it would have a useful effect on the statute book if drafters were allotted a fixed maximum number of words to use each year: once they had used their full allocation, each extra word used by them in drafting would result in a small deduction from their pay at the end of the year. This would concentrate the mind on the importance of brevity in drafting.

All of which goes to show that different kinds of mind—and at its best the Office of the Parliamentary Counsel contained an interesting diversity of minds and approaches—are suited to different projects. As with any other kind of technical artist, different drafters will be better suited to different kinds of work, and allocating the right project to the right person is in itself a considerably demanding skill.

Eventually, one produces a first draft. Here too, however, tastes and opinions vary as to when it is the right moment to show one's draft to the Department. My own preference was to expose a draft as early as possible, if necessary describing it as a preliminary sketch; I found that to be the most efficient way of drawing out structural difficulties from the Department at an early stage; and I never minded being told if I had made fundamental errors. Others, however, tended to prefer to keep their draft to themselves until they were reasonably sure that it was fit for purpose. Although again there are no rules about which approach is best, mine has two advantages: first, it makes use of the Departmental lawyers as well as one's own assistants in devilling the draft from an early stage; secondly, it is often the only way to meet the increasingly demanding timetables imposed on the drafter.

Exposure to criticism

Irrespective of the point at which one is prepared to expose one's draft to the Department, at that point one must accept, and if necessary force oneself to welcome, comments and criticisms. Although it is less pronounced than it once was, there is still a general tradition of deference towards Parliamentary Counsel in Government Departments as a whole. Paradoxically, I have the impression that the attitude to Parliamentary Counsel felt, but not expressed, within Departments is less appreciative than it once was, particularly amongst administrators; but Counsel are still generally approached outwardly with something of deference.

This is not, and I think never was, a good thing. It is always preferable to treat people with courtesy. But deference is something else, and, if it is ever appropriate to show it at all, the object of it has to earn the right to it by proving his or her worth. Merely because somebody is working in the Office of the Parliamentary Counsel does not make his or her opinions on any subject more likely to be right than anybody else's; although it will, on comparatively rare occasions, give him or her the power to follow them even in defiance of the majority. The Departmental lawyers with whom I have had the most enjoyable and productive relationship over the years, have also been those who were most ready to attack, question and insist upon defence of my drafts. Dealing with a Departmental lawyer who simply accepts everything you say, and buys everything you produce, is like trying to fight with a marshmallow. The drafting process is at its best when every aspect of the draft is being tested against sharp and penetrating analysis and challenge. A Departmental lawyer, or administrator, who accepts without question everything emanating from Parliamentary Counsel, effectively subverts the process and deprives the system of its efficacy.

The same, incidentally, is true within the Parliamentary Counsel office itself. The senior-devil relationship ought again to be one of dynamism and mutually respectful provocation. Very often one tries out a new idea, or an extreme approach, precisely for the purpose of provoking one's devil into challenging it; one then meets the challenge and debates the usefulness of the idea or approach, until it has either been destroyed or affirmed. A devil who simply agrees with one is largely useless.

Having begun the process of exchanging drafts and comments with the Department, one simply continues until the process is complete or one has run out of time. As to the first possibility, contrary to some people's expectations, it is possible to take a draft to the point at which further polishing will only make it worse. Too little thought is the enemy of good drafting; but too much thought can be an equally damaging problem. After a while, one loses objectivity and grasp on the overall picture, and starts obsessively to move and change words without any good reason, doing either no good or actual harm. To put it simply: pedantry good, neurosis bad.

As to running out of time, in recent years it has become the norm rather than the exception for a Bill to be introduced into Parliament before it is completely ready. Despite occasional remonstrations, Parliamentarians on all sides appear to have accepted that Bills will be brought in half-baked, and a raft of Government amendments will be tabled to attempt to finish the cooking during the Parliamentary process.[6] Worse still, from the democratic point of view, it has now become routine for Bills of any size to include a power for the Minister to finish the job, in effect, by subordinate legislation: these powers to make ancillary and supplementary provision have largely been accepted without major controversy, although one might think that they were an affront to the entire democratic process. If a Bill requires further work, including consequential work on other parts of the statute book, that work should be undertaken before the Bill is introduced into Parliament, and not after: otherwise, in being asked to approve the Bill, Parliament is not being shown the whole picture of the legislative changes proposed.[7] The affront is compounded by the fact that Departments no longer appear to regard it as anything to be ashamed of to admit openly that an Act a few weeks old needs to be corrected by statutory instrument if it is to work properly; nor do they appear to expect any difficulty about having the necessary corrections regarded as consequential or incidental provision.[8]

---

[6] This is not, however, something that can be achieved satisfactorily—see further Ch.19.

[7] For specific discussion of a controversy in relation to a particular form of a power of this kind see further Ch.23; what that incident shows, however, is that as a general rule these provisions have come to be accepted, and it is only the occasional change of form that gives rise to controversy.

[8] See, for example, the Explanatory Memorandum to the Equality Act 2010 (Consequential Amendments, Saving and Supplementary Provisions) Order 2010 (SI 2010/2279): "2.1 This Order makes minor amendments to the Equality Act 2010 ("the Act"), and minor amendments and repeals to other primary legislation, which are consequent on, or supplementary to, commencement of the Act. The amendments to the Act are supplementary to commencement, in that they give full effect to one of the main purposes of the Act, namely to harmonise and restate equality law. The amendments achieve that by making minor corrections and by updating certain references to reflect recent amendments to some of the current equality provisions."

16 INTRODUCTION OF BILL

The stage in outline

Every Bill has to begin by being introduced in, or presented to, one of the Houses of Parliament. For a Government Bill, this is achieved by a Minister of the Crown giving notice on Day 1 of presentation of a Bill, presenting the Bill on Day 2, and having it printed by the House on Day 3.[1]

Introduction, and the technical First Reading that immediately follows it, are entirely formal stages, that do not occupy any debating time on the floor of the House, and are not put to a vote.[2] There is therefore no particular pressure on the number of Bills that can be introduced, and a great many Bills are introduced by private Members, without any realistic prospect of proceeding further than introduction, but for the sake of attracting a little publicity by the mere process of introduction.

Indeed, as part of a long-running and carefully planned campaign to change the law, the introduction of a few abortive Bills can be a useful way of focusing attention on an issue, and of preparing to attract support for an eventual private Member's Bill brought in under the Ballot with some reasonable chance of success. In particular, the process known as the 10-Minute Rule Bill,[3] can provide a

---

[1] The three principal qualifications to this are as follows: (1) in the House of Lords there is no Day 1 Notice of Presentation; (2) Finance Bills are technically brought in on resolutions of the House, which is why the Budget debate centres around a series of Ways and Means Resolutions proposed by the Chancellor of the Exchequer; (3) not all Bills are printed on Day 3—it is possible, and increasingly common, to arrange for them to be printed on Day 2 immediately after presentation.

[2] With the potential exception of 10-Minute Rule Bills, on which a vote is possible, as described above.

[3] So-called, of course, because the maximum amount of time that can be spent debating it is 20 Minutes!

significant injection of publicity: it allows the presenter to give a short speech in favour of the Bill, at a time straight after Questions when there may still be a few Members and even Ministers present, or at least leaving the Chamber slowly enough to hear a word or two; and the press gallery may not yet be entirely deserted.

Other Bills may simply be presented by being handed in at the "Back of the Chair". Those Bills will receive no automatic debate, and almost without exception will proceed no further. That will not, of course, prevent the Member who hands in the Bill from issuing an exciting-looking press release to his or her local newspaper: "Local MP acts to change the law about . . .".

Technically speaking, Bills do not need to be introduced into the second House: once a Bill has been passed by the House of Commons it is automatically sent to the House of Lords, where it waits to see if any peer is prepared to pick it up and run with it; the same applies in reverse for Bills sent from the House of Lords to the House of Commons.

Which House?

Technically speaking, almost any Bill can start in either House. The main exception is Finance Bills, which for technical reasons are more or less bound to begin in the House of Commons.[4] Other Bills with significant public finance components are also likely to start in the House of Commons.

There used to be a working presumption that Bills that contained a large amount of "lawyers' law" would begin in the House of Lords. Although that presumption may take some time to die, it owed its origins to the presence of the Lord Chancellor in the House of Lords as the Speaker of that House, as well as to the presence of the Law Lords and, more importantly (since the serving Law Lords by convention did not speak on Bills), a number of retired Law Lords. Now that the Lord Chancellor is a Ministerial post combined with

---

[4] In particular, the mechanism of the Provisional Collection of Taxes Act 1968, by virtue of which Budget increases can be given immediate effect, works only for a Bill starting in the House of Commons.

the Secretary of State for Justice, and is as likely to be found in the House of Commons as in the House of Lords, and now that the Law Lords have formally migrated to the Supreme Court, there may be thought to be less reason for starting Bills of this kind in the House of Lords.

Those presumptions apart, the decision as to which House to start in is generally made more by reference to general Business Management considerations than by reference to the content of each particular Bill. For example, the most obvious requirement of the Government's Business Managers at the start of each Parliamentary Session is to have a roughly similar amount of legislative business starting off in each House: if the House of Lords is kept waiting, doing little in the way of legislation, for the first couple of months of a Session while the Commons passes a stream of Bills, that is likely to place considerable strain on the Lords' timing later in the Session.

Another factor in determining the first House is likely to be the home of the senior Departmental Minister responsible for the Bill. A Secretary of State whose seat is in the House of Lords is likely to want any flagship Bill from the Department to start in that House, to enable him or her to make the opening speech at Second Reading and, hopefully, attract media publicity. Whether or not he or she is successful in arranging that will, however, depend on the Business Management considerations already discussed and, to some extent, on how much weight attaches within Government to the wishes of that particular Secretary of State.

Timing

Once upon a time, a Bill was prepared with care until such time as it was ready for introduction, and then it was introduced. Such halcyon days are long gone. Nowadays, a central unit within the Prime Minister's office in No. 10 Downing Street determines the optimal dates for introduction of Bills, by reference to the unit's intentions for media handling and publicity. If the Bill happens to be ready by that time, all well and good. If not, it is likely to be introduced anyway, and a raft of Government amendments will doubtless be necessary in order to put it into the state in which it would have been ready for introduction. That is, of course, only one of the reasons why Bills are often introduced in an imperfect state.[5]

The timing of introduction has also been affected by the recent experiments in carry- over from one session of Parliament to another.[6] Whereas it was once the case that anything not ready to be introduced by about February was pretty much too late for that Session, unless it was very small or extremely urgent, it is now possible to introduce a large and complicated Bill at more or less any point during one Session with a view to having it carried over to the next.

In theory, of course, the increased possibilities of carrying-over are a victory for democracy, in the sense that it is possible to provide plenty of time for debate without being constrained by the approach of the end of the Session. In practice, however, recent experience has been rather the reverse: having all Bills die at the end of each Session was an important constraint on the Government's power to legislate, possibly the only really effective constraint on the power of a Government with a large House of Commons majority. Even a relatively small Opposition was able to impose a degree of restraint, by negotiating over the progress of Bills as the end of each Session approached. The more use that is allowed to be made of carry-over, the easier it will be for Governments to ignore the usual channels and any attempt by the Opposition to negotiate. It will be interesting to see what use is proposed to be made of carrying-over by the coalition Government formed in 2010, particularly since they made an early announcement that it was not their intention to impose programming restraints on the amount of time allowed for debating Bills.

Conclusion

The main way in which the circumstances of a Bill's introduction are likely to affect the shape of the emerging Act is that the less ready the Bill really was for introduction the more defective the final product is likely to be. A defective foundation can only be remedied to a

---

[5] See further Ch.14.

[6] For more details of the present technical possibilities of carrying over see *Craies on Legislation*, 9th edn.

very limited extent by alterations in the plans as the building is constructed, and the same goes for Bills.

For reasons of scope, where it is known that material on a particular subject will be wanted for addition to a Bill during its passage, it is common to include what is referred to as a "marker clause" on introduction; this is in effect a dummy clause, which is not intended to remain on enactment, designed merely to hold a slot for the subject to prevent challenge on scope grounds when the Government are ready to introduce the real provision by way of amendment. So the Government sometimes introduces Bills not merely knowing that certain provisions may require perfection by way of amendment, but actually without having any intention of certain provisions remaining in the Bill at all.

The courts have already become more comfortable than they might have been once with the idea of examining what happens to a Bill during its passage in Parliament and, in particular, its amendment history, for the purposes of construing the Act that emerges from it.[7] There may be room for taking notice also of what goes on in relation to a Bill shortly before its passage and, in particular, the circumstances of its introduction. For example, where a Bill is introduced relatively late in the Session and there is evidence that a provision included on introduction was never intended to be more than a marker, being replaced in its entirety in Committee or on Report, that might affect how the courts treat anything that may have been said about the provision at Second Reading, perhaps according it weight in construing the eventual replacement provision despite its different shape.

---

[7] See further Ch.30.

17 SCOPE

Introduction

Each House of Parliament has rules about the scope of Bills before it,[1] designed to prevent debating time allocated to one issue from being swamped by attempts to introduce quantities of material on another subject altogether.

As a general rule, amendments may not be tabled to a Bill that are outside its scope. That rule is, technically at least, enforced rigidly by the Speaker and by Chairs of Committees in the House of Commons, as a matter of order. In the House of Lords, there is considerably less discipline in matters of that kind, but at least in clear cases of abuse the House has effective methods of self-discipline to prevent Bills being diverted from their principal objects.

Sufficient discussion of the technical application of the rules of scope and relevance in each House to thoroughly confuse the reader will be found in *Erskine May*.[2] In practice, this is one of the many aspects of Parliamentary procedure that is more a matter of feel and experience than of the application of rigid rules.

How does the scope of Bills affect the content of Acts?

The best way of answering this question is probably to start by giving one of the most extreme examples. Section 145 of the Nationality, Immigration and Asylum Act 2002 created offences of trafficking in prostitution. Subsection (1) created an offence of trafficking someone

---

[1] In the House of Lords, scope is technically known as "relevance"; although members of the House of Lords are as likely as others to forget the distinction and to refer to scope, a much more commonly used expression.

[2] Although as I write, a new addition of *May* is in preparation, and it is to be hoped that on this and a number of other subjects it will bring greater clarity, hopefully by trying less hard to be comprehensive.

into the United Kingdom. Subsection (2) created an offence of trafficking someone within the United Kingdom, but only where the
person had first been the victim of a subsection (1) offence. One might
well ask, if there is to be a new offence of trafficking a prostitute
from London to Birmingham, why should it matter whether or not
someone else has previously trafficked the prostitute from outside the
United Kingdom into London? The answer is that of course it does
not matter, but in the context of a Bill about nationality and immigration it was impossible, because of the rules of scope, to include provision about the trafficking of prostitutes without restricting it to cases
with some kind of international connection: the restriction is clearly
artificial, but that does not prevent it from sufficing for the purposes of
the House rules on scope. The Nationality, Immigration and Asylum
Bill was the first Bill available for creating a new offence, and it was
quickly repealed and replaced by a fully generalised provision in the
Sexual Offences Act 2003.[3]

Of course, such extreme examples as this are very rare. But it serves
to illustrate a point, that when practitioners and courts are faced with
a provision that appears unexpectedly narrow, having regard to what
might be expected to be the underlying policy, they would do well to
ask themselves whether the rules of scope as applied to the Bill for the
Act in question might have imposed a relevant constraint.

So what?

If a court decides that the extent of a provision was indeed dictated by
the requirements of the rules of scope—and this might well be one of
the cases in which the rule in *Pepper v Hart* would permit recourse to

---

[3] At the Second Reading in the House of Lords of the Bill for the Nationality,
Immigration and Asylum Act 2002 the Minister, Lord Filkin, said: "We are
committed to strengthening the law to clamp down on the evil crime of trafficking women and children for the purpose of sexual exploitation. We have
acted quickly by including in the Bill measures to close the loopholes that allow
foreign nationals and those from the EU to be brought into or through the UK
for this purpose. We will do more in other legislation subsequently." *Hansard*,
HL Vol.636, col.1093 (June 24, 2002).

Hansard[4]—the question arises as to what effect, if any, that should have on the court's decision.

In essence, of course, the reason why Parliament has chosen to legislate in a restricted way is irrelevant, once it is accepted that the restriction is clearly established by the choice of words used. It is inconceivable that the courts would ever say "Well, we know that Parliament had really wanted to legislate about dogs as well as cats, and the only reason why it was prevented from doing so was that the Bill for this Act was only about cats and not about dogs, so we will apply some kind of purposive rule so as to include cats as well as dogs in the enacted provision".[5]

If anything, the impact of the discovery of information about scope on the construction of legislation would be likely to be the reverse. Imagine, for example, an argument about an undefined reference to "animal" in an ancillary provision of an Act otherwise dealing expressly with dogs alone. It is conceivable that there might be some arguable ambiguity about whether the reference to "animal" was intended to be read entirely generally, or whether it was intended to be coloured by surrounding express references to dogs. If the ancillary provision in question had been added by amendment during the passage of the Bill, it might be argued that the legislative intention can be deduced from the fact that the rules of scope would have prevented a provision of substantive generality[6]; and if there were any direct or indirect reference to the limitations imposed by the rules of scope, such as were found in relation to the nationality example above, that might well be sufficient to decide the question.

That apart, it is possible that simply knowing the effect that the

---

[4] Or one of those cases where the court denies that the rule in *Pepper v Hart* applies but proceeds to look at *Hansard* anyway; see, for example, *Earl Cadogan v Sportelli* [2008] UKHL 71, per Lord Neuberger of Abbotsbury, [113]–[114].

[5] For an unsuccessful, and rightly so, attempt to encourage the courts to understand the notion of purpose of this in this way, see the discussion of the *Haw* case in Ch.28.

[6] The point would be less clear in the case of a provision that had always been in the Bill since introduction, because the scope of a Bill is determined by reference to the sum of its provisions when introduced.

rules of scope may have had upon the shaping of a particular provision may help practitioners, and the courts, to achieve a quick and clearer understanding of the terms of the provision. Being able to give oneself a firm answer as to why a provision was drafted in a particular way, can, if nothing else, save practitioners considerable time that might otherwise be spent in wondering why it was not drafted differently.

18 HYBRIDITY

Introduction

The rules of hybridity are possibly one of the most complicated areas of Parliamentary procedure.

As for scope, the reader will find a highly technical explanation of the rules set out in *Erskine May*; but it is difficult or impossible to apply these rules as a technical and academic exercise without the kind of appreciation of their flavour and purpose that comes from experience. A former Clerk of the House of Commons once told me that in his view the rules of hybridity were more a matter of smell than anything else; and I knew precisely what he meant.

In essence, the purpose and effect of the rules of hybridity are as follows. They exist to ensure that Parliament does not legislate in such a way as to prejudice the private interests of particular individuals or businesses, at least without giving those individuals or businesses an opportunity to make representations beforehand. If a Bill is found to be hybrid, therefore, before it can pass through the usual stages of examination of the provisions of a public Bill, it is subjected to a process, based on that used for private Bills, during which individuals and businesses that claim to be adversely affected by the Bill can petition a Committee of Parliament to explain what those effects would be and why they are unfair or otherwise inappropriate.

It is important to understand that merely prejudicing private interests does not make a Bill hybrid. The Government can introduce legislation which will cost people a great deal of money and interfere with their property in intrusive ways, but provided that all people, or all members of each relevant class of person, are treated in the same way, hybridity does not arise. One of the technicalities that can prove difficult to determine is what amounts to a relevant class for this purpose. But the essence of the idea is that hybridity is there to prevent public Bills from singling out particular individuals or businesses for disadvantageous treatment, at least without giving them an opportunity to be heard.

The issue of whether a Bill is hybrid is determined by the House Authorities.[1] In practice, before a Bill is formally referred for examination on the point, informal discussions will have been held between the House Authorities and Parliamentary Counsel.[2]

How does hybridity affect the shape of Acts?

The hybrid Bill procedure is extremely lengthy, and involves the Government in considerable expense. It is so lengthy that it is very difficult for a hybrid Bill to pass through all its stages in a single Session; which is why hybrid Bills have always been an exception to the rules that public Bills die at the end of a Session and are not carried over to the next.[3] For these reasons, apart from Bills whose entire purpose is to affect public works (such as the construction of a new rail link with the Channel), the Government will go to considerable lengths to avoid having one of their Bills adjudged to be hybrid.

The most obvious way of avoiding hybridity is to take a proposition that in reality is aimed only at one or more members of a relevant class, but to generalise it so that it on its face it affects all members of the class equally. A Government Bill to privatise the property of Daniel Greenberg Dog Control Ltd would be hybrid; but a Government Bill to privatise the property of all animal control companies would not be; and whether or not a Government Bill to privatise the property of all dog control companies would be hybrid, would depend on the House Authorities' appreciation of dog control companies as a distinct commercial class. So the first method of avoiding hybridity is to cast one's net widely.

The obvious problem with that, however, is that the Government may not want to privatise all animal control companies, or even all dog control companies. If the target in reality is Daniel Greenberg

---

[1] As to whom, see Ch.9.

[2] Although the informal discussions may not be the last word on the matter if, in particular, a Bill is challenged on grounds of potential hybridity during its passage through either House—see, for example, the Local Government Bill 2010.

[3] As to recent changes to these rules, see Ch.16.

Dog Control Ltd alone, one might think a hybrid Bill therefore inevitable. Not so. The first possible way of avoiding hybridity would be to frame the provision in question as a power, allowing the Secretary of State to privatise the property of any dog control company that he or she chooses. On the face of the Bill, therefore, this would be a completely general power, that did not single out any particular private interests for prejudicial treatment. But that would not necessarily be the end of the story: the House Authorities would need to be convinced (a) that the power was in practice capable of being exercised in respect of a complete and genuine class, and (b) that there was no settled intention to exercise the power in respect of only one or more particular members of a genuine class. Of course, if it were known that the only real intended target were Daniel Greenberg Dog Control Ltd then the second condition could not be satisfied.

The result of all this is that when confronted with a provision which appears to give power to do by subordinate legislation something that one might have expected to be done, at least as to its principal details, on the face of the Act itself, one can ask oneself whether the reason for doing the entire process by subordinate legislation is to avoid a possibility of hybridity.

Nothing, of course, turns on this as to the validity of the provision in question. Hybridity is only a rule of the two Houses of Parliament. Even if a Bill that manifestly should have been treated as hybrid were allowed to proceed as a normal public Bill, after Royal Assent the courts would, on fundamental constitutional principles, not allow themselves to examine the nature of the proceedings leading up to Royal Assent, and the Act would be treated as being just as valid as any other.

Validity aside, however, it may be helpful for practitioners and judges to bear hybridity in mind as a possible explanation for an apparently unusual or unexpected power, or for a provision that is cast in more general terms than one might have thought necessary or appropriate having regard to the underlying policy.[4]

---

[4] A good example of this would be s.132 of the Serious Organised Crime and Police Act 2005. Although apparently aimed at banning demonstrations near Parliament generally, examination of the *Hansard* debates shows that in

De-hybridising provisions

It is arguable that hybridity has really had its day, and that the modern procedures of administrative law are better able to safeguard private interests from improper interference by the Executive than a complex procedure centred around committees of politicians. Although the courts may not and should not become involved in reviewing the legitimacy of Parliament's legislative intentions,[5] the political decisions underlying the policy of a hybrid Bill should be susceptible to judicial review, as should decisions on the exercise of any power granted by public general or hybrid Bill. And, of course, the incorporation into UK law of the European Convention on Human Rights by the Human Rights Act 1998 has introduced significant protection against arbitrary interference with people's rights to private property, which can be policed by the courts even against an express provision of an Act, and which therefore occupies, but more effectively, a large part of the field of rights that the hybridity process was designed to protect.

The emptiness of the principles of hybridity is perhaps best demonstrated by the fact that although the House of Lords operates a hybridity procedure for statutory instruments that are subject to affirmative resolution, it has become a matter of routine for the enabling Act conferring a power that might be exercised in a hybrid manner to include an express de-hybridising provision, providing that any instrument that would be subject to the rules of hybridity is to

---

reality Mr Brian Haw was the only intended target of the new legislation. So much so, that Crown Counsel tried to argue that a purposive construction of the legislation, aided by examination of *Hansard*, would be bound to include Mr Haw within its remit (see further Ch.28). The legislation is, however, in entirely general terms. The risk of an allegation of hybridity may have been one reason for this; or there may have been other legal reasons why a more closely-targeted provision was thought vulnerable, possibly on human rights grounds; or it may have been felt that despite the specificity of the acknowledged policy intention, targeting Mr. Haw alone would be likely to lead to others quickly seeking to replace him.

[5] Although this statement—which a few years ago would have been a truism—is now subject to significant exceptions, in relation to the European Union and the European Convention on Human Rights.

proceed as if it were not. These provisions are routinely included, without giving rise to serious protest or even attention. If there were any reality in the efficacy of hybridity as a protection for private interests, one could expect that de-hybridising provisions would be treated as an abomination, whereas in fact they no longer even raise a yawn.

The Modernisation Committee of the House of Commons which was established by the incoming Labour Government in 1997 achieved some notable successes, perhaps the most significant of which was the abolition of the rule requiring Members who wanted to raise Points of Order during a division to wear a top hat, one being specially kept near the Speaker's Chair for that purpose.[6] If the Committee were to be re-established and were looking for any more pressing items for its continuing agenda, the question of hybridity would be one that could afford profitable inquiry. To establish a modern system that recognised the importance of identifying and protecting private interests from unintended or improper consequences of otherwise general legislation would be a significant advance.

---

[6] No—not a joke, unhappily; see Select Committee on Modernisation of the House of Commons, Fourth Report, March 9, 1998, paras.63–65.

19 AMENDMENTS

Introduction

Bills can be amended at various stages during their passage through either House of Parliament. A Bill that starts in the House of Commons is then sent to the House of Lords, which can amend it; those amendments go back to the first House and have to be agreed before they are made. The same process applies in reverse to a Bill that starts in the House of Lords.

Technical discussion of what is possible by way of amendment will be found in *Erskine May*.[1] The essence of the system, however, is that amendments have to be made by combinations of three operations: the removal of text, the addition of text and the substitution of text. These three tools have to be applied to the Bill as it was introduced or last amended, in a relatively economical way so as to minimise the amount of Parliamentary time taken up in debating them and in order to satisfy other practical constraints (such as the need to be able to explain their effect in terms sufficiently clear to lead to their being agreed to). There are restrictions on the times at which amendments can be tabled, and on the topics that may be covered.[2]

The technicalities of the amendment process can leave a significant mark on the shape of the Act that emerges from Parliament; and it is the purpose of this chapter to identify some of the principal ways in which this can happen.

By way of final introduction it is worth noting that the courts are increasingly prepared to investigate the technicalities of an Act's Parliamentary history in construing it;[3] they are, in particular,

---

[1] See Ch.2 above.
[2] See further Ch.17.
[3] See for example *Lewisham London Borough Council v Malcolm* [2008] UKHL 43, [77]–[81] per Baroness Hale at (dissenting).

prepared to turn their mind to the possible implications of a particular provision having begun life as an amendment,[4] and they are even prepared to construe an Act with an eye on what did not happen by way of amendment as well as with an eye to what did happen.[5] An understanding of exactly how amendments do and do not work is therefore increasingly important for those construing statutes.

What effect does the amendment system have on the shape of legislation?

Very often one looks at a provision of an Act of Parliament and says to oneself "what on earth was the Parliamentary drafter thinking about?" For example, it may be that the provision seems completely out of line when compared with other provisions in the Act. Or the provision may include material that appears structurally inept.

Where this happens, there are two options open to the reader. First, one can simply mutter "Parliamentary Counsel are not what they were". Alternatively, one can check *Hansard* to see whether the material in question was inserted by way of amendment.[6]

There are two reasons why the making of amendments to Bills during their Parliamentary passage may result in legislation that looks, or even is, less well drafted than the surrounding material. The two reasons are worth taking separately.

---

[4] The two most obvious implications being (a) that it may be drafted in a way that is at variance with other provisions of the Act simply because of the lack of drafting expertise on the part of the person preparing the amendment or through inadvertence, and not necessarily because a substantive departure was intended from the policy of other provisions of the Act, and (b) that other parts of the Act may fail to reflect the amended provision if the need for consequential amendment were overlooked or as a result of the lack of a practical opportunity to table the necessary consequentials.

[5] See, for example, Lord Carswell in *R. v JTB (R. v T)* [2009] UKHL 20, [38]–[40]; See also *Adorian v Commissioner of Police of the Metropolis* [2009] EWCA Civ 18, [35]–[39].

[6] And then, if it wasn't, mutter "Parliamentary Counsel are not what they were".

Government amendments

Amendments moved by the Government are drafted by Parliamentary Counsel; generally by the same Parliamentary Counsel responsible for drafting the Bill itself in the first place. In theory, therefore, there is no reason why amended material should be any less well drafted than the rest of the Bill.

In practice, however, there are generally political constraints on the amendment process that can have a significant impact on the shape of the resulting legislation. Put simply, amendments take time, whether on the floor of either House or in Committee, and it is the job of the Whips and other Business Managers to keep a tight control on the amount of time that is used for the passage of each Bill. There is therefore a general and unspoken assumption that Counsel are requested to make any required policy changes on which they are instructed to draft amendments using the minimum number of amendments and the smallest amount of structural disruption to the Bill.

This is very often like being told to take a hippopotamus and convert it into a giraffe, while breaking as few bones as possible. This is easier to do than one might think, but the result is rarely going to look like one of the more elegant products of evolution.

Having discovered that a particular piece of legislative material was inserted by way of Government amendment, the reader will have any structural infelicity explained to him or her, and there should be no further consequences for construction of the legislation. The same material will be relevant for determining the intention of the legislature in relation to that material as in relation to the rest of the Bill, with the addition, in the case of *Hansard*, of the debates on the amendment. The mere fact that material was added by way of amendment should not excuse any lack of overall substantive coherence; and one would expect, therefore, a court to reject the suggestion that a definition that is expressly limited to Part 1 of the Bill should be applied to material occurring in Part 2, merely because it was inserted at a late stage by way of amendment by which time the drafter may have forgotten which definitions were Part-specific. That may in practice be the true explanation: but it would be insufficient to override the clear and express will of the legislature to limit the definition in its application to Part 1[7].

Non-Government amendments

Non-Government amendments are, however, a different story. Although they may have been drafted by Parliamentary Counsel and handed out by the Government to interested back-benchers to move, in most cases they will have been drafted by the back-benchers themselves[8], by interested groups briefing the back-benchers, or possibly by lawyers acting for one of those groups[9].

The result is that it is more likely than not that a back-bench amendment will be technically defective in some way or another. Neither the back-benchers nor the run of their policy advisers are experts in the technicalities of legislation. Indeed, since only a very small proportion of amendments tabled or moved are expected to become law, there is no particular need for them to be technically sound. All that matters is that they should demonstrate the political point being made sufficiently clearly to enable Ministers to respond to it. Even where a Minister is sympathetic to the underlying principle of amendments, the almost invariable response is to agree to take the point away and to bring forward a Government amendment, drafted by Parliamentary Counsel, at a later stage in proceedings on the Bill; in response to which offer back-bench Members or peers would be expected to withdraw their amendments, and almost always would.

Even front-bench Opposition amendments are rarely drafted in a form that is technically perfect; and, again, since few of them pass into law, it does not generally matter.

So as a rule non-Government amendments do not survive to affect

---

[7] That need not mean, of course, that the expression as appearing in Part 2 might not fall to be construed in the same way as in Part 1; nor is it inconceivable that the courts might decide to apply a cross-contextual application of the definition having regard to all the circumstances of the Act; but the mere fact of being an amendment ought not to figure in those circumstances.

[8] Perhaps with help from the House Authorities; see Ch.9.

[9] See further Ch.7.

the shape of the Act that emerges. But there are exceptions. In particular, where the Government do not express sympathy with the underlying principle of an amendment, the Opposition front-bencher, or the back-bencher, proposing it may nevertheless push it to a vote, and may win.[10] The result of that occurrence will be to make the amendment, in its technically defective form, part of the Bill and, therefore, part of the eventual Act.

Even then, all is generally not lost. By convention, the Government accepts responsibility for ensuring that when a Bill becomes an Act upon Royal Assent, it does so in a form that is technically adequate to achieve the intended purpose, both for the Government's own policy and for any non-Government policy that may have found expression by way of a successful non-Government amendment. So Parliamentary Counsel will be asked to prepare any necessary amendments to remedy defects of the original non-Government amendment, and to make any consequential amendments necessary.

A problem arises, however, if the non-Government amendment is carried at the last amendable stage of the Bill, leaving no opportunity for the Government to table remedying amendments.

This arises only rarely, for practical reasons. In the case of an amendment made at Third Reading in the House of Lords, although there is no further stage in that House at which amendments can be tabled, there is at least an opportunity for further Commons proceedings. If the Bill originated in the House of Commons then any amendments made by the House of Lords have to go back there for approval, and that is the stage at which remedial work can be done by the Government. While if the Bill originated in the House of Lords, then it has to pass through all stages in the Commons and the defective material can be remedied there. The same considerations apply in reverse for amendments made on report in the House of Commons, that being the last amendable stage in that House.

Defective material will be left in the Bill, therefore, only in the relatively infrequent case where there is no opportunity to table rectifying amendments at a later stage in the same House, and considerations

---

[10] Particularly, traditionally, in the House of Lords, where there is not necessarily a reliable Government majority.

of Parliamentary timing make it impossible or seriously undesirable to deal with the matter by way of consideration of that House's amendments in the other House.

Despite all this, however, remedial work done by the Government to successful non-Government amendments will for practical political reasons be necessarily exiguous, as is the case for Government amendments themselves, as has been explained above. Again, therefore, when faced with material which the Parliamentary history shows to have been inserted by way of non-Government amendment, practitioners and the courts will have to ask themselves whether it is possible that certain apparent results may be attributable more to technical defects in the drafting than to determined policy.

No amendments

Paradoxically, although amendments are sometimes responsible for an apparently bizarre form of a particular piece of legislation, the inability to make necessary amendments can sometimes have the same, or a worse, effect. Apart from the reluctance of Ministers to allow the necessary consequential amendments to reflect Government or non-Government amendments, in the case of some Bills the responsible Ministers, which may mean in practice either the relevant Departmental Ministers or the Whips or other Business Management Ministers, decide that for reasons of timing or practical politics no amendments at all are going to be made.

In fact, they decide that routinely on almost every Bill, but the line is very rarely held beyond the first amendable stage! At Legislation Committee the drafter is always asked whether the Bill is ready for introduction or whether it will require amendment and, depending on the political strength and degree of interest on the part of the Chair of the Committee for the time being, the Committee will very often demand an assurance that the Bill will be complete and correct before it is introduced. The Legislation Committee occasionally goes to the extreme of refusing permission for the introduction of a Bill that is insufficiently ready for Parliamentary Counsel to be able to indicate that a significant number of amendments is unlikely, with the result that the Bill loses its "slot" for introduction and has to be introduced later in the Session, which in extreme cases (such as in the last Session of a Parliament when time is anyway short) could be fatal. In most cases, however, the drafter will assure the Committee that the Bill is in a fit state for introduction—but almost no Government Bill goes through all its stages without being amended at any of them. A handful of amendments is the norm, and on a large and technically complicated Bill, prepared in today's invariable rush, to make hundreds of amendments is unhappily by no means unusual.

When Ministers decide against amendments and actually show signs of meaning to stick to their decision, the result may be that the drafter can breathe a sigh of relief and relax, knowing that he or she is not going to be asked to improve upon what they have already prepared with sufficient care. Sometimes, however, the timing and other constraints on the process leading up to introduction will have made it necessary for the drafter to introduce the Bill in a condition which will certainly require amendment.[11] Then, for reasons that may have nothing to do with that particular Bill, Ministers decree that there are to be no amendments.

What happens then depends on the factors to be balanced in the particular circumstances. If the amendments are so important that some or all of the Act will simply not work properly if they are not made, Counsel will have to require the Departmental Bill team to brief the Minister accordingly, and the no-amendment decree may have to be revoked to a limited extent: that will not please the Minister, however, and he or she may well demand a risk-analysis to determine just how much harm would be done if the Bill were enacted without the amendments. The result will depend on a balancing exercise—which only the Minister can undertake—of the political damage likely to be caused by amendments (which might include a risk of losing the Bill altogether for lack of time) against the likely practical results of passing the Bill in a defective form.

---

[11] It is by no means unknown to hand in the introduction text to the House on a particular day, and on the same day to send to the Department the first set of draft amendments, dealing with matters that had to be held over from the pre-introduction instructions because of the lack of time or other resources to get them right, or even sufficiently likely to be right to make them worth exposing to the public, before introduction.

Bills are rather like wallpaper in this respect. The professional decorator who wallpapers a room will always be aware of a number of
wrinkles, mis-matchings and other imperfections in the result; only
the worst, however, will be apparent even to a reasonably discriminat-
ing client. The decorator has a choice to say nothing and reckon that
anything that the client does not notice, does not exist for any practical
purpose; but there is always the risk that the client, or a more discern-
ing friend or acquaintance of the client, will notice the defect at some
time in the future. In the case of wallpaper, it is only the reputation of
the decorator and his or her chances of further work that are likely to
be at stake; in the case of a Bill the calculation is a little more delicate,
because the potential risks of the resulting Act failing to work at all or
as intended have implications beyond the drafter's professional reputation. Be that as it may, every honest and competent drafter will be
aware of imperfections in his or her own work, and will often become
aware of them in time to recommend that they be perfected through
amendment; where amendment is politically impossible or undesirable,
the drafter has to decide whether the defect is the kind of imperceptible
wrinkle which only becomes a cosmetic problem if the decorator is
unwise enough to point it out, or whether it is potentially sufficiently
significant to amount to a substantive deficiency which honesty com-
pels him or her to ensure that the Department—who will have to operate the legislation and face any challenges to it—are made aware of.
The choice is not always entirely easy.

Requirement for Parliamentary Counsel's approval

There is a rule of Government that a Minister may not accept a
non-Government amendment verbatim without the approval of the
Parliamentary Counsel in charge of the Bill.[12] Since this is a rule per-
petuated by each successive Legislation Committee, the result is that
a Minister actually lacks the authority required in accordance with the
doctrine of collective Cabinet responsibility to accept an amendment
without Parliamentary Counsel's approval.

On the face of it, this is another point at which the unelected and

---

[12] See the Cabinet Office's Guide to Legislative Procedures (see Ch.2 above).

only semi-accountable Parliamentary Counsel really "come into the battle". In practice, however, the rule is of less importance than it might seem. For one thing, Ministers rarely actually want to accept an amendment in its entirety, without being seen to improve upon it slightly themselves.

On other occasions, of course, there is a political or presentational reason why a Minister does want to simply accept an amendment. When that happens, Parliamentary Counsel would have to have a very strong reason indeed for persuading the Minister to resist the amendment. Indeed, it has been known for the rule to be flouted and amendments to be accepted, where they appear to be unexceptionable.[13]

Handout amendments[14]

An amendment that has been drafted by Parliamentary Counsel and given to a back-bencher to table is known as a "handout amendment". Politicians have not always been entirely honest about handouts, wanting to claim credit for the actual crafting of an amendment; most, however, acknowledge technical support from wherever it has come, whether from the Government or from an outside interest group that provided briefing.

On occasions it is the Government that wishes to hide its involvement in the production of amendments. This can arise particularly in relation to a private Member's Bill which the Government wishes to oppose without being seen to do so. Although in recent years Ministers have seemed to be aware of the importance of admitting involvement in the production of amendments whenever it has taken

---

[13] More often than not, the rule is disobeyed because the relevant Minister is not aware of it and Counsel has insufficient warning of its breach to be able to insist upon it; occasionally, however, the Minister decides that in the political circumstances of a particular amendment nothing short of simple acceptance of it verbatim will satisfy its supporters or avert what might be a significant setback, such as a Government defeat involving significant numbers of rebels. Although this happens only very rarely, for obvious reasons it is more likely to occur in the House of Lords than in the House of Commons.

[14] I say a little more about this topic in Ch.10.

place, and of neither encouraging nor colluding with private Members in concealing the provenance of amendments, the issue still occasionally causes difficulties and in relatively recent times has even been responsible for a Ministerial resignation.[15]

To and fro

Every Bill has to be agreed by both Houses before it can be enacted.[16] Although we talk colloquially about amendments being made to a Bill in each of its two Houses, technically it is only the first House that can actually amend the Bill by its own action; the second House is really only making suggestions to the first House, and those suggestions become amendments to the Bill only when the two Houses agree on them.[17] This is apparent from the fact that while the Bill that goes from House 1 to House 2 is the Bill not as introduced but as amended in that House, House 2 sends back to House 1 not an amended Bill, but a list of "amendments" made in House 2 and marked by reference to the Bill as it emerged from House 1.[18]

---

[15] See the following passage from the *Daily Telegraph*'s obituary of January 8, 2005 for Sir Nicholas Scott: "But his past came back to haunt him in 1994, when he was effectively forced to resign as Minister for the Disabled, largely as a result of a storm of protest stirred up over his role in the wrecking of a Private Member's Bill of Rights for the disabled. . . . His downfall in 1994 was precipitated by his revelation that he had misled the House in claiming that wrecking amendments to the Labour-inspired Civil Rights (Disabled Persons) Bill had not been Government-inspired. He resigned at the next reshuffle."

[16] With the obvious exception of the rare Bills passed under the Parliament Act 1911 without the cooperation of the House of Lords.

[17] This reality is somewhat obscured by the practice of each House, when considering a Bill that has come from the other House, of tabling amendments to the Bill and printing it after the Committee Stage (and Report in the Lords) as amended, as if they had control of the Bill in the same way as the first House; but the reality is reasserted when the Bill finishes its passage in the second House—it is not printed as amended at its final stage in that House, and is not printed as amended again until Royal Assent.

[18] Like many technicalities of Parliamentary procedure that reflect history or underlying logic, this causes a considerable amount of trouble, probably more

The "to and fro" stage[19] is a process of enormous potential complexity, compounded by the fact that it is more often than not played

---

than it is worth. House 2 proceeds with the Bill as if it were amending it: so it prints a Bill following Committee as amended, and amendments for the Report stage are tabled by reference to the as amended Bill. The same goes for Third Reading in the House of Lords (in the House of Commons, Third Reading is not an amendable stage). So Committee Amendment 1 might amend clause 1 so as to insert subsection (1A); Report Amendment 1 might amend subsection (1A) so as to substitute a new paragraph (a); and Third Reading Amendment 1 might remove three words from new clause 1(1A)(b); but when the Bill returns to House 1, someone has to go through and produce a list of amendments that includes a single composite amendment to clause 1, encapsulating the effect of all three amendments. For a Bill of a couple of hundred pages, to which a few hundred amendments are made over the three Lords stages—neither of which is by any means unusual—this means that a considerable amount of tricky work is required. Even the Public Bill Office Clerks, who are extremely skilled in this kind of work, frequently make an error in producing the composite list; by which I mean that I several times spotted an error that they had made—so if one assumes, which seems reasonable, that I probably missed one or two as well, the likelihood is that there are some provisions on the statute book that do not reflect the Bill as it was actually passed, but which represent a minor error in the composition of the final set of amendments. It is actually quite unlikely that anyone after Royal Assent would be in a position to discover a mistake of this kind, since most of the people closely involved in the minutiae of a technical Bill are likely to have moved on to other things, and it is astonishing and slightly troubling how quickly one forgets the details of something that one lived and breathed only a few months earlier. So when faced with a provision that looks most unlikely to have been intended to have been passed in that form—particularly if it forms part of a complicated part that is relatively trivial in policy terms—one might do well to go back over the chain of amendments to the Bill (using the amendment papers preserved in the Parliamentary papers and available online) to check whether the Act actually reflects what happened in Parliament. As to what would happen if one could establish that it did not, the circumstances would dictate the most likely result, which would probably be a combination of the constitutional proprieties according to which the courts will not interfere with or question Parliamentary proceedings and the common sense reality whereby a proved clerical mistake could not be allowed to cause injustice or serious inconvenience.

[19] Frequently referred to by Parliamentarians in public, highly humorously, as "ping-pong".

out at considerable speed and under constraints of considerable political pressure,[20] including the pressure imposed by the knowledge that if the Bill is allowed to reach stalemate over even a single amendment, the whole Bill falls.[21] It can also involve a certain amount of making the game up as one goes along.[22] From the point of view of the practitioner or other interested reader of a statute, therefore, it may be useful to bear in mind that if a provision owes its origins to an amendment created or altered during the to and fro process, there is more reason than normal to assume that it may have been crafted in some haste and under some pressure; a court considering whether a provision is a mistake that is correctable by the courts under the *Inco* rule[23] may be more ready to make a finding of a drafting error in relation to a complicated matter dealt with in haste at to and fro than might be the case for a provision that was in the Bill since introduction.[24]

---

[20] Particularly at the end of a Session, it is not unknown for a Bill to go back and forth between the two Houses several times on a single day.

[21] See further Ch.9.

[22] By the time one gets beyond the "Commons amendment in lieu of Lords amendment on which the Lords have insisted" stage, or an equivalent level, one is already into territory which if not untrodden is possibly uncharted, and as to which whatever charts may have been constructed on a former Bill are likely not to be capable of being found in the Public Bill Office filing Cabinets with the necessary speed for tabling; so the titles of amendment papers, and even the form of the amendments, are in effect made up by reference to broadly comparable precedents and general first principles.

[23] See *Craies on Legislation*, 9th edn, Ch.15.

[24] On the other hand, as to amendments in general, the courts are likely to be more reluctant to assume inadvertence or error in relation to precise wording "deliberately" tabled by way of a separate amendment to the Bill, than in relation to provisions that formed part of the Bill on introduction: while it is unreasonable to assume that in practice every word of a 300-page Bill on introduction was considered and checked with the ideal care, an amendment's distinct prominence, and the fact that it requires to be crafted separately by reference to the latest text of the Bill, might be thought to make it less likely to have been produced without being weighed carefully (other than in a to and fro situation or another instance where timing considerations put the drafter under pressure, such as if several hundred amendments were tabled for one stage of the Bill, as sometimes happens).

Conclusion

The courts have shown themselves increasingly ready to consider issues of the Parliamentary history of legislation. The fact that material has been inserted by way of amendment during a Bill's passage could be relevant in a number of ways, and practitioners have to be capable of discovering when this was the case and making appropriate submissions to the courts about construction.[25]

---

[25] See, for example, Lord Carswell in *R. v JTB (R. v T)* [2009] UKHL 20, [38]–[40]; *Adorian v Commissioner of Police of the Metropolis* [2009] EWCA Civ 18, [35]–[39]; and *Lewisham London Borough Council v Malcolm* [2008] UKHL 43; [77]–[81]; per Baroness Hale (dissenting). For an interesting instance of a court having regard to the *withdrawal* of an amendment at a stage in the Parliamentary process of a Bill, for the purposes of construing the resulting Act, see *Mucelli v Government of Albania* [2007] EWHC 2632 (Admin), [60], per Richards LJ; but note that the danger of this kind of construction is that the court may not be seised of all the reasons why a particular attitude to an amendment was taken by its proponents or opponents; and even if the reasons are transparent, it would be dangerous, and contrary to generally understood principles, to equate the legislative intent with the subjective intentions of a particular set of players in the course of the proceedings in one House.

20 QUEEN'S CONSENT

Introduction

Queen's Consent should not be, but often is, confused with Royal
Assent. The latter is the constitutional process by which a Bill
becomes an Act. The former is a procedural rule of each of the Houses
of Parliament, which has no legal significance once a Bill has been
enacted.

Details of the rules determining when and at which stage Queen's
Consent, or Prince's Consent, require to be signified in relation
to a Bill will be found in *Erskine May*.[1] Like the rules of scope
and hybridity, however, their practical application depends a good
deal on experience, and their relevance is determined by the House
Authorities, generally after discussion with Parliamentary Counsel.

The essence of the rules about Queen's Consent is that Consent
is required to be signified in relation to Bills that either (a) affect the
Royal Prerogative, or (b) may have a significant effect on the Queen's
personal interests.

Effect on the form of legislation

Prerogative consent is unlikely to have any influence on the shape of
legislation. In particular, since the practicalities of Consent impose
no kind of burden on Government or Parliament, and occupy no
significant amount of time, the formation and drafting of legislation
is never influenced by the desire to avoid the need for this kind of
Consent.

The other kind of Consent, private interests Consent, may have
an effect. Where private interests may be affected, the Government
is encouraged to make contact at as early a stage as possible with

---

[1] See Ch.2 above.

the Palace's professional advisers.[2] There then follows a process of negotiation to ensure that the Bill does not unwittingly have any effects that are objectionable. That might require, for example, adjustment of the phrasing of any provision about application to Crown land.

Constitutional justification

The process of negotiation that takes place in determining possible issues of private interests Consent is delicate. On the one hand, it is no more conceivable that the Queen would decline to give Consent to a Bill on the grounds that it potentially injured her property interests than it is that she would refuse Royal Assent to a Bill passed through Parliament. Although both are theoretically possible, their effect as a matter of constitutional law so far exceeds the amount of influence that is thought tolerable for the Sovereign in a Parliamentary democracy that action by a reigning Queen or King to refuse Consent or Assent would probably be the last political action of any kind that they were permitted to take. In other words, the power to refuse Consent or Assent is only permitted to remain in the Sovereign's hands because there is no practical possibility of its being exercised, and if it were to be exercised it would be rapidly removed, one way or another.

Despite that, however, there is a big difference in the legitimacy of the exercise of influence in relation to Consent and Assent.

Royal Assent is a question of legislative power, which vests solely in Parliament as a fundamental principle of the Parliamentary Sovereignty on which our democracy is founded; to refuse Royal Assent to a Bill would be an intolerable attempt to undermine the legitimacy of Parliament.

Consent, however, relates to the principles surrounding the bargain that was made in 1760, when George III in effect handed over most of his land to be managed on behalf of the Government with revenue accruing to the Treasury, in return for fixed annual payments. Despite

---

[2] See the Cabinet Office's Guide to Legislative Procedures (as to which see Ch.2 above).

its antiquity, the effects of that bargain are still felt in solid terms in the payment of Civil List salaries; and the understanding that Parliament will not legislate in such a way as to damage the Sovereign's remaining private financial interests without Consent is part of the delicate balance arising out of the original bargain.

There is therefore nothing unconstitutional about the Queen and her financial advisers negotiating the terms of a Bill insofar as it affects her finances, while it would be constitutionally improper for her to attempt to influence the contents of a Bill on general political grounds.

21 FINANCIAL RULES OF THE HOUSE OF COMMONS

Introduction

The House of Commons asserts financial privilege which, broadly speaking, means that it arrogates to itself the right to control taxation and public expenditure.

In addition to the financial privilege of the Commons, the Government asserts some rights to control measures that would impose taxation or entail significant public expenditure. That is achieved principally through the use of Money Resolutions, which are required to cover provisions in Bills that would give rise to significant public expenditure, and Ways and Means Resolutions, which are required to cover provisions that amount to imposing charges by way of taxation.

The detailed rules of the House of Commons financial procedures will be found in *Erskine May*.[1] This chapter focuses only on one or two aspects that have the potential to affect the shape of legislation.

Sink clauses

The "sink clause" is a device that has always been well known to the drafters of legislation, but which appears to have been a sufficiently well-kept secret to be capable of baffling lawyers and judges until extremely recently.

When a Bill is introduced into the House of Commons and contains provisions which will in due course require the cover of a Money Resolution, the initial print of the Bill shows those provisions in italics, so as to suggest that they do not formally form part of the Bill

---

[1] See Ch.2 above.

until they have been franked by the cover of a Resolution.[2] That works perfectly well when the provisions imposing a charge on public funds are relatively few and discrete. Very often, however, public expenditure permeates the Bill so that if one were to identify and italicise all those provisions that are capable of imposing a charge on public funds, vast swathes of the Bill would be italicised. In order to avoid that, a provision is introduced towards the end of the Bill, providing that all expenditure under the Bill is to be paid out of "Money Provided by Parliament". The provision is substantively inert, since in the absence of any other express provision for, for example, direct charge upon the Consolidated Fund, there is no other way that the charges could be met other than by Money Provided by Parliament.[3]

In the case of *R. (on the application of Friends of the Earth) v Secretary of State for Business, Enterprise and Regulatory Reform*[4] the courts were confronted with a provision of this kind, and were invited to consider it in the context of an argument that there was an implied duty for the Government to exercise powers conferred by the Act concerned, on the grounds that the provision "indicated that Parliament understood that the Act might have financial consequences".

The judge read out a passage from *Craies on Legislation* describing sink clauses as being of no legal effect and concluded:

"if the author of this work is correct in this passage (and there is no reason to think that he is not) it might be helpful if the use of this type of provision in legislation is reviewed so as to avoid possible confusion in the future".

---

[2] It therefore being the case, for example, that if the Bill reaches Committee without the resolution having been obtained, the Chairman is unable to put the question on Clause Stand Part in relation to those provisions.

[3] "Money Provided by Parliament" is the legislative expression used to describe "Voted Money"—money provided by the House of Commons in response to Estimates, through the mechanism of Consolidated Fund Bills and Appropriation Acts.

[4] [2008] EWHC 2518 (Admin).

An alternative solution, of course, is to ensure that practitioners and the judiciary are sufficiently familiar with the key concepts of Parliamentary procedure which influence the shape of legislation to avoid confusion being caused by what is, undoubtedly, a very useful device, in the present state of the Commons rules on Parliamentary procedure. At conferences of legislative drafters[5] sooner or later somebody gives a talk deploring the lack of education about the way legislation works in the standard syllabuses of universities and professional courses.[6] As well as being given adequate information about how to read and apply statutes, law students should be taught enough of the rudiments of Parliamentary procedure to be able to identify provisions, such as sink clauses, that are inserted for a procedural rather than a substantive reason.

That is particularly important in the case of the financial rules of the House of Commons since they are also important for an adequate understanding of the basics of public finances. The financial privilege of the House of Commons, the nature of Votes and Estimates of public expenditure, Consolidated Fund Acts and Appropriation Acts, and financial resolutions, all form as much part of the mechanism of public money as do budgets and Finance Bills. As all lawyers are expected to be educated in the rudiments of public and administrative law, they should at least be aware of the basic mechanisms that control public finances.

---

[5] Yes, they do take place, and there is no reason why the idea should be funnier than conferences of engineers or any other highly technical profession.

[6] They are quite right: it is ridiculous that law students continue to sit routinely through a great deal of tuition about how the common law develops and works, and are given perhaps one or two perfunctory lectures about how to read a statute, when approximately 95 per cent of law is now regulated by statute and statutory instruments. I doubt if one lawyer in a hundred could recall from memory a single provision of the Interpretation Act 1978, or identify from memory more than three of the entries listed in its Schedule of definitions; and yet trying to read a statute without thorough knowledge of the Interpretation Act is like trying to decipher a map without having the key to its symbols: you may frequently get to the right destination, but you are likely also frequently to go wrong with disastrous results.

SECTION 4
PROBLEMS

22 INTRODUCTION

Until this point my principal purpose has been to identify the different influences on the shape of legislation exerted by different people and different aspects of the legislative process. I now turn to a number of problematic issues, each of which needs to be confronted by the legislative drafter. For example, each legislative drafter must decide for himself or herself what approach to take to theoretical questions about the complexity of language; and the answers of each drafter will fundamentally shape the legislation for which he or she is responsible.

The practitioner and the judge confronted with a piece of legislation to construe and apply need to be aware of the principles by reference to which it was constructed. Apparent choices of language will be more or less significant according to whether they appear to follow a trend and give effect to a particular principle, or run counter to that trend or principal, perhaps by reason of inadvertence.

The courts are nowadays more ready than they once were to designate an expression or provision as a drafter's mistake, and to correct it.[1] In part, the ability to recognise something as a mistake depends on, or will at least be assisted by, being able to recognise the normal principles according to which each drafter operates. The purpose of this chapter is therefore to describe some of the principal issues that confront drafters and how they determine to approach them on each occasion.

---

[1] See further Ch.28.

23 PRIMARY AND SECONDARY LEGISLATION

Introduction

Striking the right balance between primary and subordinate legislation has been a matter of Parliamentary and other controversy for many years. The Donoughmore Committee[1] was already able to report that there was "a considerable body of literature on the subject"[2] when it was appointed to:

> "consider the powers exercised by or under the direction of (or by persons or bodies appointed specially by) Ministers of the Crown by way of (a) delegated legislation, and (b) judicial or quasi-judicial decision, and to report what safeguards are desirable or necessary to secure the constitutional principles of the sovereignty of Parliament and the supremacy of the Law".[3]

The fundamental issues have not changed since Donoughmore, which therefore remains a very important work on the subject. Useful discussion is also found in the *Renton Report*[4] and in the *Hansard Society Report*.[5] As in previous chapters, this chapter aims to concentrate on adding practical description and discussion to the pre-existing literature.

---

[1] *Committee on Ministers' Powers*, April 1932, Cmd.4060.
[2] Para.2.
[3] Para.1.
[4] See Ch.2 above.
[5] See Ch.2 above.

How is the choice made?

Given the amount of controversy that arises in Parliament and elsewhere about the delegation of legislative power, one might assume that there would be Government guidelines by reference to which it would be determined in the case of each Bill what provisions must be specified in full detail on the face of the Bill and what matters can appropriately be left to subordinate legislation.

The reality, however, is that the decision is taken entirely ad hoc and by reference only to the very vaguest and most informal of principles.[6] Nor is there any kind of central control or monitoring of the use made of subordinate legislation: a Department's memorandum to the

---

[6] The Cabinet Office's Guide to Legislative Procedures says the following (2004 edn, para.8.18):

"8.18 Matters of detail are often set out in Schedules to a Bill; or they may be left over to be dealt with by statutory regulations or other forms of subordinate legislation. The following are some of the points which Parliamentary Counsel and the department may need to take into account in preparing the Bill:

- the matters in question may need adjusting more often than it would be sensible for Parliament to legislate for by primary legislation;
- there may be rules which will be better made after some experience of administering the new Act and which it is not essential to have as soon as it begins to operate;
- the use of delegated powers in a particular area may be well precedented and uncontroversial;
- there may be transitional and technical matters which it would be appropriate to deal with by delegated powers.

On the other hand,

- the matters, though detailed, may be so much of the essence of the Bill that Parliament ought to consider them along with the rest of the Bill;
- the matters may raise controversial issues running through the Bill which it would be better for Parliament to decide once in principle rather than arguing several times over (and taking up scarce Parliamentary time in so doing);
- Parliament will take a close interest in the nature and extent of Parliamentary control over subordinate legislation, so careful consideration should be given to this question."

Legislation Committee before introduction of a Bill is likely to draw attention to the use proposed of delegated legislation, particularly if anything unusual or extreme is involved, and in cases of the latter kind the Department may have consulted the Law Officers at some point during the preparation of the Bill, possibly at the instigation of Parliamentary Counsel. But these are things that may happen, rather than things that must happen as a matter of required procedure.

The decision on each occasion is therefore in practice made by those preparing the Bill, which in turn means, in practice, either Parliamentary Counsel or one or more Departmental lawyers. Where the instructions to draft a Bill indicate the Department's wishes as to which matters are to be left to secondary legislation, the degree of scrutiny given to those wishes depends on the individual personality of the Parliamentary Counsel to whom the Bill has been assigned. I have the impression that some Counsel routinely accept the wishes of a Department on this matter, while others routinely question the Departmental judgment and challenge it whenever they think appropriate.

My own attitude was more or less to disregard the Department's wishes in the matter, and to start from first principles considering what matters I thought could best be left to secondary legislation, and what matters should be set out in the Bill.[7] Overall, my recollection is that I far more often invited Departments to leave details which they had proposed to include on the face of the Bill to be dealt with by delegated legislation, than the other way around. Despite Parliamentary perceptions, for the most part Departments are still relatively cautious in the use they make of delegated legislation. To put it another way, wherever Departments know in advance the details of

---

[7] Although in practice, at a later stage in the development of the Bill, it was frequently necessary to compromise or even to abandon the principal approach, if it was simply impossible to obtain instructions on the details for the face of the Bill in the complete absence of settled Departmental policy. In those cases one would be more or less forced to delegate power to deal with matters not by reference to their suitability for delegation but by reference to the simple impossibility of settling the details in time for the inclusion on the face of the Bill. I do not, however, recall being compelled to do this in any case where I considered the delegation unconstitutional or otherwise seriously improper.

particular matters they are tempted to instruct Counsel to put them on the face of the Bill, often forgetting that the necessary flexibility to meet real-world changes over time makes it preferable for everybody to relegate comparatively unimportant detail to secondary legislation. As a result, I would say that in general Acts of Parliament still contain far too much unimportant detail about matters that would be better contained in statutory instruments, or, indeed, left entirely to be dealt with administratively. It is only when important matters have still not been decided by Government before the time at which the Bill requires to be introduced that Departments are tempted, and frequently succumb to temptation, to leave to secondary legislation matters that really deserve to be set out on the face of the Bill.[8]

The comparatively informal method of making a decision as to what to delegate results in enormous variation between different Bills produced by different Departments and drafted by different Parliamentary Counsel. The Lords Select Committee discussed below has changed the position a little, since Departments now have to defend their decisions as to delegation to a Committee which operates with at least something of a corporate memory and a consistency from Bill to Bill. But the Committee is not equipped to aim towards any kind of formal imposition of consistent standards.

The role of the Lords Committee

A Select Committee to consider the propriety of proposed powers to legislate was established only as recently as 1994; even now, it is a Lords Select Committee, rather than a Joint or Commons Committee, which might lead one to believe that the issue is not taken very seriously by politicians and Departments. That would be a mistake. The Committee, now known as the Committee on Delegated Powers and Regulatory Reform, is possibly one of the most effective and influential in the entire Parliamentary system, within its relatively contained remit.

Empirical proof for this observation could easily be found by searching recent Lords' debates on Bills in Committee and on Report,

---

[8] See further the passage on Skeleton Bills below.

and spotting how many times the Committee's reports are referred to in debate, and how often successful amendments are brought forward either by members of the Committee or by the Government expressly in reaction to a Committee report. It is also evident from the general rule which is operated to the effect that stages of Bills are not taken until the Committee has had an opportunity to consider the Government's memorandum and to produce a report on the proposed delegated powers.[9]

More generally, however, it is sufficient to note how seriously the Committee is taken in the Government's preparations for introducing a Bill. The Cabinet Office *Guide to Legislative Procedures*[10] says as follows:

"Departments must consider what degree of Parliamentary scrutiny will be appropriate for any delegated powers in the Bill, and produce a Delegated Powers Memorandum for Legislation Committee justifying the inclusion of any delegated powers and addressing any concerns that might be raised. The Memorandum must be published on introduction in the first House (whichever one that is) and formally submitted to the Lords Delegated Powers and Regulatory Reform Committee."[11]

In addition, a typical Lords Handling Strategy, seen by Legislation Committees as a key document particularly for controversial Bills or Bills needing to be passed with some degree of expedition, will stress the approach to be taken to handling the Delegated Powers Committee.

As with a number of Committees, the Government will always take care to provide ample documentation to the Committee at an early stage. There is always a memorandum provided to the Committee

---

[9] This includes, where appropriate, cases where the Government has tabled amendments conferring a number of new delegated powers and has submitted a supplementary memorandum dealing with them, in which case the Committee will where reasonably practicable produce a supplementary report in reply.

[10] See Ch.2 above.

[11] Para.3.13.

with each Bill on introduction to the Lords or when it reaches the Lords from the Commons; and informal advance contact with the advisers to the Committee is far from uncommon. This is certainly advantageous to the Committee, although there is always the danger with Government that the ample resources of the civil service make it possible to drown correspondents with paper, making it difficult for the Committee to burrow through the complexities of the memorandum to discover the real points of likely contention. From time to time matters which one might have expected to be issues of interest or controversy for the Committee are passed over in silence, and one suspects that even with a powerful and determined secretariat the Committee has simply overlooked something that may have been, without sinister intention, hidden from sight due to the length of the Bill concerned and the complexity of its accompanying memorandum.

It is probably fair to say that the most important proof of the effectiveness and influence of the Committee is that there is a working, although informal, presumption that its recommendations are to be accommodated unless there is a strong reason for resisting them. One could contrast that with the Departmental attitude taken to the Joint Committee on Statutory Instruments (JCSI); although that Committee has a similarly technical remit, it has at some points in its history been seen to wield its non-power with little discrimination, as a result of which its influence has been limited. Although the reputation and influence of the Committee has varied considerably over the years, as a general rule an adverse report of the JCSI is not necessarily greeted with dismay in a Department (although the reaction depends considerably on the nature of the report and the preoccupations of the Department); it is not uncommon for Departments simply to determine to ignore express criticisms or recommendations of the JCSI. By contrast, it will be far from easy to persuade a Minister to accept a recommendation simply to ignore a criticism of the Delegated Powers Committee, and he or she will want to be provided with some convincing arguments before going into bat with instructions simply to reject the Committee's report.[12]

---

[12] The main reason for this is, of course, simply the fact that Ministers know that they will have to face members of the Select Committee in the course of

Affirmative v negative resolution

One of the common themes of reports of the Delegated Powers Committee is to the effect that a power that the Bill makes subject to negative resolution should instead be subject to affirmative resolution. The Government's memorandum to the Committee will generally try to justify any choices of negative resolution, and by and large the rules of thumb operated by the Committee are now sufficiently well known for Departments to be likely mostly to "get it right" first time.[13] Sometimes, however, the Committee will feel that the Government should have jumped the other way, in which case depending on the apparent strength of their feeling the Government is likely either to table or accept amendments to change the scrutiny procedure.

A common approach in recent years has been to require affirmative resolution for the first exercise of a power, and negative thereafter. It is not entirely logical that this device should satisfy as often as it appears to. To some extent, of course, it depends on the good faith of Ministers not to start off with a harmless "dummy-run" subject to affirmative resolution and then bring out the real, and objectionable, scheme by way of a second instrument subject to negative resolution only. It is, however, probably sensible to rely on good faith to that extent; the political realities are such that it is most unlikely that a Department would try to get away with a ruse of that kind, and any obvious abuse could be countered anyway by finding time in the Lords to debate a prayer against the second instrument under the negative resolution procedure.[14]

The stronger objection to the first-only affirmative approach is that if the House wants to see and vote on how the power is going to be exercised in the first place, it should logically equally want to see

---

debates on the Bill, while in the case of negative resolution statutory instruments the instrument on which the Joint Committee reports is unlikely to be subject to any Parliamentary proceedings and the Minister will therefore not have to "go into bat" on it at all.

[13] See, for example, *Craies on Legislation*, 9th edn, Ch.1.3.

[14] For descriptions of how the negative and affirmative procedures work see *Craies on Legislation*, 9th edn, Ch.6.

and vote on any major revisions in the future that completely alter the nature of the subordinate legislative scheme. Given that some provisions already leave it to the Minister to choose between negative and affirmative procedure,[15] perhaps we will see in the future provisions that require a Minister to use the affirmative procedure both for the first instrument and for any later instrument which the Minister thinks makes significant structural changes to the existing scheme; while leaving a lot to Ministerial discretion, I have a feeling that in practice a provision of that kind could be made to operate fairly effectively. It would certainly be interesting to see whether the idea commended itself to the Delegated Powers Committee, for if it did it would be likely to be taken up and implemented.

The JCSI is also entitled under its terms of reference to comment on an inappropriate choice of Parliamentary procedure, in cases where both affirmative and negative resolution are possible and the decision as to which to employ is left to Ministerial discretion. A Department deciding which to advise Ministers to use on a particular occasion is likely to approach the legal advisers to the Joint Committee to enquire in advance as to the likely attitude of the committee to a particular choice.

Super-affirmative procedure

In recent years a new kind of procedure for Parliamentary scrutiny has begun to be used for particularly serious cases of delegation of power—known colloquially as super-affirmative procedure.[16] One well understands why this procedure came into being: it arose principally as a response to the traditional and often-expressed frustration on the part of Parliamentarians that by moving a matter from the face of the Bill into delegated legislation it was put beyond the reach of amendments. Although as a rule the super-affirmative procedure

---

[15] For example, the European Communities Act 1972 s.2(2).

[16] See further *Craies on Legislation*, 9th edn, Ch.6.2; in reality there is no one standard form of this super-affirmative procedure, but there are certain common denominators, notably the opportunity for Parliament to comment formally on a draft, and a requirement for extensive consultation.

does not allow amendments to be tabled to statutory instruments in the same way as they are tabled to Bills, the presentation of a draft to Parliament allows, in effect, a similar kind of opportunity for Parliament to suggest detailed improvements. It is not quite the same as being able to table formal amendments, but it does go a long way towards meeting the argument.

There are, however, difficulties with the super-affirmative procedure. For one thing, its sheer length and complexity significantly erodes the advantages gained by using delegated legislation to handle particular matters; which makes it less likely that relatively minor amendments that are necessary to meet real-world changes will be made, because of the consequent time and trouble for the Department.

Clearly, the super-affirmative procedure is an elegant and effective solution to the problem of allowing the delegation of powers for practical reasons in circumstances where the importance or sensitivity of the substance would ideally indicate primary legislation.[17] Provided that the new procedure is kept strictly for rare and extreme cases of this kind, it will have been a useful innovation. The more it is used, and the more it comes to be used for cases of doubtful necessity, the more Ministers will feel obliged to use it more generally, and the greater the risk that it will do more harm by way of preventing appropriate use of delegated powers than it does good by increasing the degree of Parliamentary and public scrutiny.[18]

---

[17] So, for example, in the case of Legislative Reform Orders, if one takes the view that it is appropriate to allow them to be made at all, which not everybody does, it is clearly appropriate and indeed necessary for them to be subject to a procedure more exacting than the ordinary draft affirmative procedure.

[18] The Cabinet Office's Guide to Legislative Procedures does not encourage the proliferation of the use of super-affirmative procedure: it says: Departments should avoid including such provision in Bills (or conceding amendments to that effect), since this adds to the complexity of Parliamentary procedure and has a considerable downside for future business management. The only circumstance in which Departments should contemplate allowing for Parliament to amend secondary legislation is when the matter would previously have been legislated for by Act." (2004 edn, para.8.25).

Skeleton legislation

Much has been said in Parliament and elsewhere[19] about the unde-
sirability of taking the delegation of power to such an extent that
the primary legislation becomes a mere skeleton, with all the flesh to
be provided by statutory instrument. Without wishing to rehearse
the arguments here, skeleton legislation does present particular problems both for Departments and Parliamentary Counsel, as well as for
Parliamentarians.

The pace at which new legislation is expected, by Government principally, to be developed and enacted, increasingly frequently makes it
simply impossible for the details of a new system to have been established before the Bill providing for it is introduced and passed. One
can argue—and many do—that this is simply unacceptable; and that
if Government does not have time to work out the details of what it
wants to do, then it should not bring in the Bill to do it. Unhappily,
however, that argument is becoming increasingly unrealistic. And
perhaps the fault is not entirely that of successive Governments: it
could be that the ridiculous pace at which we all live and expect to
live today results in an expectation on behalf of the public that new
legislation, once announced, will be brought in and enacted within
a period of weeks. It could be that the kind of inter-Departmental
committee or collaborative working party that might once have been
asked to spend months or even years developing policy before the Bill
was introduced, is simply no longer going to be tolerated by people in
general except in the most extreme of circumstances.

Whatever the reason and whosoever the fault, it is often the case that
for practical purposes there is no alternative but to legislate by way
of broad powers. The introduction of the Community Infrastructure
Levy in the Planning Act 2008 is a case in point: it is an instance of
skeleton legislation at its worst, or at any rate at its most extreme,
but the political demands were such that the policy could not have
been achieved in any other way. However, it is worth recording that
inevitably one wastes a huge amount of endeavour in trying to draw
the powers sufficiently broadly, while still giving enough flavour of

---

[19] See, for example, the *Hansard Society Report* (see Ch.2 above), p.64.

what is intended to make the delegation just about acceptable to Parliament; and at some points in the process of the preparation of a Bill of this kind one is likely to ask oneself whether effort and work might not actually have been saved if one had bitten the bullet and instead of taking powers actually sat down to produce at least the bulk of the regulations on the face of the Bill itself. There is also, of course, the danger that the broader the power one takes, the less the courts will find that it is suitable for the particular kind of use that one wants to make of it; that is likely to be particularly the case in the field of fiscal or criminal law, and the less one is able to know of the details of the legislation in advance, the more the risk that full implementation will be prevented by any defect or perceived defect in the powers taken.

Considering the increasing number of Bills or parts of Bills that are accurately described in Parliament as skeleton legislation, and that are therefore the subject of controversy in Parliament, it is surprising how rarely Parliament exerts its power by simply refusing to pass powers that amount to an inappropriate degree of delegation. The reports of the House of Lords Select Committee frequently draw attention to inappropriate cases of delegation, although they most commonly focus on the issue of the procedure for Parliamentary scrutiny of the eventual delegated legislation that has been proposed. The Government have in recent years taken the attitude that where the Delegated Powers Committee recommends that a particular matter should be made the subject of affirmative resolution rather than negative, they will in general accede to this request and either accept opposition amendments to that effect or table their own. I have the impression that, as a result, a bloodless skirmish is frequently fought over the appropriate procedures for Parliamentary scrutiny in cases where the real battle ought to be over whether the matter is appropriate for delegation at all: it is certainly the case that Departments sometimes propose that a particular matter should be set out in the Bill by a power subject to negative resolution procedure, but concede affirmative resolution if the matter is raised by the Delegated Powers Committee. If the Secretary of State wanted to take power to cut people's heads off for parking on double yellow lines, as a matter of tactics he would probably be best advised to take the power in a Bill and make it subject to negative resolution, or, perhaps a mere requirement to lay before Parliament, and produce a lengthy memorandum for the Delegated Powers Committee explaining why this choice of procedure appeared appropriate; he or she would certainly lose that particular battle with the Committee and then concede to affirmative resolution, but might thereby have diverted attention successfully from the real question of whether a power of this kind is appropriate for delegation in the first place. While that is obviously an extreme and facetious example, I have seen cases that were not a million miles from it, and it is certainly interesting how rarely Parliament has, whether or not at the Committee's instigation, simply refused to enact a power at all in any form on the grounds of its being inappropriate for delegation.[20]

The rise and rise of delegation

In the last few years of my time as Parliamentary Counsel I had an increasing feeling that there was coming to be a consensus, albeit an unspoken consensus, within the public service that primary legislation is an unrealistically wieldy way of running the country and that Ministerial diktat is so much more effective for everybody. One might say that on this matter Sir Humphrey Appleby and Jim Hacker are finally pulling together in the same direction, and finding no opposition in Parliament or the people, because Parliamentarians are increasingly elected or appointed from people with the same kind of political understanding, leaving citizens with fewer and fewer Parliamentary champions to oppose the creeping usurpation of legislative power.

My principal proof for this rather disturbing theory is the chain of general powers to legislate on a virtually unconstrained range of topics that began with the Deregulation and Contracting Out Act

---

[20] For an interesting example of a case where the Government made a tentative approach to the Select Committee about the possible introduction of a very extreme case of delegation, was rebuffed and in effect accepted the rebuff and did not attempt to take the power, see the correspondence over the Mental Capacity Bill set out in Extract 8A in the Appendix to *Craies on Legislation*; 9th edn.

1994, entered a broader phase in the Regulatory Reform Act 2001 and found its broadest form yet in the Legislative and Regulatory Reform Act 2006. The result of where this chain of increasing powers has ended (for now) is that the essential requirement is for a Minister to be able to identify something as a "burden", having done which he or she can then almost entirely bypass Parliament and legislate in a form as powerful as an Act but with much less scrutiny.

It is, of course, true that many beneficial measures can be passed into law in this way which would otherwise languish for lack of being of sufficient political priority to merit a place in any Government's legislative programme. But the same would be true of a power to legislate by Ministerial diktat without any degree of control at all; on the whole, and as presently constituted, the Government could be trusted in practice to misuse the power only rarely and in relatively minor ways. But that is not the point of Parliamentary sovereignty: the essence of our democracy is that all legislative power vests in Parliament alone, and that it should be delegated only, in essence, under tight Parliamentary control and for the purpose of giving more efficient and detailed effect to provisions passed by Parliament. Almost anything in law can be described as a "burden" on someone or another; and a power to legislate the main trigger for which is the ability to identify removing a burden, even if it is replaced with another burden on someone else, is arguably a step too far in constitutional terms for a Parliamentary democracy.

On many occasions over the years I have sat in the Officials' Box in Parliament—particularly in the Lords—and heard back-benchers oppose the taking of powers on the grounds that,

> "although of course the present administration can be trusted not to abuse the power, one cannot be certain about future Governments, and this is a power that a future Secretary of State might be tempted to misuse".

And yet although this argument is still heard, the protests are made increasingly weakly with the consciousness of participation in a lost battle, the front-benches increasingly rarely support it, and, ultimately, however it has been allowed to come about, we have reached a stage where truly extraordinary powers—such as the power to invent an entirely new tax on planning development by statutory instrument,[21] or to legislate with the power of an Act in a whole range of deregulatory directions—have come to be delegated, in a way that would have been thought completely impossible by Parliamentarians, politicians and civil servants, a relatively small number of years ago.

The solution

If I am correct in identifying a disturbing acceleration of open-ended powers to make subordinate legislation, the situation is not entirely without precedent. It was because of a similar, although smaller-scale, worry about the growth of legislative delegation that the Donoughmore Committee was established in 1929.[22] That Committee held a wide-ranging inquiry hearing evidence from experts on all "sides" of the question, and made a number of reasoned and balanced recommendations.

A similar exercise would be a splendid idea today. If the House of Lords' Select Committee on Delegated Powers had sharper teeth and a slightly wider remit, it could perform this function on a continuing basis; as things are, however, nothing short of an inquiry with a serious injection of influence of those who are neither politicians, civil servants nor even Parliamentarians, is likely to rein in the present trend effectively. The reason for this is that, unlike the situation in 1929, we are now faced with a position in which the "bottom line" of delegation likely to be acceptable to Parliamentarians and politicians is already far beyond what the public may wish to permit. The Cabinet Office has had a dedicated deregulation unit for some years, and successive Governments have committed to the concept of deregulation; yet despite this we have a suite of powers for secondary legislation that gives an unprecedented breadth and depth of legislative power to Ministers alone.

I do not feel it an exaggeration to put the position as high as the following: if an anti-democratic and dictatorial regime were to acquire significant political power in the United Kingdom, it would be able to

---

[21] Part 11 of the Planning Act 2008—the Community Infrastructure Levy.
[22] See Ch.2 above.

bypass Parliament and legislate in an extreme and controlling way on a troublingly wide range of subjects, all through reliance on powers that have been duly granted by Parliament, with very little real controversy. The history of totalitarian regimes shows that they generally prefer to assert legitimacy for their actions under the pre-existing law wherever possible, and that they are adept at using and building upon pre-existing legal powers of all kinds, of which the power to legislate is one of the most potentially dangerous.[23]

---

[23] Although not necessarily the most dangerous: for example, one of the present powers that would provide a particularly welcome opportunity to an Executive composed of, or containing, totalitarian elements, is the power of the Secretary of State to deprive a person of British citizenship, under s.40 of the Nationality Act 1981 as substituted by the Nationality, Immigration and Asylum Act 2002. s.4 and amended by the Immigration, Asylum and Nationality Act 2006 s.56. This allows the Secretary of State to deprive a person of citizenship if "satisfied that deprivation is conducive to the public good". Taken with the law of deportation, this produces the combined power to deprive any person of citizenship and then deport him or her so long as the Secretary of State is satisfied, in effect, that the country would be better off without them! The main restriction (at present) is that the power may not be used to make a person stateless: but, apart from the large number of people who have an alternative citizenship available (such as Jews, who have the right of immigration into Israel), this would mean that if, for example, the UK first obtained the agreement of a third country to offer citizenship to an undesirable resident of the UK, perhaps on unattractive terms, the power could then be used to expel the person from this country and force them to enter the other. At present, the European Convention on Human Rights would impose certain constraints on how this power is exercised; but even with the Convention as incorporated in UK law at present, the power would still have considerable potential effect.

24 PLAIN ENGLISH

Introduction

Every drafter has to decide for himself or herself what kind of style to use for legislation. It is increasingly taken for granted that any good modern drafter will be committed to the concept of using "plain English", although each drafter is likely to have different ideas about what that means.

There are three common myths about the use of plain English in legislation: first, that it is a modern idea; secondly, that people like it; and thirdly, that it works.

In fact: plain English is an old idea; many of the people who claim to want it don't like it when they get it; and it has severe limitations on its usefulness many of which are not properly recognised.

An old idea

A former First Parliamentary Counsel once observed that one of the earliest examples of good legislative drafting is the Ten Commandments. Certainly, they are short; and they convey at least a good part of their probable intended meaning with a reasonable degree of certainty and clarity. It is also certainly notable that whenever one looks at legislative codes of any kind that have stood the test of time, they are distinguished by the use of short propositions,[1] language that was contemporary and a clarity of the underlying purpose and intended effect that remains palpable.

As to guidance on legislative drafting, I know of no work on the subject, of whatever antiquity, that does not stress the importance of using short and simple propositions, and readily intelligible language.

---

[1] Although the extent to which the propositions are separated by punctuation, and the form of that punctuation, varies with fashions of "plain English" over the centuries.

The drafter who deliberately indulges in perceived archaisms in a vain attempt to impress the audience is just as out of touch with good practice of 50 or 100 years ago as he or she is with good practice of today's drafting.

People don't like it

So plain English is not new, and has always been urged as good drafting practice on the assumption that readers of legislation will prefer it. But I have always had the impression that the users of legislation appreciate plain language less than drafters expect them to, and sometimes less than they themselves pretend to. Genuine forces for change have a habit of playing out faster in the private sector than in the public sector, where commercial pressures are able to exert faster and stronger influence. One would therefore expect that if the demand for plain English were as high as some of the campaign groups arguing for it appear to suggest, the drafting of commercial documents by private lawyers would have been compelled by market forces to adopt plain and simple language as a matter of routine. It is true that in the commercial sector a clearer and simpler style is more frequently employed than was once the case for all kinds of documents, including commercial agreements. Even there, however, the inroads on old practice have been slower and less dramatic than one might have expected; and when it comes to "real" law—complicated commercial agreements and the like—there rarely appears to be any serious attempt or pressure to produce intelligible documents.

I received clear proof of my impression that plain English is less fashionable than some of its exponents like to suggest when in April 2009 the Department for the Environment, Food and Rural Affairs published a consultation paper on a draft Flood and Water Management Bill. For the first time (so far as I know) the substantive consultation paper included a set of questions specifically addressed to the style of the draft; and the draft had been obviously constructed with a view to adhering to the precepts of plain English so far as possible. The sentences used in the draft were short and staccato; and the language was generally basic and lacking in words with a particularly "legal" feel. This was acknowledged in the response of, for example, the Law Reform Committee of the Bar Council of England and Wales. They said:[2]

> "We approve the modern drafting style. We consider that while remaining concise, the draft successfully avoids archaic and potentially ambiguous words: with a general use of "must" rather than "shall" etc. and avoidance of "above" and "below" and excessive use of (say) "by reason of subsection (1)" . . . We thought the wording generally expressed in plain language was simple and clear: e.g., s 7: 'things that might be done in the course of flood or coastal erosion risk management . . . moving things onto, off or around a beach, or carrying out other works . . .'"

So the professional lawyers liked it. Oddly enough, however, a number of the consultees who represented what might be regarded as the "ordinary" reader of legislation, admittedly not private individuals but small or medium-sized businesses in the water industry, took specific objection to the use of plain English words such as "thing" and "thinks". One or two went so far as to say expressly that they thought they gave the Bill an insufficiently "legal" feel. They were not objecting on the grounds of inaccuracy or inefficacy, but simply because sometimes people like the law to be dressed up a bit. Whatever the Government and the Bar Council may think, citizens like to see their judges in clothes that represent something of the majesty and distance of the law itself: in a similar way, apparently, they like to see legislation dressed up a bit, so as to emphasise that it is something out of the run of ordinary documents.[3]

---

[2] See www.barcouncil.org.uk [accessed November 10, 2010].

[3] This attitude is also found widely among Parliamentarians: see, for example, the resistance to using "thinks" as a simple replacement for "is of the opinion that" or "considers", and other similar instances, recorded in *Craies on Legislation*, 9th edn, Ch.8.1.

It doesn't work

If those are indeed the true feelings of a number of ordinary citizens, they are certainly right to recognise that legislative drafting is unlike the production of any other kind of document. Although it is open for debate how much the differences should be emphasised by deliberate use of formal language where an informal alternative will serve the same purpose with the same degree of accuracy, it is certainly the case that the nature of legislation imposes severe constraints on the extent to which plain and simple language can, or even should, be used.

In particular, it can be dangerous to use plain English, if the result is to mislead readers into thinking that they have understood more of the law than they actually have. In many cases, therefore, one wishes that there were particular legalistic expressions that could be used in legislative drafting that had no close equivalent in normal English language. For example, legislation talks to a great extent about rights and duties imposed upon "persons". A lay reader of legislation might come across a reference to a "person" and say to himself or herself "yes, I know what a person is; it means a human being". A professional lawyer reading the same legislation would be likely to say to himself or herself:

> "Ah, I know more than the lay reader does: I am able to realise that this is a reference to legal persons, that is to say things with legal personality".

In fact, both of these readers would be wrong. A reference to a person in legislation has to be read in the context of Sch.1 to the Interpretation Act 1978, by virtue of which a number of things, including unincorporated associations, which do not have legal personality, are included. If one could only use a word like "snurkle", which has no meaning at all in ordinary English, one would at least clearly advertise to the reader that one was using a concept which was not found in ordinary speech and was peculiar, not merely to the law, but to the language of legislation.

To the question "then why not do without the Interpretation Act and simply spell out exactly what you mean in ordinary language on each occasion?" the answer is, of course, that this approach would make every single section of every single Act a great deal longer and a great deal more complicated. And this illustrates the second reason why the limitations on the proper use of plain English in legislative drafting are greater than is generally recognised by the public, or admitted by those who argue for the use of plain English as though it were some kind of theological desideratum. There are many concepts in the law that are complex and technical, and which change their precise meaning frequently as a result of developing case-law or for other reasons. A good example is legal professional privilege, to which the legislative drafter adverts when he or she provides that a person need not answer questions of a kind that he or she could not be compelled to answer in civil proceedings. That is an effective shorthand way of attracting a large, complex and constantly shifting body of law.

When plain English exponents try, as they sometimes do, to rewrite legislation in plain English so as to show us all how much better it could be done, they tend to confine themselves to making minor adjustments of provisions that are already reasonably comprehensible; as soon as they come to any one of the many complicated and technical concepts such as legal professional privilege, they, not unnaturally, throw up their hands in despair, admit defeat and replicate the original wording. When one points this out to them, the normal reaction is along the lines of "well, of course, there are limits on plain English": indeed there are, and in the context of legislation those limits are so severe that one frequently wonders whether it is worth attempting to render any of it into plain English, if the result is merely to tantalise readers and make them think that they are well on the way to understanding the provision for themselves, only to come across a complicated provision that infects what came before and makes them realise that they have probably understood nothing. (Or, worse, as I say above, to mislead them into thinking that they have fully understood the provision by the use of words that do have a natural English meaning, but are being used in a technical legal sense that is hidden from the average reader.)

All of which results in the wise lay-reader acknowledging that, as Harold Macmillan once put it:

"in order to achieve precision in legislation which is complex and often technical, it is not always possible to avoid an impression of obscurity"[4].

Two processes in one

Some of these problems and limitations arise from the fact that when one is drafting legislation one is actually doing not one job, but two, rolled into one: one is making the law; and one is communicating it. But although the same document serves both purposes at the same time, it is important to remember that they are distinct exercises, and that what may serve the purpose of one very well may be contrary to the interests of the other. In particular, the first purpose is pre-eminent: what matters most is that the law as made should be clear and precise. If it can be communicated at the same time in words that are clear to the likely reader, so much the better. But there are other ways of communicating the purpose and effect of legislation, other than by the words used to make it.[5] There are no ways, however, of correcting the legislation itself (other than by formally amending it) once one has used words in making it that do not have a precise resonance within the legal structure.

Whose plain English is it anyway?

One of the sub-myths about the use of plain English in drafting leg-islation is that there is a single target audience of "ordinary people" who have a right to be able to understand legislation, preferably with-out professional assistance.

The reality is that the target audience of legislation depends entirely on its context. It is important, for the sake of the efficacy of the rule of law, to ensure that legislation is communicated in language that will so far as possible be understood by those to whom it is principally addressed; subject always to the need to give priority in producing the

---

[4] See *Tributes to the Earl of Stockton (Harold Macmillan) Hansard,* HC Vol.108, cols.30–31 (January 12, 1987).

[5] See further the discussion about the origin of Explanatory Notes in Ch.25.

text of legislation to the first process, that of making accurate law, over the task of communicating it.

A law prohibiting people from taking dogs into parks has a direct impact on individuals who keep dogs, and effective rule of law demands that they be able to discover reasonably easily the existence, nature and extent of the law. The law should therefore be cast in terms which so far as possible are capable of complete understanding with a normal command of conversational English.[6]

If, however, it is necessary for the achievement of the policy to deploy a concept that has no precise equivalent in conversational English, the drafter does no service to the reader by employing a word which is sufficiently near to an ordinary English term to be likely to mislead readers into thinking that they have understood the law more completely than is in fact the case. If the complexity of the law makes it necessary for a citizen to have advice as to its effect, no service is done by making it appear deceptively simple. Of course, whether it is proper to have much in the way of law that is so complex that it cannot be readily understood by all citizens is another question.

A law taxing profits made from transactions in petroleum futures is aimed at only a very limited number of people, and it is neither necessary nor desirable to set out to make it intelligible to everyone. The attempt would be doomed to failure, since the very concept of transactions in futures is complex; it would succeed only in making the legislative proposition less clear to those at whom its communication is principally aimed. As to the use of jargon, if the oil futures industry has a set of terms which are clearly understood by all concerned, the law may as well reflect reality by employing the industry's jargon to describe the industry's affairs.

A similar situation arises frequently in tax legislation which is aimed at preventing avoidance by use of a particular accounting mechanism. Instead of using concepts from the unreal world of

---

[6] What Lord Mackintosh of Haringey rather amusingly described as "demotic English", when defending the use of ordinary English words like "thinks" rather than more lawyerish equivalents such as "in the opinion of"; see *Handard*, HL Vol.651, col.432 (July 10, 2003).

legislation to attempt to find some interface with the equally unreal world of accountancy, and hoping that anyone watching from the real world will have some inkling of what is going on, the most effective approach, and the clearest approach for the key target audience, is to adopt the relevant jargon used by the accountancy profession. That is the most efficient way of clarifying the target for the benefit of those targeted; and explanatory material can be used to try to give some vague idea to politicians and others of the technical battle that is being fought out between these two unreal and complicated worlds.

So is Plain English a complete non-starter?

No. But like everything else it has to be understood in the context of the fact that the only rule of legislative drafting is that there are no rules of legislative drafting. To attempt to fight an ideological campaign about the use or avoidance of particular words and expressions in the arena of Acts of Parliament is unlikely to assist, or as we have seen even to please, the average reader. The only question that the drafter should ask himself or herself on each occasion is:

> "what is the clearest and simplest way of presenting the material that I am required to enact and communicate so as to ensure that its key target audience knows what is expected of it and is able to comply?"

Linguistic dogma, social politics and philological academia have no part to play in this exercise.

The result is that drafters should apply principles of plain English drafting as they have been expounded by the great drafters for centuries, not in order to satisfy particular social or political pressures, but because clear and simple law is the only effective kind.

Since there are clear limitations on the extent to which good legislative drafting can utilise natural English expressions in the natural English way, it is also important for explanatory material to be provided, and for people to receive proper training in how to read and understand legislation. Explanatory material will be particularly but by no means only of importance to citizens who are not legally qualified, and it should, at least, put all the readers of the law in a position either to understand it or to appreciate the need for expert professional help.

As for legally qualified readers, their basic legal education ought to fit them, more than it generally does at present, for understanding most legislation. Undergraduate law courses still focus principally on tools used in the development of the common law. As the number of areas of law which depend heavily or even significantly on common law dwindles towards extinction, it becomes increasingly important to focus on understanding how legislation works. It is not sufficient to provide a few high level lectures on the application of ancient maxims such as the Mischief Rule. Students must be brought face to face, much more than they are at present in most law schools, with examples of legislation as the lifeblood of law, and learn under experienced tutelage how to grapple with the complexities and technicalities of legislation. All too often, students emerge from the entire professional training process with no adequate perception of most of the difficulties, still less with serviceable keys to their solution.[7]

---

[7] This proposition can be easily tested: try asking a roomful of qualified lawyers to explain the distinction between territorial application and extent; or what a legislative reference to service "by post" is required to be taken to mean.

25 EXPLANATORY MATERIAL

Introduction

As has been discussed in the previous chapter, the nature of legislation imposes constraints on the techniques it can use in communicating and explaining itself. Obscurity of legislation may be due to poor drafting or to the Parliamentary or political constraints under which it was produced: but it may also sometimes simply be a function of the dual nature of the exercise, whereby one is forced to make the law and communicate it at the same time and in the same document.

There therefore is, always has been and always will be an important role for explanatory material, to sit alongside the text of legislation itself and, with greater or lesser authority depending upon its provenance and intention, to help readers to understand the legislation.

This chapter briefly explores the role of explanatory material and discusses some of the opportunities and problems that it presents.

Explanatory Notes

The best-known and most-used "official" form of explanatory material alongside Acts of Parliament today are the Government's Explanatory Notes. Although technically they are not authoritative, and they routinely protest their lack of authority at the start of each new set of notes, the fact that they are in reality produced by the Government quickly and predictably led the courts to disregard that protest and to treat them as, at the very least, one of the most promising sources of background material in the context of which the legislative intention may be deduced.[1]

Explanatory Notes in their present form owe their origin to a memorandum presented by the then First Parliamentary Counsel,

---

[1] See *Craies on Legislation*, 9th edn, Ch.27.1.

Sir Christopher Jenkins KCB, QC, to the House of Commons Select Committee on Modernisation of the House on June 23, 1997. He wrote:

> "Unlike other forms of writing, a Bill is not there to inform, to explain, to entertain or to perform any of the other usual functions of literature. A Bill's sole reason for existence is to change the law. The resulting Act *is the law*.
>
> A consequence of this unique function is that a Bill cannot set about communicating with the reader in the same way that other forms of writing do. It cannot use the same range of tools. In particular, it cannot repeat important points simply to emphasise their importance or safely explain itself by restating a proposition in different words. To do so would risk creating doubts and ambiguities that would fuel litigation. As a result, legislation speaks in a monotone and its language is compressed. It is less easy for readers to get their bearings and to assimilate quickly what they are being told than it would be if conventional methods of helping the reader were freely available to the drafter.
>
> This difficulty is compounded if drafting and lay-out are poor. But even the best drafting and best lay-out cannot eliminate it. It is therefore important to find other ways of helping the reader.
>
> The Committee may therefore like to consider how Members and subsequent readers of Bills and Acts could be helped by material which does not itself form part of the law, but is provided alongside the law."

This to some extent, of course, understates the extent to which legislation can and always has used literary techniques to clarify its own meaning.[2] But it is certainly true that to a considerable extent the nature of legislation handicaps it in facilitating its own exposition.

---

[2] See, in particular, Ch.26.

What effect have Explanatory Notes had?

Explanatory Notes are written by human beings and are therefore, like human beings, of variable quality.

At the beginning of the project to recommend the introduction of Explanatory Notes, frequent mention was made of the Financial and Explanatory Memorandum that then routinely accompanied Bills and was printed with them; although these memoranda were also for the purpose of explaining the effect of the Bill, they had come to be treated as a wholly perfunctory exercise that did little more than repeat the basic proposition of each section without attempting to explain it. The new Explanatory Notes were designed to provide real explanation and thorough background, and not merely to repeat bits of the Bill.

This aim has on some occasions been accomplished. The Explanatory Notes for the Gambling Act 2005 are, for example, without doubt of genuine assistance to anyone who wants to understand the underlying intention of, and social and legal background to, the Act. They are clearly a work of great care in which an enormous amount of time and effort has been invested.

But they are the exception rather than the norm. The predictable reality of Explanatory Notes is that familiarity has bred contempt, and the vastly overworked Government lawyers and Bill team administrators are rarely able to devote anything like the time and energy to the production of the Explanatory Notes that their original intention merits and requires. All too often, they emerge in as bland and pointlessly repetitive a form as was the case for the earlier memoranda, whose defects were to be remedied by the introduction of the new system of Notes.

It should also be noted in passing that although the theory, which is widely publicised, is that Explanatory Notes are passed by Parliamentary Counsel, both in the case of Notes to the Bill and in the case of Notes to the eventually emerging Act, the reality is that the pressures on the time of Parliamentary Counsel are generally at least as great as those on Departmental lawyers and administrators, so that they are rarely able to do very much to ensure that the Notes are helpful as well as accurate (and it is not always possible even to ensure that they are accurate). When faced with the need to produce

accurate Notes in as short a time as possible, the easiest way of achieving it is, of course, to stick as closely as possible to mere description
of the provisions, without taking the time to add much or anything in
the way of explanatory and background material; but it is, of course,
precisely that material that is likely to be most valuable for the reader,
and that was the originally intended principal purpose of these Notes.

Constraints of Parliamentary rules

There is another reason, not always appreciated, why the Explanatory
Notes tend to be more bland than might be helpful. The notes to the
Bill, both as introduced into its first House and as sent to its second
House, although written by the Government are published by each
House of Parliament alongside the Bill.

Parliamentary rules, therefore, determine what material may be
included. Most significantly, there is an understandable rule that the
Notes are to be confined to material that explains the effect of the Bill,
rather than seeking to justify it.

The problem is that one can give a broader or narrower interpretation to what amounts to justification. The House Authorities
have tended over time to become increasingly strict in applying this
rule and in eliminating anything that they regard as argumentative.
While one can fully appreciate the desire of the House Authorities
not to allow Parliamentary resources and facilities to be susceptible to
exploitation for the purposes of Government propaganda, the result
of a very strict application of this rule is frequently to deprive readers of material that might help them to understand the fundamental
social purpose of the provision concerned, and which would therefore
help them to be able to assess to what extent that purpose is achieved.

The Explanatory Notes prepared for the Act as passed are not
subject to these theoretical limitations. They are published by the
Government alone and there is therefore no bar to the inclusion of
any material that the Government thinks likely to be helpful to the
reader. Nevertheless, it is rare that much if any background material is
added to this final version of the Notes. In part, this simply reflects the
fact that if Government lawyers are busy during the production of the
Bill and have little time for the Explanatory Notes, they are generally
even less likely to have time to embroider the Notes for an Act after

Royal Assent, by which time they will probably have been moved on to a multitude of other projects. There is also possibly something of a self-denying ordinance that restrains the Government from wanting to turn the final version of the Notes into overt propaganda.

Estoppel function

Despite the various problems associated with Explanatory Notes and resulting in their frequently being much less helpful than was hoped when they were introduced, they are generally serviceable to some extent and can, on occasion, be enormously helpful.

There is one way, in particular, in which Explanatory Notes can be of very specific importance to practitioners and judges in construing an Act. As in the case of the rule in *Pepper v Hart*, as well as serving to elucidate the intentions of the legislature, explanatory material of this kind can be used to set up an estoppel against the Government.[3] If the Minister in speaking to a particular provision gives what amounts to a firm undertaking that it will, or will not, be used in a specified way, the courts have shown their willingness to regard this as establishing a legitimate expectation, or a kind of estoppel, that will generally prevent the Government (including a later Government) from departing from this undertaking. In the same way, if Explanatory Notes express an intention that the provision is to be used, or not used, in a particular way, it will be reasonable to expect the Government to be held to this intention.

Other kinds of explanatory material in Acts

A traditional dogma that underpins the argument in Sir Christopher Jenkins' memorandum to the Modernisation Committee asserts that the nature of legislation imposes a constraint that prevents it from including any material that is inert, in the sense of not being intended to have distinct legal effect. The argument goes that the courts will be invited to give some legal effect to the material, and that whatever effect they choose is bound to be wrong, since none at all is intended.

---

[3] See *Craies on Legislation*, 9th edn, para.28.1.9.

There is, of course, a great deal of truth in this argument. We have
already discussed some of the constraints imposed by the nature of
legislation on what it can and cannot do: and adding additional material for some extraneous reason is always going to be, at best, risky.

But one should not overstate the point.[4] In particular, one needs
to recognise that Acts of Parliament had included a considerable
amount of inert material for many decades. To give one example,
when one Act refers to a section of another it is customary to
include a parenthetical reference to the contents of the provision
referred to: it is generally accepted that parenthetical references of
this kind are not intended to have any kind of legal effect, so much
so that it has traditionally been the practice of the House Authorities
to permit them to be altered by editorial action at the request of
Parliamentary Counsel rather than through formal amendment, if
it turns out that they are, or become, inaccurate.[5] Section headings,
too, and italic cross-headings of groups of sections, are also generally inert: again, the House Authorities have traditionally permitted
amendment by editorial action, arguably with less justification in
this instance, there being a number of decided cases in which the
courts have had regard to headings of this kind for the purpose of
construing legislation.[6]

Departmental guidance

Against the background of an apparently growing willingness of
the courts to allow themselves complete freedom in the range of
background material to which they will have regard in construing
Acts, it is not surprising that Government Departments have from
time to time invited the courts to have regard to Departmental
publications in construing the Acts to which they refer. Nor have
the courts in principle been unwilling to look at material of this
kind: so far as concerns formal Departmental publications such as

---

[4] And, lest I should seem to be setting up a straw man, I acknowledge that
most of the exponents of this point do not overstate it (although some do).

[5] As to the wisdom of this practice, see Ch.9.

[6] See *Craies on Legislation*, 9th edn, Ch.26.1.

White Papers and Green Papers, or other formal publications such as Law Commission Reports, the courts have been looking at them in the course of construing legislation for several decades. In principle, there is no reason why mere informality of production should make the courts less willing to have regard to a Departmental publication.

There are, however, limits on the kind of use to which the courts are prepared to put Departmental material; or perhaps it would be more accurate to say that there are limits on the weight that courts are prepared to give to it. Occasional attempts are made to invite the courts to have regard to Departmental material for the purpose of, in effect, giving the Government "another bite at the cherry" by way of informally rectifying aspects of the legislation that do not properly reflect what the Government intended, or perhaps with hindsight would like to have intended. Those attempts are firmly rebuffed by the courts, and rightly so.[7]

Conclusion

The courts always do and must begin the task of construing legislation by looking simply at the words used to express it[8]; anything beyond that is an admission of failure on the part of the drafter to communicate the law in a manner so clear and effective that it requires no external assistance.

On the other hand, even when the courts or other readers describe themselves as pursuing a "literal" approach, it is both desirable and inevitable that the words used will be read in their context,[9] and the drafter will rarely be able to encapsulate the entire legal, policy and social context of the legislation in the words used to enact it.

So there will always be an important place for explanatory material of various kinds, to help readers of all kinds—of whom the courts are only a sub-set and, at that, a sub-set that ideally will not be troubled to construe a particular provision—to understand and apply

---

[7] See *Craies on Legislation*, 9th edn, Ch.27.1.
[8] See *Craies on Legislation*, 9th edn, para.16.1.1.
[9] See *Craies on Legislation*, 9th edn, paras.18.1.1–18.1.3.

legislation.[10] The legislative drafter therefore needs to see himself or herself as part of a partnership, bearing principal responsibility for the accuracy and clarity of his or her drafting, but accepting that the product will be construed in the light of a range of background and explanatory material, produced both before and after enactment. That material must never become an excuse for making the legislative product any less clear or self-contained than is reasonably possible, and drafters must guard against any attempt to rely upon it in that way; but the knowledge that Explanatory Notes and other authoritative kinds of material are available can help the drafter to avoid the opposite temptation, which is the temptation to strain the boundaries of what can properly be done with legislative text itself beyond what the nature of legislation can bear, in a misguided attempt to help the reader.

---

[10] For example, the Westlaw Annotated Statutes service—of which the present writer is the General Editor—aims to provide navigational tools, technical explanations and background material designed to help readers to find their way through the increasingly large and complex maze of United Kingdom legislation.

26 THE USE OF EXAMPLES

Introduction

As a particular issue within the general question of the inclusion of explanatory material,[1] from time to time consideration is given to whether or not it is desirable for legislation to give examples of its own application.

The case against

Broadly speaking, the case against the inclusion of examples is the same as the case against the inclusion of all material that is not intended to have direct legislative effect. The argument goes that the more additional words are included, the more scope there is for the courts to be invited to give them a construction which subverts the intention of the primary legislative material itself.

The case in favour

The case in favour of the inclusion of examples relies on not overstating the importance of the argument against it, but balancing the risks against the clear benefits of using examples to clarify the intended application of particularly complex legislation, or to resolve issues of application at the margins and thereby prevent the need for later resolution of perceived ambiguity.

It also needs to be appreciated at the outset, that legislation has been including examples, in effect, for decades. Whenever a list or series of subdivisions in a provision is introduced by the words "in particular"—which happens frequently—the legislation is in effect giving a list of particular examples. Drafters have always been warned that the principal risk of specificity of this kind is that the courts will

---

[1] As to which, see Ch.25.

draw inferences about the exclusion of anything that one might have expected to see but which is not included expressly.[2]

That is a real risk, but, again, one that needs to be balanced against the benefits, and not treated as an automatic veto. For example, if an Act is conferring a power to make subordinate legislation in very broad terms, the mere fact that the power is drawn very widely will tend to discourage the courts from allowing the power to be used for anything very extreme. In those circumstances, therefore, it is wise to invite the Department to specify a list of particular and potentially extreme things that they know already they want to do, or may want to do, with the power, thereby placing those beyond doubt. Although that might have a marginal effect on the limitations that the court might impose upon the breadth of the power itself, the result is still to ensure that the power is more serviceable than it would be if it were left in entirely broad terms. This is a balance that must be struck on each occasion, by reference to the circumstances of the case and not to dogma.

It also must be recognised that examples, expressly described as such, have been used in legislation from time to time; and if they have had the kind of apocalyptically disastrous effects that the dogmatic opponents of the inclusion of inert material prophesy, I for one am not aware of them.[3]

Conclusion

For some reason, the inclusion of examples is a technique that, at least when used expressly with the word "example", frightens people more than many other kinds of drafting innovation. Ironically, however, there is possibly no innovation that could do more to help the readers of legislation and bring additional clarity to the statute book. When we teach, we expect to give examples as a matter of course, to aid our students in understanding our arguments, theories and explanations.

---

[2] "Expressio unius est exclusio alterius"; see *Craies on Legislation*, 9th edn, Ch.20.1.

[3] See, for example, the Consumer Credit Act 1974; the Adoption Act 1976 s.42; and the Child Support Act 1991 s.42.

So long as we qualify an instance by describing it as an example, we do not expect our intelligent students to make the mistake of thinking that we are describing the only, or necessarily an entirely typical, case. We expect them to be able to understand that an example is precisely that—a helpful illustration of our words, and not an attempt to limit them by reference to all facets of the example.

Of course, legislation is not the same as teaching or any other form of communication; it is a strange hybrid exercise that both makes the law and communicates it in a single document. But although it is not only communication, it is partly communication: and we should not deny ourselves the use of one of the most powerful tools of communication simply because it requires to be used with care, and occasionally qualified with discretion.

I recently drafted a statutory instrument that had to reflect a European Union development by qualifying the text of many thousands of references throughout the statute book and statutory instrument book. Faced with the unappealing prospect of a few hundred pages of individual textual amendments—which in practice would have been bound to include omissions and inaccuracies, even with the most reasonably realistic degree of care—I decided to construct a few basic propositions which would account for well over 99 per cent of the enactments to be amended, leaving the last few to be dealt with in a Schedule of particular amendments. Having done so, I asked myself and others whether the propositions were sufficiently clear and precise for commercial editors and other readers[4] to be able to absorb them easily and apply them accurately. As to this, the verdicts were divided, although the preponderance of opinion was in favour; certainly there was nothing like enough opposition to convince me to go for the several-hundred-page option; but the informal consultation did leave me with a feeling that a degree of additional assistance for the reader would be a good idea. Examples were the obvious answer: the provision of one or two worked examples of each general proposition

---

[4] Although in practice this was precisely the kind of technical instrument which only commercial editors, and not many of them at that, would be concerned with; another reason for saving a few hundred pages of statutory instrument if at all possible.

rendered it pellucid. So I produced a few examples and turned them into a Schedule, introduced by a laconic provision simply to the effect that "Schedule 1 gives examples of the application of articles 1 to 7". Then I showed it around, and it was as if I had suddenly introduced a series of jokes of dubious taste—even those who had previously been perfectly happy with the provisions on their own and found them sufficiently clear without the examples, were uncomfortable about the innovation purely on the grounds that it was an innovation.[5]

Examples are the most undeservedly criticised tool of legislative communication. We could do with a few senior judges commenting on how useful they would have been in aiding the construction of a provision, wondering aloud from the bench why drafters don't use them, and reassuring the drafting world that the judiciary can be trusted to make appropriate and discrete use of them, as they have in fact been doing with all the "in particulars" and other covert examples since drafting began.

Until then, however, examples are likely at best to be relegated to Explanatory Notes or other material, where they continue to be helpful but, because they are not expressly authoritative, less helpful than if they were included in the text.

---

[5] Not a complete innovation, as noted above.

27 THE PESTILENTIAL POWER OF PRECEDENT

Introduction

Innovation is the lifeblood of good legislative drafting. Expressions, techniques and practices endure long past the point at which they have ceased to be fit for the purpose for which they were designed. But the powerful pull of precedent encourages people to continue to follow blindly the paths forged by earlier generations of drafters, without considering the extent to which circumstances have changed. Someone has to be prepared to turn off the established path and to start down an avenue that better delivers a result in the contemporary context.

Example—the abolition of chapter numbers

A good example is the abolition of the use of chapter numbers in legislation. When an Act of Parliament is given Royal Assent it is assigned a chapter number, based on a system of renumbering for each calendar year since 1965, and using regnal years before that. These numbers have been without practical utility for several decades, almost without exception.[1] Some years ago I decided to stop using chapter numbers for the purpose of general legal writing, since I could

---

[1] I can only think of two exceptions, neither of them very impressive. The first is that a small handful of statutory editors around the country, probably numbering no more than five in all, may have found it useful to use chapter numbers when giving effect to a Repeal Schedule; but now that everybody is working entirely electronically there is no obvious advantage even to that. The second, which is mostly fanciful, is that if a provision were drafted in terms of having an effect on all other Acts passed before it but no others, it would be important to know the precise order in which Royal Assent had notionally been given to a number of Acts on the same date, and the chapter numbers would be determinative of that (although in fact the chapter numbers are themselves reflective in that context of the order in which Royal Assent has been, normally, signified by the Royal Commission, which in turn reflects the order given in their letter of instructions).

no longer imagine that they were genuinely useful for any reader: in the preface to the first supplement to the seventh edition of Stroud's Judicial Dictionary in 2007 I said as follows:

> "I have finally decided to omit chapter number citations for Acts of Parliament. They are no longer likely to be of significant assistance to any reader. Even someone consulting the Queen's Printer's annual printed volumes of Acts will find an alphabetical index at the front of each volume; and the greater number of people using commercial or electronic versions of Acts will normally expect to gain access using titles alone. It is probably time for chapter numbers to be dropped from all routine use (including, arguably, in cross-references within Acts, particularly now that they have moved from the margin to the text itself and so disrupt the reader's visual flow for no practical purpose)."

But I continued to feel obliged to use chapter numbers in legislative drafting, simply because everybody else did. From time to time I complained weakly, but it was not until 2009 that I had a bright idea about how to get rid of them. My idea was to stop using them: and I did this in the Bill for the Banking Act 2009. I relied on the hope that by the time anybody noticed what I had done, it would be too late for anybody to claim with any degree of credibility that it mattered. Nor was I disappointed. The Bill passed all its draft stages without the Department or anybody else apparently noticing or caring; it passed its first House of Parliament, the House of Commons, in similar style; and it was, predictably, not until it reached the House of Lords that anybody noticed, or at least cared enough to raise the issue.

I was asked whether I thought an innovation of this kind could reasonably be carried through in such an informal and impromptu manner, to which my reply was that I was not intending to innovate for anybody other than myself, and that so far as the drafters of other Acts of Parliament were concerned they were entirely at liberty to continue using chapter numbers for as long as it seemed good to them to do so. I did, of course, undertake that if anybody in authority instructed me to continue using them I would do so, even to the extent of reinserting them into the present Bill, should anybody seriously think it sufficiently worthwhile. Not surprisingly, nobody could really argue that this would be a sensible use of anybody's time, and the Bill proceeded without chapter numbers, on the basis that it was, rather quaintly, "an experiment".

I am delighted to be able to record that shortly after that, which is to say within a few months, the "experiment" was universally adopted, and chapter numbers are no longer found in Westminster Acts.[2]

The perceived dangers of innovation

Innovation has a tendency to frighten the horses.

That need not necessarily matter if the Ministerial horse that one is riding oneself has the will to calm the stampeding herd, and the context is one in which a certain amount of political energy can be expended on that process. Lord Mackintosh of Haringey wins my personal award for willingness to face the opposition and to stand up for good innovation in the proper context.[3] In a debate on the Railways and Transport Safety Bill he defended "thinks" against suggestions that "considers" would be more usual legislative language, on the grounds that—

". . . we are happy to engage Parliamentary Counsel who use ordinary English—what I would call demotic English—in the drafting of the Bill. I believe that "thinks" says what it means and is the right word to use, rather than "is of the opinion" or some more pompous phrase".[4]

In a later episode, however, despite citing Lord Mackintosh in support of another attempt to use "thinks" in legislation,[5] Treasury Ministers

---

[2] The Scots still use them, but perhaps not for much longer, since they are generally ahead of the English in modernisation projects.

[3] *Hansard*, Vol.651, col.432 (July 10, 2003).

[4] My admiration for Lord Mackintosh on that occasion is only slightly diminished by the knowledge that in his use of the word "demotic" he was perhaps demonstrating an imperfect grasp of the need to communicate in modern parlance.

[5] *HM Revenue and Customs and the Taxpayer: Modernising powers, deterrents and safeguards A New Approach to Penalties for Incorrect Tax Returns; Responses to the 19 December 2006 Consultation Document*, March 2007.

were eventually persuaded to give in to the forces of darkness and abandon "thinks" at least in that context, faced with implacable insistence that it implied a lower threshold. So one wins some and loses some: but if one keeps trying, every time a "thinks" slips into the statute book it makes it more defensible next time.

So strong can the prejudice against innovation be that it can sometimes force the legislator to perpetrate bad law simply because it attracts less attention than good law. A good example of this occurred in the House of Lords proceedings on the Bill for the Nationality, Immigration and Asylum Act 2002[6] where the Government were defeated heavily on the proposal to introduce a power to make consequential and incidental provision: as a number of peers noted, the power was drawn to similar effect as, if not narrower effect than, a number of precedents; but its novelty of form was the subject of intense suspicion and criticism, and was sufficient to persuade a majority to approve an amendment to prevent it from being used for certain parts of the Bill.[7]

Purpose clauses and overview clauses are two other examples of recent innovations that have caused sufficient alarm in certain circles to make them slow to catch on. Even the relatively harmless index of defined expressions, for which Lord Brightman campaigned so hard for many years, was, simply because it was an innovation, resisted by

---

[6] See *Hansard*, Vol.640, col.309 (October 31, 2002).

[7] The fall-out from that affair was also interesting. The House of Lords Select Committee on Delegated Powers considered the episode and was at first minded, in particular, to recommend a standardisation of powers of this kind into a particular form. Partly as a result of information about the importance of intelligent diversity provided by Parliamentary Counsel, however, the eventual Third Report of the Delegated Powers and Regulatory Reform Committee on Henry VIII powers to make incidental, consequential and similar provision (HL Paper 21) did not include a recommendation in those terms. The Chairman of the Committee, Lord Dahrendorf, speaking to the Report in the House of Lords (*Hansard*, HL Vol.643, col.168 (January 14, 2003)) acknowledged that "There is possibly a risk that the "one clause fits all" principle would in some cases lead to a wider empowerment of the Executive than is either necessary or desirable."

some, and to this day has not become a routine addition to every Bill, despite its obvious harmlessness and utility.

Should we be bolder?

Contrary to the impression I may have given so far, my answer to this question is, no. Innovation for its own sake would undoubtedly be a more dangerous force in legislative drafting than is an entrenched reaction of opposition to novelty.

In fact, I think that until recently we had the balance about right. The Office of the Parliamentary Counsel had a strong majority of conservative operators, whose regard for precedent was high and whose instincts were to be suspicious of innovation, but not to such an extent that they were incapable of being persuaded.

The result was that in the productions of a small minority of drafters at any one time, innovations and experiments came and went. Very often, the perpetrators themselves became bored of, or unconvinced by, their own experiment after one or two attempts. The important thing was that nobody else in the Office was forced, or even particularly encouraged, to follow suit. The result was that an experiment would catch on if the colleagues of the experimenter, and in particular his or her junior assistants from time to time, liked the innovation and determined to use it for themselves. If not, it might continue to be used by its originator for a while, even for a number of years; but sooner or later it would die away, if only on the retirement of the drafter concerned.

So experiments and innovations had to be good if they were to survive; but there was no law against them. This seems to me to be ideal: it provides the conditions under which fluid development of legislative drafting can take place, but puts each development to proof of its own usefulness, requiring it to be judged by other drafters.

What has happened in very recent years, however, is that there has been a positive force against innovation, which has certainly been detrimental to the development of legislative practice. A committee was even established within the Office of the Parliamentary Counsel to issue recommendations to the Office at large on questions of style, partly for the purpose of ensuring greater consistency. The very idea of having a group of colleagues tasked with telling everybody else what they should or should not do was anathema when I joined the Parliamentary Counsel Office in 1991: and it should be anathema still.

The illusory value of consistency

One of the arguments when the drafting group within the Office of the Parliamentary Counsel was established was that inconsistency in minor points of style detracted from the reputation of the Office and was potentially confusing to the reader.

I never accepted either of these arguments.

Even the most megalomanic of drafters has to accept that when it comes to significant substantive provisions there can be no simple precedent; nor is there any value in superficial similarity between two provisions. As I may have said already in one or two places in this book, the only rule of legislative drafting is that there are no rules of legislative drafting. The drafter must consider on each occasion in relation to the material before him or her, "what is the simplest and clearest method of presenting this material to my target audience on this occasion?" Any rule or dogma that detracts from consideration of this question, or that constrains the choice of answers, is deleterious to good drafting.

So if one accepts that consistency of form is not to be found in provisions of serious substance, what is left? The answer is, provisions of triviality such as the form in which one introduces Schedules. So one drafter might prefer the formula "Schedule 1 shall have effect"; while another might prefer the more modern "Schedule 1 makes provision about dogs"; and yet another might prefer something post-modernist like "Schedule 1 is the first Schedule to this Act". It is not possible that any reader could be misled by the difference of styles into thinking that a difference of substance is intended. As to reputation of the Office, the reader comparing these three styles would be likely to gain the impression that the Office is staffed by individualists, whose individualism is given free rein: what could possibly be better than that?

Alas, although that would once have been an accurate impression, there are increasing attempts to impose styles and approaches by the enumeration of rules set down from a purely theoretical perspective.

This increasing tendency has two principal dangers.

First, there is no reason to suppose that the approach imposed from above will necessarily be better than any of the other approaches variously preferred by individual members of the Office. In particular, unless there are systematic arrangements for the testing of different approaches on representative groups of ultimate target audiences of Acts, no one can claim greater authority for his or her preferred approach than anyone else. As has been seen in connection with the use of plain English,[8] professional drafters are not always accurate in predicting what the target audience will prefer, even when attempting to provide an approach that they hope will suit them best.

Secondly, imposing standard solutions even to trivial drafting issues is the surest way to prevent the kind of development necessary to keep legislative language in step with changes in language generally. The drafter who first coined the approach "Schedule 1 shall have effect" was probably reflecting the plain English of his or her day; at any rate, there was nothing surprising or uncomfortable in those days in the imperative use of the word "shall".[9] It might not therefore have been unreasonable for that drafter to turn to his or her colleagues and insist, supposing him or her to have been in a position to do so, on their following suit. The form could have been written down in some Manual or book of office practice, and followed slavishly by drafters ever since. The problem with that, is the boiled frog syndrome.[10] If

---

[8] See Ch.24.

[9] There is, of course, a more general debate about whether "shall" is still fit for purpose today as a feature of the legislative landscape. My own belief is that its very archaism is useful in highlighting to the reader that it performs a function unlike any function performed in normal speech. See further *Craies on Legislation*, 9th edn, para.8.1.9.

[10] This is an extremely important syndrome, well known to all those of us whose wives teach Psychology A-Level. In the boiled frog experiment, you take two frogs and two saucepans of water. The first frog is dropped into a saucepan of boiling water: the instant his flippers touch the water they sense its heat, an instinct causes him to spring to safety, and he survives. The second frog is placed in a saucepan of cold water, which is then gradually heated to boiling point: the frog senses the increasing heat, but is never able to identify a point at which it has become unbearable, so he stays put, and is boiled to death. (This experiment can be conducted equally well with female frogs: in

it is necessary to overturn an established rule in order to change the practice, at what point does the young and tender drafter feel that the expression has become so archaic to make it necessary and appropriate for him or her to challenge the established practice? Particularly since an Office that indulges in written rules and manuals is unlikely to have an atmosphere that encourages innovation. The result is that nobody either notices the need to, or dares, challenge the existing practice, and it remains until it has well outlasted its fitness for purpose.

Far better to have an office where people are encouraged to innovate freely. Someone with a taste for wackiness will therefore invent an approach like "Schedule 1 is the first Schedule to the Act"; his or her colleagues will see it and ignore it; and it will gradually fall into desuetude, where it belongs. Another colleague will come up with one of the many other more modern methods which are less wacky, and will find that a number of his or her colleagues follow suit. Gradually, therefore, and without compulsion, the language of legislative drafting will move on. A much more satisfactory result for the reader of legislation than an artificially imposed superficial consistency, which will rapidly fall out of date.

Manuals

It will easily be discerned from what I say above, that manuals of drafting are simply a menace, that sap the will to innovate, and encourage people to believe that one can learn to draft by following a set of rules.[11]

---

this footnote references to the masculine include references to the feminine, and cognate expressions are to be construed accordingly.)

[11] The best "manuals" of legislative drafting are in fact not manuals in the sterile sense discussed above at all—in fact, they are a helpful series of articles exposing and expounding different issues in legislative drafting, so that the drafter can review the arguments and devise a solution apt for the material with which he or she is presently confronted. See, in particular, various manuals produced under the aegis of the Institute of Advanced Legal Studies, such as the *Manual in Legislative Drafting* edited by Constantin Stefanou and Helen Xanthaki, published by the Department for International Development in 2005.

28 MISTAKES IN LEGISLATION

Introduction

There was a time when the courts appeared most reluctant to believe that the drafter of an Act had simply made a mistake.

Perhaps the point should be put rather differently: presumably, judges have always been aware that drafters are fallible; but there was a time when they seem to have felt that attributing an apparent infelicity or absurdity to simple inadvertence on behalf of the drafter was too easy a "way out", and risked allowing Parliament to escape the full consequences of its own supremacy. The supremacy or sovereignty of Parliament means that it is open to Parliament to legislate in any way that it chooses: but having chosen to legislate in a particular way, Parliament is stuck with that. Parliament ought not to be released from the consequences of its legislation by protesting "that's not really what we meant" where it clearly is what they meant, but is not what they should have meant, or what they would have been taken to mean if the drafter had expressed the thought properly in accordance with his or her instructions.

If that correctly explains judicial reluctance to dismiss an apparent defect of substance in an Act as a drafting mistake, then the reasoning is clearly as relevant today as it ever was. Be that as it may, judges do appear readier today than they once were both to identify something as a mistake on the part of the drafter and, more significantly, to be more prepared to remedy the mistake by judicial action.

This chapter explores a little of the background to how mistakes happen, how they are treated when they occur, and how they should be treated.

The law as to mistakes of drafting

The state of the law in relation to the correction of drafting mistakes by the courts is discussed in detail in *Craies on Legislation*.[1] In essence, we have reached the stage where the courts are now prepared, despite the traditional reluctance of the judges to interfere with Parliament's role of law-making,.to mend defective law, where the defect is beyond reasonable doubt, and there is equally little doubt as to its precise solution.[2]

The courts remain rightly nervous of this enterprise, and one would hope that the judicial reluctance to encroach upon the Parliamentary prerogative of legislating will continue to make them nervous. When in doubt as to whether or not a particular result derives from a drafting mistake, it is to be hoped and expected that the courts will always err on the side of caution, and decline to interfere to remedy the possible mistake.

It is, after all, always open to Parliament to legislate to correct an error: and not only can Parliament legislate fast if it needs to, it can also legislate with retrospective effect insofar as necessary.[3] So it is

---

[1] 9th edn; see Chs 15 and 20.

[2] For a recent example, see the following passage of a decision of the Sheriff Court—*Dundee City Council, Petitioners* Sheriff Court (Tayside, Central and Fife) (Dundee), 17 May 2010, 2010 G.W.D. 18-357: "The right of the court to correct obvious drafting errors undoubtedly exists—see the discussion in *Craies* para.20.1.9 ff. In my opinion, the legislative intention is achieved by adding in article 17(1) the words, 'or on or after' after the word 'before' in the first line thereof and by adding the words 'or is made' after the word 'is' in the same line. If that is done, the freeing order, if granted on or after 28 September will be deemed to be a permanence order with the detailed provisions set out in article 17(2)." This illustrates the extent to which judicial rectification of drafting mistakes is no longer treated by the courts as a daring exercise of constitutional importance, but as merely an everyday occurrence to be taken in the judicial stride.

[3] For a recent example of an Act passed at great speed to avoid unwanted consequences of a judicial decision see the Terrorist Asset-Freezing (Temporary Provisions) Act 2010, the background to which is set out in the Government's Explanatory Notes; note also that although retrospective legislation is controversial and the circumstances in which it is thought proper are limited, one of

never reasonable for the Government to say to the courts "you must intervene to correct the mistake because otherwise untold damage will be done". Even where the legislative route might in the circumstances prove an imperfect solution, it is impossible to conceive a situation in which the damage caused in that way would outweigh the damage caused by the constitutional impropriety of the courts taking upon themselves the right to legislate.

We therefore appear to have arrived at what seems to be the most proper position, whereby the courts will intervene to correct a simple drafting mistake if to refuse to do so would simply be to put everybody to a lot of clearly unnecessary inconvenience to correct it in a legislative manner; but beyond that they will not go.

Temptation to push the doctrine

It remains tempting, however, for Governments, and indeed others, to push at the boundaries of this doctrine and attempt to pressurise the courts into "correcting" things that are not simple mistakes within the classic understanding of that term; or to correct clear mistakes in ways that would require more creativity than the courts can justify given their lack of democratic accountability.

The best illustration of this temptation, and of the difficulty in which the courts find themselves when faced with it, is to analyse one of the most important recent cases dealing with the correction of drafting mistakes, albeit that it was not generally recognised at the time that this is what the case was in fact about.

Mr Haw and Parliament Square

The case arose in relation to s.132 of the Serious Organised Crime and Police Act 2005. That section was introduced for the purpose of

---

the mitigating factors generally relied upon in fiscal contexts to justify retrospective legislation is a Ministerial announcement on Day X that an Act will be passed as soon as possible to change the law with retrospective effect from Day X—a properly publicised announcement of that kind avoids the principal injustices of retrospection.

tackling the longstanding demonstration organised by Mr Haw in Parliament Square. That intention was clear from the discussion in Parliament and a number of pieces of background material.

The section began as follows:

"132 Demonstrating without authorisation in designated area
(1) Any person who—
  (a) organises a demonstration in a public place in the designated area, or
  (b) takes part in a demonstration in a public place in the designated area, or
  (c) carries on a demonstration by himself in a public place in the designated area,
is guilty of an offence if, when the demonstration starts, authorisation for the demonstration has not been given under section 134(2)."

From reading the above it will be immediately apparent to the alert reader that the drafter made a mistake.[4] If the whole purpose of this section was to prevent Mr Haw from continuing his demonstration, it was clearly inept for the operation of the section to depend upon something that must be done "when the demonstration starts". Of course, since the section was intended to operate on new copycat demonstrations that might arise, it was not unreasonable for it to include provision requiring something to be done before the start of a demonstration. But the drafter either should have included a reference to the continuation of a demonstration in the alternative, or should have made express provision for transitional cases (or ensured that the transitional provision in a Commencement Order had express vires to make retrospective provision).

---

[4] In so far as it is accepted that this was indeed a mistake, it illustrates the limitations on the drafting process—the drafter of the Act was one of the most experienced and able members of the Office of the Parliamentary Counsel, and probably because of that was subjected to extraordinary pressures of timing in the production of the Bill for this Act, as a result of which arose this slip which every one of his or her colleagues would instantly recognise as a "there but for the Grace of God . . ." moment.

When this became apparent the Government's first approach was to attempt to remedy the mistake by including transitional provision in the relevant Commencement Order that would have had the effect of making the section apply retrospectively to demonstrations that had already begun.[5] The Commencement Order was challenged by way of judicial review and rightly struck down by the Divisional Court. In argument before the court Counsel for the Crown was most urgent that the court should adopt what was described as a "modern, liberal, purposive construction".[6] She argued strongly that various published materials made it clear that the principal target of the provision was Mr Haw, and that the courts were bound to give effect to the legislative intention in allowing that target to be hit. The court refused to do so, however, on the grounds that whatever the Government's intention may have been in relation to Mr Haw they had simply not produced legislation capable of achieving that intention. As Smith LJ said[7]:

> "In my judgment, even if this were not a penal statute, there is no room for a modern, liberal, purposive construction.[8] The words of section 312 are clear and they give effect to a perfectly sensible

---

[5] It is, of course, standard practice for Commencement Orders to be given express power to include transitional provision. The purpose of that, however, is to make provision adapting the new law to transitional cases that are undoubtedly caught by it. A mere power to make transitional provision does not itself confer the power to stretch the new law back in time and catch retrospectively cases that, on the clear wording of the new law itself, would not be caught.

[6] [2005] EWHC 2061 (Admin) per Smith L.J. para.42.

[7] Para.58.

[8] Although even this is something that the courts will be prepared to do if instructed expressly by Parliament. Hence s.3 of the Human Rights Act 1998 (c.42), which in effect requires the courts to construe all statutes—even those passed before 1998—in the context of the United Kingdom's obligations under the European Convention on Human Rights; this requirement has been construed by the courts as requiring them to give weight to the text of the Convention Rights even at the expense of a certain degree of violence to clear words used—see, in particular, *Ghaidan v Godin-Mendoza* [2004] UKHL 30.

purpose, even though demonstrations which began before 1 August are not caught."

As I said about that case elsewhere[9]:

"No case could better illustrate either the inherent limitations on purposivism in the United Kingdom courts, or the fact that the increasing trend towards openness in regard to evidence as to context may not be relied on so as to substitute the Government's clear policy intentions for the clear meaning of the legislation that they have caused to be enacted for the purposes of achieving it. Construction of legislation in its proper context is one thing: allowing a recorded intention of the legislature to override the natural meaning of the words used is quite another."

The Court of Appeal reversed the Divisional Court's decision and held that the provision did indeed apply to Mr Haw.[10] One can appreciate the Court of Appeal's difficulty in this matter. On the one hand, it was clearly monstrous to suggest that the courts should do violence to the language of the statute in recognition of the fact that the drafter had simply failed to achieve what everybody involved had expected to be achieved. On the other hand, the general Parliamentary expectation had indeed been clear, and it might be thought equally scandalous for mere inadvertence on the part of the drafter to defeat that expectation.[11] The court attempted to cut through the conundrum by purporting to give, not a purposive construction that disregarded the clear terms of the Act, but a contextual construction that has regard to the clear terms of the Act but construes them in the light of their context. The court said as follows[12]:

---

[9] See "All Trains Stop at Crewe: The Rise and Rise of Contextual Drafting", (2005) 7 *European Journal of Law Reform* 31–46.

[10] [2006] EWCA Civ 532.

[11] Although, as I say above, the answer to that is that it would have been open to Parliament to pass remedial legislation, having retrospective effect, as quickly as they liked.

[12] [2006] EWCA Civ 532, [22]–[23].

"It appears to us that when the Act is construed in its context and having regard to the plain intention of Parliament as deduced from the Parliamentary language, including the disapplication of section 14 of the 1986 Act, section 132(1) on its proper construction includes demonstrations actually starting before the commencement of the Act as surely as those starting after. Those starting before, like the respondent's, are deemed to start at commencement; and in such cases the words "when the demonstration starts" refer to the time of commencement. The provisions of section 133 and 134 then work perfectly satisfactorily by reference to such a start date. This is the construction which we understand was favoured by Simon J in paragraph 76. It is important to observe that we have reached this conclusion on the basis of the statutory language construed in its context. . . ."

It is of course important to realise that the courts do and should always give a contextual construction to the words before them, and that the academic debate about literal or purposive construction translates, in the real judicial world, into a debate about what evidence the courts are prepared to have regard to in determining the context within which legislative language is to be construed.[13] But it stretches credulity to regard "starts or continues" as a mere contextual construction of "starts". The reality of the situation was that the Government, and therefore Parliament, simply got it wrong. They failed to legislate in a way that was capable of covering the transitional case, despite the fact that it was the single transitional case that those involved were most anxious to deal with. It can be argued that the rule of law, and the distinction between the role of Parliament and the role of the courts, would have been better served if everyone, Government included, had simply recognised this as a mistake from the beginning, and had adopted a legislative solution insofar as that was desired.

---

[13] See further "All Trains Stop at Crewe: The Rise and Rise of Contextual Drafting", (2005) 7 *European Journal of Law Reform* 31–46.

Identity Cards Act 2006 s.44

The case of Mr Haw is thus a useful cautionary tale for drafters and
others involved in the legislative process. Another similarly useful cautionary tale can be found in relation to the Identity Cards Act 2006,
and the error identified and corrected by the courts in *R (on the application of the Crown Prosecution Service) v Bow Street Magistrates'
Court.*[14] The essence of the case was the question whether a number of
people charged with serious offences in relation to forgery of passports
were entitled to be acquitted, which in turn depended on whether old
offences under an Act of 1981 had been repealed by the 2006 Act,
before the commencement of the replacement offences provided for
in the 2006 Act.

Although the statutory provisions are of some complexity, the
question at the heart of the case was relatively simple, and turned on
the effect of commencing a repeal Schedule. As a matter of simple
statutory interpretation the court found no difficulty in determining
that the statute had clearly repealed an earlier offence, despite the
fact that it was clear that this could not have been a sensible policy
intention, and that the drafter had simply made a careless mistake.
Indeed, it was the very obviousness and carelessness of the mistake
that led the court to believe that it was capable of rectification by
judicial action.[15]

This is therefore an important cautionary tale for drafters because
it illustrates how simple carelessness can subvert the rule of law, and
lead readily to a situation in which acknowledged criminals are able to
walk free. In drafting, it is often tempting to feel that one is part of a

---

[14] [2006] EWHC 1763 (Admin).

[15] "42 I am also satisfied that, as a result of an error and inadvertence on
the part of the draftsman and Parliament, the terms of section 44(3) of the 2006
Act failed to give effect to that intended purpose because section 44(2) was not
excluded from the list of excepted provisions specified in brackets in section
44(3) and the exclusion of Schedule 2 from the bracketed list of exceptions was
insufficient to achieve the intended purpose, particularly having regard to the
terms of section 44(2) itself. In my view, this is a plain case of a drafting mistake. 43 For those reasons I am satisfied that the first two conditions identified
by Lord Nicholls in *Inco Europe* are clearly satisfied in this case."

subtle political and Parliamentary game being played almost entirely for the benefit of Parliamentarians and politicians. It is insidiously easy to forget that what we do affects the real world, and that however trivial the point may appear to be, nothing is trivial to the citizen who is affected by it. When a criminal walks free because of an ineptly drafted statutory provision, future victims of that criminal are likely to feel that the drafter has served them badly.

How do mistakes happen?

Drafters are human beings. They have their good days and their bad days. Each of them has strengths and weaknesses. It is therefore incumbent upon the system so far as possible to make best use of each drafter's strengths, and mitigate so far as possible the risks arising from each drafter's weaknesses.

In the traditional structure of the Office of the Parliamentary Counsel the primary safeguard against mistakes was the "four eyes" principal. As has been discussed above,[16] the Office was traditionally structured in teams of two, for the most part, each containing a senior and a junior. When the teams operated properly, nothing would be sent out by either member without having first been thoroughly checked by the other; and this check was being carried out by someone who increasingly knew and understood the way in which the other worked, and was therefore increasingly capable of challenging their work and exposing deficiencies.

Ideally, a system of that kind should be capable of spotting a careless mistake of the kind made in the case of the Identity Cards Act 2006, and rectifying it before it reached Parliament.

There are, however, a number of reasons why that sometimes does not happen. The speed required of drafters today sometimes makes it impracticable for a draft to be thoroughly scrutinised by the other member of a team before it is issued to the Department; and once it has been issued, it becomes increasingly difficult to recapture the objectivity required for scrutinising it point by point. On other occasions, it may be simply arrogance on the part of a senior drafter that

---

[16] See Ch.4.

leads to failing to give a junior the proper opportunity to scrutinise it; and it may be laziness on the part of the senior to fail to scrutinise the draft of a junior properly. It can be tempting to decide that a particular junior has progressed to the point at which his or her drafting is basically sound and therefore requires minimal supervision; but cases such as the Identity Cards Act 2006 show that the drafter's work continues to require as much supervision as it can get, up until the day of retirement.

Conclusion

Legislative drafting is an enterprise of such supreme importance, not merely at a high level of constitutional theory but as a matter of interference in people's daily lives, that the potential effect of human weakness must be minimised so far as possible. The traditionally effective mechanisms used to ensure this seem to have produced remarkably few instances of clear drafting mistakes in Acts of Parliament over the decades. The case of *Inco*,[17] and the frequency of its invocation since being decided, might appear to suggest that drafting mistakes are becoming more frequent.

---

[17] *Inco Europe Ltd v First Choice Distribution* [2000] 1 WLR 586 HL—the case in which Lord Nicholls established three conditions which must be satisfied before the courts will correct an obvious drafting error.

29 PURPOSE CLAUSES

Introduction

For some time there has been a popular theory among critics of Parliamentary drafting that there is a fundamental flaw of approach that leads to a vicious cycle of complexity and uncertainty. The argument is, in essence, that the approach taken in drafting UK legislation is to attempt to make express provision for every conceivable eventuality. This, it is argued, leads the courts to take a strict approach to construing legislation; and it encourages professional advisers and others to attempt circumvention by side-stepping the precise cases covered by the legislation, while continuing to indulge in activities that ought to be covered by its fundamental purpose.

If only, the argument continues, statutes were drafted as statements of broad policy and purpose, the courts could give effect to that purpose in a flexible and creative way, and evasion would thereby be made more difficult.

The fundamental misconception in this argument is, of course, that legislation is not drafted merely so that it can be made to work effectively in partnership with the courts. If a provision comes to the courts to be construed, the drafter has already, to a considerable extent, failed. The aim of the drafter is to provide certainty about the law on the face of the legislation itself, so that a citizen, or at the very least a citizen with professional advice, can ascertain the applicable rights and duties without having to seek the court's interpretation of legislation on each occasion.

In addition to this misconception, as I have already discussed,[1] the courts are rightly reluctant to be creative in the matter of applying legislation. It is Parliamentarians and not the judges who, as the elected and accountable representatives of the people, are entitled and obliged to make law for the good government of the country. The

---

[1] See Ch.28.

dangers of the judges usurping that role are obvious and potentially extreme.

So the idea that all would be well if we stopped producing complex legislation and relied instead upon a few broad statements of purpose, is a clear non-starter.

However, the fact that an idea is frequently proposed by those who clearly fail to understand it, does not mean that it is without merit altogether. Statements of purpose do have a place in legislation, and this chapter aims to discuss briefly what that place might be.

Another myth

Like the use of plain English,[2] there is a commonly held myth that the use of statements of purpose is a radical innovation in statutory drafting. This myth appears to be believed both by many proponents of the approach as well as by most of the opponents.

The reality is, however, that in one form or another legislation has for centuries indulged in statements designed to make the underlying policy purpose of the legislation clear; and the courts have routinely allowed themselves to have regard to those statements in construing legislation.

Years ago, this function was fulfilled by the routine inclusion in an Act of Parliament of a preamble. The great advantage of the preamble was that its placing showed that it contained material that was different in kind from the material forming part of the legislative provisions themselves, and that it was intended to flavour them, and provide background to their construction, rather than to take parity with them (which always creates a risk of inconsistency).

Preambles as a routine component of United Kingdom statutes were abandoned some time ago. Their abandonment has, however, been regretted by the courts. In the case of *LCC v Bermondsey Bioscope Co*[3] Lord Alverstone CJ said:

"I quite recognise that the title of an Act is part of the Act and that it is of importance as showing the purview of the Act: and

---

[2] See Ch.24.
[3] [1911] 1 KB 445, 451.

I may express in this connection my regret that the practice of inserting preambles in Acts of Parliament has been discontinued as they were often of great assistance to the courts in construing the Acts."

Far from being a radical new device, therefore, statements of purpose are in fact a belated attempt to revive a technique that the courts, or at least some of them, wish had never been lost.

Using purpose clauses

The advantages and disadvantages of the use of purpose clauses in legislation are discussed in detail in *Craies on Legislation,*[4] and no purpose would be served by repeating them here. The discussion in *Craies* also draws attention to recent uses of the technique.

In essence, the official position of the Government today is that they are neither for nor against purpose clauses as a matter of dogma, and that while purpose clauses have an important part to play on occasion, they also have recognised risks and should therefore be used with caution. The reality is that some drafters are more wary of purpose clauses than others, and therefore whether material is introduced in the form of a purpose clause has more to do with the attitude and approach of the individual drafter than anything else.

As the discussion in *Craies* shows, Parliamentarians have consistently been in favour of the greater use of purpose clauses. The courts have never shown themselves to be troubled by purpose clauses in theory, and are seen on most occasions to derive assistance from them. And insofar as plain English proponents and other lay users of legislation express opinions, they are generally in favour of the greater use of purpose clauses. When almost everybody is in favour of a particular technique, including many of those entitled to an opinion, there must surely be a presumption that it is advantageous.

Of course, there are dangers associated with the use of purpose clauses that drafters will be particularly attuned to. And it is a significant part of the drafter's job to protect Parliamentarians and others

---

[4] 9th edn; see Ch.8.1.

from dangers of this kind, including dangers arising from techniques that people claim to admire.[5] But one must not exaggerate the dangers, particularly if by doing so one frustrates the legitimate choices of politicians and other users of the statute book. As with other material that goes beyond the mere expression of substantive law,[6] the inclusion of purpose clauses does have the potential for creating uncertainty and inconsistency. As a result, there will be occasions when purpose clauses are simply inappropriate, because the advantages that they could confer do not outweigh the dangers in the particular case. But there will be other cases in which a purpose clause is clearly not going to disturb underlying certainty of the legislation, so far as it can be achieved anyway, but will add important flavour that will help readers, including but not limited to the courts, to orientate themselves correctly at the beginning of their reading.

There will also be cases where the dangers associated with including a purpose clause can be significantly reduced if it is carefully phrased and presented. It is, after all, easier simply to reject a technique of which one is suspicious, than to learn how to use it effectively and safely. Purpose clauses are popular, and they have been used sufficiently often in recent years for it to be clear that they are here to stay: it is therefore the clear duty of each drafter not to determine not to use them on theological grounds, but to study their use and abuse with a view to becoming able to use them as effectively and harmlessly as possible.

Overview clauses

A sub-set of the debate about purpose clauses is the debate about overview clauses. Purpose clauses are substantive law: they direct the courts to have regard to specified matters when construing the legislation; or they give similar directions to specified statutory bodies in carrying out functions; or they exert some other specified influence on one or more specified classes of reader, and thereby affect the state of the law.

---

[5] Parents, children and fish-fingers come to mind.
[6] See further Chs 25 and 26.

Overview clauses, in contrast, are clearly inert. They simply inform the reader of what he or she is about to find later on in the Act or Part concerned.[7] It can be argued that these clauses are simply unnecessary; that the traditional arrangement of sections at the beginning of each Act serves the same purpose; or that readers are capable of carrying out their own overview before returning to read the material more carefully. Whether they are strictly necessary or not, however, overview clauses appear to be popular with at least some classes of reader. And, unlike purpose clauses, it is more or less impossible to conceive of any situation in which they can do harm (at least, if properly drafted).

One might therefore expect that overview clauses will become increasingly common in statutory drafting. Contemporary business and other documents increasingly commonly begin with a summary, to orientate readers and to make it easier for them to know whether they need to read the document, or particular parts of the document, at all; there is no reason why legislation should not perform the same function and help the reader at the outset.

---

[7] For example, the Banking Act 2009 has an overview clause at the beginning of each significant set of sections.

30 PEPPER V HART

Introduction

As is well known, in 1993 the House of Lords finally accepted that given the increasingly wide use made by the courts of background material for the purpose of establishing the context within which the words of legislation require to be read, it was surprising that in cases of difficulty of identifying the legislative intention the courts denied themselves, for constitutional reasons that did not appear particularly compelling, the opportunity to consult *Hansard*, a document that one might expect to be one of the most fertile—if not the most fertile—source of direct indications by the legislature of its purpose.

In fact, the evidential value of quotations from *Hansard* is generally very weak, for a number of reasons.

It is not the place of this chapter to give an account of how and when *Hansard* is used by the courts under the rule in *Pepper v Hart*.[1] The courts have spent a considerable amount of time considering how *Hansard* should and should not be used by them, and there are various judicial pronouncements, as the pendulum has swung gently backwards and forwards, for, against and then for again, reliance on the rule. These pronouncements are recorded and discussed in those publications that analyse the judicial operation of the rule in depth, and I will not repeat that process here. But I do want to take this opportunity to offer a few observations about what effect the rule in *Pepper v Hart* has had on the shape of legislation.

When the rule was first propounded, a number of people speculated about what effect it might have on the way in which the legislative process is conducted; but for the most part attention was focused on the behaviour of Ministers in Parliament, rather than on the drafting

---

[1] For an account see *Craies on Legislation*, 9th edn, Ch.28.

process. Insofar as anything was said at all about the latter, it was confined to a simple assertion that nothing would change.[2]

"Can we Pepper v Hart it?"

The House of Lords decision in *Pepper v Hart* was treated by Government Departments initially as something of a threat, and a nuisance. In particular, the fear was that every Ministerial statement would have to be scrutinised for accuracy and potential nuance with greater rigour than had previously been the case. It was probably inevitable that it would not be long, however, before Departments came to see the decision primarily as an opportunity. In particular, Departments faced with difficult points of drafting, where it seemed hard to ensure precisely the right flavour in the choice of words used, soon began to suggest that reliance could be placed on *Pepper v Hart* to ensure the intended construction of the provision concerned.

There are, of course, two obvious objections to this course of proceeding. First, it is an essential condition of the rule of law that citizens should have reasonable access to an authoritative text of the law that applies to them.[3] In the same way that it is, at least, monstrously unfair for citizens to be bound by laws that they cannot readily discover, it is equally improper for citizens to be bound by a text, the precise meaning of which can only be ascertained by reference to a passage of Parliamentary debate, of which there is no reason to assume that the citizen could possibly be aware, and which they would find difficult to locate even if aware of its existence. The idea that citizens, or even their professional advisers, should be reasonably expected to scour *Hansard* for possible elucidation of every single law that applies to them is manifestly absurd.

Secondly, questions of accessibility aside, the fact remains that *Pepper v Hart* is, at best, a very imprecise tool in the hands of the

---

[2] See, for example, the House of Lords Written Answer HL Deb (April 5, 1995) WA 25: "Textual clarity and precision, and the avoidance of ambiguity, will continue to be high priorities in drafting legislation . . . ."

[3] See Ch.24.

legislature. For one thing, the rule can be invoked only in accordance with the test set by the House of Lords in *Pepper v Hart* itself, which confines it mostly to the resolution of ambiguity: since it is for the courts to determine what amounts to sufficient ambiguity for the rule to be invoked, there is always a risk in leaving a matter to be clarified under the rule, that the courts will determine that the text on its face is already unambiguous (but not necessarily bearing the meaning that the Government would like). That consideration apart, once the rule has been invoked there is no guarantee that even relatively clear and precise statements of the Minister in the House will be construed in precisely the way that the Government would like, in finessing the actual text of the Act.

So for most purposes the proper answer to a Departmental suggestion that a point might be left to be "*Pepper v Hart*'ed" is that it is the responsibility of the Government to produce legislative text that is clear on its face, and not to be content with material that is known to be unclear, in the hope that the courts will pick up the pieces and provide clarity by reference to research that may or may not be carried out comprehensively by lawyers and others affected by the law.

That said, since as has been stated the only rule of legislative drafting is that there are no rules of legislative drafting, it is not surprising to learn that there can be cases in which deliberate advance reliance on the rule in *Pepper v Hart* is not inappropriate.

The best example is where the Government wishes to rely on the estoppel element of the decision in *Pepper v Hart*. In essence, from its earliest days the decision has had two purposes, although only one is generally recognised by the legal profession at large. The first purpose is the resolution of admitted ambiguity. The second purpose is holding the Government to undertakings given during the passage of the legislation.[4] It is not unreasonable for the Government to give an undertaking during the passage of a Bill, knowing and intending that it will be capable of being relied upon under the rule in *Pepper v Hart*, particularly where the matter is of sufficient political importance for it to be reasonably likely that professional advisers will take note of

---

[4] See *Craies on Legislation*, 9th edn, para.28.1.9.

the passage concerned.[5] It is important, however, to be sure that in such cases the material being added by way of undertaking is not an attempted elucidation masquerading as an undertaking. So, for example, if the Act states that the Secretary of State may make regulations prohibiting people from taking dogs into parks, it would be entirely reasonable for a Minister to give an undertaking, intending it to be relied upon, that there is no intention ever to use the power in relation to little furry fluffy things, only in relation to nasty big snarly snappy things; and the more precise he or she can be about which breeds are fluffy or snappy, the more legitimate and useful the reliance on *Pepper v Hart* becomes. On the other hand, for the Minister to "undertake" to treat village greens and other open spaces as being parks, is not a genuine undertaking at all, but an attempt to identify and resolve an ambiguity through *Pepper v Hart*, where the appropriate treatment would be to resolve any genuine doubt by a clear definition.

The second case where deliberate reliance on the rule in *Pepper v Hart* may not be inappropriate is where Parliamentary Counsel has advised that there is no real ambiguity on the face of the legislation, and that an attempt to resolve a perceived ambiguity by express provision would therefore be to introduce unnecessary additional material into the Act, which always has the risk of going wrong.[6] In such a case, where a Parliamentarian is insistent that he or she perceives an ambiguity in the provision concerned, it is perfectly proper for the Minister to reassure the Parliamentarian of the Government's clear understanding of the meaning of the provision, and to note expressly that the statement is capable of being relied upon under the rule in *Pepper v Hart*, should it later happen that the courts agree with the Parliamentarian in identifying an ambiguity, contrary to the Government's understanding.

---

[5] In annotating statutes for the Annotated Statutes Service on Westlaw UK, where *Pepper v Hart* notes are routinely included, my editorial policy has from the start been to include any passage that could be seen to amount to an undertaking: so without searching *Hansard* it should be possible for professional advisers to have their attention drawn to Government undertakings when reading the up to date text of the legislation itself.

[6] See above, Ch.25.

The reality is, however, that it would be pointless to deny that the existence of *Pepper v Hart* exerts some influence on the shape of legislation: a tight-rope walker who knows there is a safety net underneath cannot prevent himself or herself from behaving differently than would be the case if there were no net. However much he or she asserts that "balance and skill will continue to be high priorities in tightrope walking", when considering whether or not to risk the extra melodramatic wobble he or she would not be human if the existence of the safety net did not exert at least a subliminal influence. So too in the preparation of legislation: even if neither the drafter nor anyone else in the Bill team consciously says "Let's leave the point fuzzy and get the Minister to say something clear that we can *Pepper v Hart*", the Bill team in particular would not be human if they did not occasionally, with a greater or lesser degree of consciousness, allow a point to drop sooner than they otherwise might, in the expectation of putting something clear in the Minister's Speaking Note.[7]

As to how wicked an attitude this is, it depends partly on how puritan a constitutionalist one is and partly on fact and degree. One can take a strong line and assert that however human the temptation may be to leave a point to be clarified through the rule in *Pepper v Hart*, it is a deliberately informal and improper delegation of the legislature's functions to the courts; one can add that it is unsatisfactory both as a matter of constitutional law and as a matter of practicality to force the reader to search in *Hansard* for the true meaning of the statute and to have recourse to the courts to establish it authoritatively.

There is, of course, a lot in these objections; but one must not overdo them. And the point can be put in a slightly different way that makes the practice appear less wicked: however much one tries to be as precise as possible in drafting laws, there is always a limit to what one can achieve. It ought always to be possible to avoid actual ambiguity, in the sense of two or more reasonably plausible meanings of a given expression, each of which would make arguable sense in the context of the policy of the Act concerned. But it is not always possible to avoid using expressions that have some potential for fine shades of meaning, all of which may be equally plausible. In those

---

[7] As to which see Ch.6.

circumstances it can be argued that one has done all one can to assist the reader by the use of the text itself, and that if one can leave some additional evidence in an authoritative form that the courts have agreed to accept as having some probative value, one may as well do so; Explanatory Notes will not always be the answer, both because of the Parliamentary rules about what can be included in them at the Bill stage and for other practical reasons; so it may be helpful to provide a neat Speaking Note for the Minister that will add, to the available evidence on the construction of the provision, a concise pointer in the direction of what was intended.

I do not recall deliberately "*Pepper v Hart*'ing" a point more than two or three times in all, and I cannot now remember with certainty any particular point on which I provided a Speaking Note for the Minister for that purpose; but I know that I did do this on a very small number of occasions, and that each time it seemed preferable to maintaining radio silence on the point.

SECTION 5
FINAL

31 OVERVIEW

When I started to write this book I was not at all sure what it would cover, far less exactly what I wanted to say about particular topics. It has turned into something of a self-propelling rant, which has been both cathartic and satisfying to write, and hopefully will not be too tedious to read.

If I were asked what I would like the reader to take away from the book it would be two thoughts.

First, that an academic knowledge of Government or Parliamentary procedures is of limited use, and may be positively misleading, unless tempered with an understanding of the political and other realities that flavour how the procedures are operated in practice; the principal purpose of sections 2 and 3 of this book has been to attempt to put some of the theories into practical context, with a view to enhancing the reader's understanding of how they actually work.

Secondly, a recurring theme has been the importance of allowing individual styles the freedom to innovate and develop, and the increasing threats that modern styles of Government and management pose to that principle.

I leave by offering one final thought.

Legislation is very important. It achieves less than some politicians would like to think, not being a substitute for or guarantee of effective administrative action.[1] But it is capable when used wisely of achieving more than many people realise. The rule of law matters enormously to society as a whole, and legislation is its backbone. Everyone involved in the process of legislation is therefore able to see themselves as engaged in a process the importance of which transcends considerations of personality or party.

More to the point, legislation covers both ends of the spectrum

---

[1] See further, for my final Denning-esque self-quote of the book, "Nothing will Come of Nothing, Daniel Greenberg laments the introduction of nonsense legislation", (2010) *New Law Journal*, July 30, p.1084.

of usefulness when a person comes to consider whether in his or her professional life he or she has contributed to, or detracted from, the general well-being: well-intentioned legislation, properly thought through and competently executed, is a powerful force for good; ill-intentioned legislation, poorly thought through or incompetently executed, can cause untold unfairness and misery.

For politicians and civil servants alike, it becomes too tempting to see legislation as a political or technical game; we need to remind ourselves constantly that although legislation may be for us one of the many games played in Parliament and Government, there is no such thing as a "minor or technical" provision that is not capable of having a serious impact on people's lives. When we allow our own ambitions or personalities to interfere with the process we do real harm, and when we exert ourselves to play our part in the process with dedication and selflessness we do real good.

32 ABOUT THE AUTHOR

Daniel Greenberg studied law at Cambridge, and was called to the Bar in 1987. He began his public service as a legal adviser in the Lord Chancellor's Department in 1988, and joined the Office of the Parliamentary Counsel in 1991. He left that Office in 2010 and now works as Parliamentary Counsel in the Parliamentary team of Berwin Leighton Paisner LLP; he is also the general editor of *Annotated Statutes*, Westlaw UK, and the editor of *Craies on Legislation*, *Stroud's Judicial Dictionary* and *Jowitt's Dictionary of English Law*.

INDEX